AF361390

PUNISHMENT AND THE HISTORY OF POLITICAL PHILOSOPHY

From Classical Republicanism to the Crisis of Modern Criminal Justice

Punishment and the History of Political Philosophy

From Classical Republicanism to the Crisis of Modern Criminal Justice

ARTHUR SHUSTER

UNIVERSITY OF TORONTO PRESS
Toronto Buffalo London

ISBN 978-1-4426-4728-2

Printed on acid-free, 100% post-consumer recycled paper
with vegetable-based inks.

Library and Archives Canada Cataloguing in Publication

Shuster, Arthur, 1980–, author
Punishment and the history of political philosophy : from classical
republicanism to the crisis of modern criminal justice / Arthur Shuster.

Includes bibliographical references.
ISBN 978-1-4426-4728-2 (bound)

1. Punishment – Philosophy.   2. Criminal justice, Administration
of – Philosophy.   3. Punishment – Moral and ethical aspects.
4. Punishment – Political aspects.   I. Title.

K5103.S58 2016   364.601   C2015-907071-6

This book has been published with the help of a grant from the Federation
for the Humanities and Social Sciences, through the Awards to Scholarly
Publications Program, using funds provided by the Social Sciences and
Humanities Research Council of Canada.

University of Toronto Press acknowledges the financial assistance to its
publishing program of the Canada Council for the Arts and the Ontario
Arts Council, an agency of the Government of Ontario.

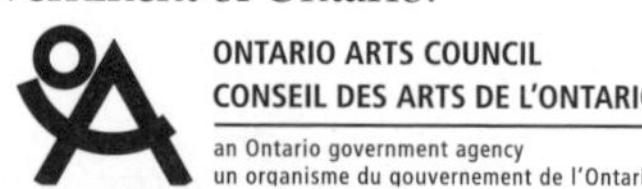

To my parents

Contents

Acknowledgments

I thank Boston College and Claremont McKenna College for their support over the years while I was completing the manuscript for this book. This book has grown out of my doctoral dissertation at the University of Texas at Austin, and anything of value in it I owe to my teachers there, whose guidance and support throughout my studies, and whose friendship since then, have been a true gift. I particularly wish to thank Thomas and Lorraine Pangle, as well as Devin Stauffer, for sharing with me their insights into the great questions of political philosophy, without which this study would not have been possible. I also thank Russell Muirhead for his valuable encouragement and sage advice.

I would also like to thank *The Review of Politics* for granting permission to use material (parts of chapter 4) that originally appeared in that journal as "Kant on the Retributive Outlook in Moral and Political Life" (Summer 2011).

A.S., August 2014

PUNISHMENT AND THE HISTORY OF POLITICAL PHILOSOPHY

From Classical Republicanism to the Crisis of Modern Criminal Justice

Introduction

When Shakespeare's tyrant Macbeth laments the meaninglessness of human existence (as he understands it) – pronouncing it to be like "a tale told by an idiot, […] signifying nothing" – he unwittingly reveals to us the importance and moral significance of crime and punishment. Macbeth's haunting soliloquy is provoked by what he believes has been a failure of cosmic justice. Early in the play, the mysterious Weird Sisters had prophesied to him that he would gain the throne of Scotland, which he coveted by fair means or foul. That prophecy is now guiding (or rather, misguiding) Macbeth to his own tragic ruin, for it has spurred him to seize the Scottish crown and thereby achieve his tyrannical ambitions. His success proves to be short-lived: his tyranny is soon brought down by those who would avenge the murdered king. He responds to these events by accusing the mysterious powers that govern man's fate of being false and fickle and in those two senses unjust. We, the audience, do not share Macbeth's bleak view of the human condition, for unlike him, we see his defeat not as a reflection of the cosmos's indifference or malevolence towards human things but rather as the fulfilment of justice: Macbeth had been tempted by the witches' prophecy to commit his crimes, but he had also been deceived by that prophecy and led unwittingly to his ultimate punishment. The justice of the prophecy, and of Macbeth's fall, seems to be confirmed by the fact that Macbeth is killed by one of his victims: the pious Macduff. By the play's end, the criminal has suffered a penalty proportionate to the gravity of his crime, his victims have been avenged, and justice seems to have been satisfied.

Is it possible that the larger teaching of Shakespeare's *Macbeth* is that the condign punishment of crime is intimately linked with our basic moral self-understanding? If Shakespeare's play had ended differently – if Macbeth's tyranny had gone unpunished – would *we* then have fallen prey to Macbeth's despair at the meaninglessness of a world devoid of justice? Before Macbeth suffers his punishment, at a point in the play where success for him still seems possible, it is Lady Macbeth who descends into despair, then madness, and eventually commits suicide. Her madness is brought about by her inability to live with her unexpunged guilt ("What, will these hands ne'er be clean?"). The Macbeths' despair is to some extent echoed by Hannah Arendt's struggle to come to terms with "the banality of evil." This striking and provocative formulation was coined by Arendt in order to describe the infamous Adolf Eichmann, the Nazi bureaucrat involved in administering German concentration camps during the Second World War, who was later captured and tried in Jerusalem. In *Eichmann in Jerusalem*, her report on the trial, Arendt describes Eichmann's actions as those of a morally obtuse, petty bureaucratic functionary incapable of appreciating the gravity of the evil he was committing. This is a source of anguish for her, for it implies that the greatest evils perpetrated by human beings on one another may in the last analysis be "banal" and thus meaningless in the sense expressed by Macbeth in his soliloquy. In this way, at least in the context of Shakespeare's dramatic expression of our experience, punishment of the unjust appears as a kind of moral necessity – required for its own sake, beyond any merely utilitarian value of the penalty as a deterrent of future crime.

Yet this poetic account of our experience, powerful as it may be, is not completely satisfying. We rightly wonder whether this poetic vision of the moral necessity of punishment can be given systematic theoretical articulation and grounding. We wonder how we might distinguish our feelings of righteous indignation from the irrational, impulsive anger that is also found in animals. (We ourselves may experience such anger whenever we fly into a momentary rage at a chair or a door we have bumped into.) Furthermore, we feel an urgent need to try to clarify what we mean when we say that justice demands restoration of a rightful "balance" and that punishment (as distinguished from some other intervention) is needed to accomplish this. Equally puzzling is the related question of what determines the "proportionality" of a punishment. We may be troubled, as well, by the complexities introduced into our thinking about crime and punishment by certain sceptical reflections about the nature of choice and moral responsibility, for careful study of the human condition reveals many ways in which our choices are constrained by forces – both external and internal – beyond our control.

The present study investigates these basic and enduring questions about crime and punishment, and its approach is normative rather than criminological, sociological, or historical (although criminological and historical issues are considered when appropriate). This study is "normative" in two senses. First, it is normative because it is fundamentally concerned with the question of the purpose or end of punishment and with its moral justification. Second, it is normative in the sense that it situates itself within the tradition of Western political philosophy and connects the theme of punishment with the larger themes of virtue, law, and the good society. This approach has the advantage of being able to tackle directly the questions regarding punishment that we have just raised. Insofar as criminology, sociology, and historical studies adopt a "value-neutral" approach to crime and punishment, aspiring to objectivity, they are inclined to dismiss ordinary moral experience (such as the experience of Shakespeare's Macbeth) as supposedly incapable of offering any real insights into the truth of these phenomena. This present study assumes, on the contrary, that it is impossible to begin to understand the human significance (the significance for human beings) of crime and punishment without paying careful attention to what we say, think, and feel about our ordinary (i.e., not disinterested) experience in these matters.

This is, of course, not the first time that these troubling questions and difficulties surrounding crime and punishment have been raised. Nonetheless, they must be raised anew, and addressed thoroughly, because it is hardly an exaggeration to say that criminal justice is today in a state of crisis. Most readers will already be aware of various political and legal controversies indicating that a number of aspects of modern criminal justice systems have come under attack. The most common target of criticism is the heavy reliance of those systems on mass incarceration. Large and costly prison complexes are now warehousing thousands of inmates serving long sentences, so that the total prison population of a modern nation can reach the hundreds of thousands, in some cases even millions. Many observers are troubled by the sheer enormity of these numbers; some go even further, accusing modern prisons of being "schools of crime" that not only fail to rehabilitate and deter but also actually "harden" criminals, who are being forced to associate only with their own like, in violent and sometimes brutal conditions. This critique of modern prisons was made most pointedly and radically by Michel Foucault in *Discipline and Punish* (1975) (discussed at length in chapter 5), which continues to inspire many "abolitionists."

Modern criminal justice systems are also being attacked for their supposed neglect of the particular needs and circumstances of individual offenders, their victims, and local communities. Indeed, correctional policy is predominantly under the jurisdiction of remote government agencies (federal, state, or provincial, as the case may be) and is administered by those agencies according to uniform penal codes that cannot possibly take into account the wide variety of local, let alone individual, factors. This state of affairs is criticized for yielding poor results overall: punishments meted out are in some cases too harsh (to deter future crime or satisfy victims), in others too lenient; local communities are deprived of their autonomy in a vital function of self-government; and as a consequence of the latter, the bonds of community disrupted by crime are not repaired.[1] In response to this problem, in the past thirty years a "restorative justice" movement has emerged in Canada, the United States, Australia, and other places whose principal mission is to challenge the modern state's monopoly over the administration of criminal justice.[2]

A third aspect of the crisis of modern criminal justice is the vexed controversy that has developed regarding whether it is excessively retributive and whether it ought to be retributive at all. In the 1970s the US Supreme Court wrestled with this issue when it was faced with the question of the constitutionality of the death penalty. In 1972, in *Furman v. Georgia*, the Court placed a moratorium on the death penalty. The question before the Court was whether the imposition of the death penalty is "cruel and unusual" and thus beyond the constitutional power of the state by virtue of the Eighth and Fourteenth Amendments of the US Constitution.[3] The five justices who made up the majority of the Court agreed that it was, but only on the narrow ground that Georgia's penal laws were causing the death penalty to be imposed in an irregular and arbitrary manner; but the justices could not agree on whether the death penalty was unconstitutional in principle. The justices' opinions revealed their awareness that whether the death penalty is "cruel and unusual" in principle depends on what makes punishment just or moral. And this was precisely what they could not agree on.

Perhaps the most interesting of the opinions in *Furman* is that of Justice William Brennan, who notes that the Eighth Amendment's prohibition of "cruel and unusual punishments" does not define "cruel and unusual." If the Court is to apply the clause faithfully, it needs a principled method for determining which specific punishments fall within the clause's prohibition in a way that reflects the broad moral commitments implicit in the clause itself and in the Constitution. But what exactly are those broad moral commitments? At bottom, Brennan believes that the "cruel and unusual" clause prohibits the infliction of punishments that are degrading to human dignity.[4] Brennan goes on to conclude that the death penalty does indeed degrade the individual, since according to him the prospect of an (otherwise unnecessary) death is so physically and psychologically painful that it makes normal human functioning impossible in the time prior to and during the carrying out of the sentence; thus, it falls under the Eighth Amendment's prohibition.[5]

Yet one might still wonder: Could depriving one individual of his or her basic dignity be morally justified by society's need for security, if it were found that the death penalty was indispensable to effective deterrence of certain crimes? Moreover, could it not be argued (as some retributivists do) that in some of the worst cases, death and nothing less is deserved because of the gravity of the crime, and that to deny this punishment would amount to denying victims, and society as a whole, the dignity belonging to *them*? Finally, it might be maintained that the worst criminal has already degraded himself to the point that all a decent society can do is to put him out of his misery, as an act of euthanasia.

Brennan himself acknowledges the existence of the possible objections we have just outlined, and his admission is illuminating:

> From the beginning of our Nation, the punishment of death has stirred acute public controversy. Although pragmatic arguments for and against the punishment have been frequently advanced, this long standing and heated controversy cannot be explained solely as the result of difference over the practical wisdom of a particular government policy. At bottom, the battle has been waged on moral grounds. The country has debated whether a society for which the dignity of the individual is the supreme value can, without a fundamental inconsistency, follow the practice of deliberately putting some of its members to death. In the United States as in other nations in the world, the struggle about this punishment has been between ancient and deeply rooted beliefs in retribution, atonement or vengeance, on the one hand, and on the other, beliefs in the personal value and dignity of the common man that were born of the democratic movement of the eighteenth century, as well as beliefs in the scientific approach to an understanding of the motive forces of human conduct, which are the result of the growth of the sciences of behavior during the nineteenth and twentieth centuries. It is this essentially moral conflict that forms the backdrop for the past changes in, and present operation of, our system of imposing death as a punishment for crime.[6]

Although throughout most of his opinion Brennan presents as sufficient and uncontroversial his standard – human dignity – for distinguishing between just and unjust punishments, here he acknowledges the existence of a more fundamental controversy over the end that punishment ought to serve. Whether or not the US Constitution's protection of human dignity against "cruel and unusual" punishment rules out the death penalty crucially depends on whether deterrence, retribution, or some other goal (or a combination of certain goals) is the politically (and constitutionally) valid end of punishment. For example, if the proper end were general security, and if the death penalty were necessary to effective deterrence, then it could not easily be argued that this penalty is "cruel," since in this case the survival of the political community would justify this punishment (without denying that it is lamentable in other respects). If, on the other hand, the proper aim of punishment were retribution, then the death penalty might be justified (and thus no longer held "cruel" in principle) as the proportional and appropriate penalty for such serious crimes as murder. In short, commitment to democracy and individual dignity is not by itself sufficient to decide the question of punishment.

While Brennan's opinion shows his awareness of the existence of the fundamental moral dispute about the proper aim of punishment, it gives little indication as to how this dispute might be decided, and on what grounds. His final position is that, historically, the death penalty has been used less and less in democratic societies (although it is still used in some), which indicates to him that the fundamental moral dispute will eventually be decided against this practice. In other words, he appears to trust in historical progress, and specifically in the progress of general moral opinion from ignorance to wisdom (as distinguished from technological progress). The reasonableness of this hopeful assumption may be questioned, and at any rate it does nothing to address the fundamental moral disagreement over the aim of punishment that still exists in fact (as Brennan himself admits). That disagreement cannot therefore be elided by reference to a possible future historical consensus, especially since, according to Brennan, it has existed "from the beginning of our [the US] Nation."

That this disagreement exists became still more obvious in the four years between *Furman v. Georgia* and *Gregg v. Georgia* (the case that lifted the moratorium on the death penalty), when Congress and more than thirty-five state legislatures re-enacted the death penalty for one or more crimes. Partly in light of this legislative response to *Furman*, the plurality opinion in *Gregg* acknowledged that retribution is one of the morally acceptable purposes of punishment, since this appeared to be the view of a large portion of the country and of its representatives.[7] Neither *Furman* nor *Gregg* nor (to my knowledge) any of the Supreme Court's major Eighth Amendment decisions that followed have resolved the fundamental moral disagreement over the end of punishment – a disagreement that all sides admit exists in the United States and other countries.

Present-day scholarship has made some attempts to address fundamental questions regarding the morality of punishment such as those raised by Justice Brennan's opinion, Foucault's book, and restorative justice advocates. An important recent development in punishment scholarship has been a resurgence of interest in retribution. This interest has largely resulted from the perceived inadequacy of utilitarian punishment theory, which had been predominant in the preceding generation of scholarship. Critics observed that this theory is reductionist (and thus unpersuasive philosophically)[8] and that furthermore, its logic – which aims to secure the greatest happiness of the greatest number – has an alarmingly "paternalistic" tendency.[9] Utilitarian punishment theories tend to view crime as analogous to disease and to view criminals as just a particularly dangerous class of ill human beings (although they are not logically committed to this position). From this point of view, the special expertise of criminologists, psychologists, and bureaucratic administrators entitles them – not judges or juries – to dictate the nature and duration of treatment ("punishment") that offenders should receive, according to the experts' calculations of maximum social utility. Since offenders may be pathologically incapable of making the right choices, and may even resist attempts to cure them – and, at any rate, since private interests may be disregarded whenever they conflict with the requirements of social utility – criminal justice experts are entitled to infringe on the autonomy of inmates and perhaps even on some of their rights. Finally, guilt, innocence, and desert would lose their conventional meaning according to this view.

Because such consequences of the utilitarian approach were unacceptable to its critics, it was suggested in much of the literature that punishment ought to aim not only at crime prevention but also at fairness, proportionality, and retribution – although the precise meanings of these commonsense notions were not always clear and much of the "retributivist" punishment scholarship that followed was concerned with defining these concepts and bringing them into agreement with liberal principles. It was hoped that in this way, the coercion to which convicted offenders were judged to be liable would be limited to what they deserved, and to no more than this, regardless of how much utility might accrue to society (or even to the offender himself) from an increase in the duration or severity of punishment.

Some retributivists further argued that besides placing a limit on penal severity, retribution satisfies justice itself, which demands the equal distribution of the burdens and benefits of civil society to all individual members. Thus whenever one person refuses to bear his share of the burden, which he does by violating the law, retribution is called for in order to re-establish the just equilibrium.[10] Some retributivists also argued for retribution on the ground that it performs the important function of expressing society's collective view of what is right and wrong, and that penalties should be designed with the aim of communicating this view, even if this should diminish somewhat their deterrent or rehabilitative effects.[11] When the strict application of the retributivist principle was challenged in scholarly debates, its defence by adherents proved less than adequate.[12] In response to this, another view became prominent in the scholarly literature that was a "mixed," or "partial" retributivist theory of punishment inspired by the earlier work of John Rawls and that of H.L.A. Hart, each of whom had called for a theory of punishment that hybridized retribution and utility.[13]

As Rawls and Hart saw it, the problem was that both utility and retribution make legitimate moral claims upon us yet appear to be heterogeneous and even mutually exclusive principles. This had led some to conclude that either one or the other principle must be true, but not both. Against this view, Rawls and Hart argue that there is a distinction to be made between principles that justify a practice and principles that justify particular actions falling under that practice, and that the principles of utility and retribution fall into these two different categories, respectively: the principle of utility answers the question of the fundamental justification of punishment as a practice or institution, while retribution justifies and regulates the administration of punishment in particular cases. To illustrate this argument, Rawls suggests that we look at each of the two questions as being addressed to a different public official: the question of general justification is addressed to the legislator, who looks to the future good, while the question of particular application is addressed to the judge, who looks backwards in time to the culpability or innocence of the accused.[14] Hart draws attention to the confused views of actual political actors (he gives the example of a British Member of Parliament), who will appeal at different times to different principles to justify their favoured policy proposals. On each occasion, the official assumes that only a single principle justifies punishment as a whole and fails to notice that at different times he is responding to different aspects of the institution in question – about its general purpose and about its case-by-case application, respectively.[15]

The Rawlsian–Hartian proposed solution to the apparent tension between retribution and utility appears to combine the best of both. This attractive solution became influential for a time, but eventually it too came under attack. For its critics, the Rawlsian–Hartian notion of "mixed" retributivism seemed artificial, for it drew convenient but spurious distinctions between questions of general justification and questions of particular application.[16] On the contrary, the critics objected, retributivists are concerned precisely with the *general justification* of punishment.[17] As one critic argues, the fundamental problem that liberal (including mixed-retributivist) punishment theorists cannot escape is that their attempt to justify punishment fundamentally in terms of deterrence makes punishment a mere tax on crime, and this disagrees with our basic moral sense that there is an important difference between taxation and punishment.[18]

Thus a truly satisfying theory of punishment – one that adequately addresses all of our basic moral concerns and questions – continues to elude contemporary punishment theory. For this reason (and for the other considerations raised here) it is necessary to return once more to the fundamental questions of criminal justice. This book attempts to do so by examining the development of the idea of criminal justice, through its crucial transformations, in the Western tradition of political philosophy. Thus, unlike most recent scholarly works on punishment, this book will not provide a novel theory of punishment (in the sense of "theory" as a programmatic set of guiding principles). Rather, it will attempt to bring into sharper focus the fundamental *questions* of criminal justice, in all of their complexity, in order to improve the quality of our theorizing on this subject and in order to further elucidate the contemporary crisis of criminal justice.

Its main thesis (alluded to in the second part of the title) is that this crisis can best be understood in light of the momentous shift in the history of Western political thought from classical republicanism to modern individual natural right and contractarianism.[19] One claim of this study is that, unlike classical republicanism, modern natural right, in its original formulation as the inalienable right to defend one's life and livelihood, necessarily implies a wholesale rejection of retributive punishment.

Before the full significance of this rejection can be made intelligible, however, the meaning of retribution must first be explicated in the context of classical political thought. The argument therefore proceeds first by examining the complex classical view of punishment, as originally elaborated in Plato's *Laws* (chapter 1). This view is complex because it contains two elements that exist in some tension with each other: the civic-republican commitment to retribution as a core aspect of political justice, on the one hand, and on the other the enlightened philosophical (Socratic) understanding of human nature, which entertains profound doubts about the coherence of retributive punishment and of what we would call "moral responsibility." That chapter argues that in order to understand properly our own concern with "just deserts," we must examine this notion in connection with the intensely civic spirit that flourishes in a small participatory republic such as the ancient Greek city-state. My analysis in certain respects agrees with, but also significantly departs from, the predominant "punishment as therapy" interpretation of Plato's teaching on punishment.[20] My argument assumes that the civic-republican spirit identified by Plato, although tempered in modern liberal-democratic societies, nevertheless persists in some form and continues to influence the public's attitude towards crime and punishment. I will argue, therefore, that the logic of this civic-republicanism, as explicated by Plato's Athenian Stranger in the *Laws*, requires retributive (non-therapeutic) punishment and regards it as morally desirable. The initially confusing tension in Plato's teaching on punishment that thereby arises – that is, the tension between its retributive and its sceptical elements – reveals itself, in the course of the analysis, to be a tension not in Plato's thought but in political life itself.

The book proceeds, next, to examine the first theory of criminal justice in the modern rationalist tradition, elaborated by Hobbes in his *Leviathan* (chapter 2). This chapter begins by analysing Hobbes's derivation of the right to punish from the fundamental natural right to self-preservation, and argues that this becomes the basis of all modern punishment theories until Kant. It then discusses the aspirational or humanizing aspect of Hobbes's purely deterrent theory of punishment, the rational limits of the sovereign's punishing power, and the collision between the sovereign's right to punish and the criminal's right to self-preservation. The chapter concludes by arguing that Hobbes's attempt to distinguish theoretically between a punishable criminal and an enemy in the state of nature fails. (This problem would continue to preoccupy later punishment theorists.) While there has been a great deal of scholarship on the penal thought of Kant and the utilitarians (especially Beccaria and Bentham), relatively little attention has been paid to Hobbes.[21] Consequently, this chapter contributes to the growing scholarship on Hobbes's teaching on punishment.

The book then goes on to show how the Hobbesian idea of criminal justice came unravelled through a series of dialectical moments in the thought of Montesquieu, Beccaria, Kant, and Foucault, respectively. Most contemporary scholarship traces the origins of the two major alternative theories of punishment – utilitarianism and retributivism – to Beccaria and Kant, respectively. While this view is not exactly wrong, it is potentially misleading, since it tends to obscure the fundamental continuity of the modern tradition of penal thought (broadly understood), in which Beccaria and Kant were collaborators in spite of their obvious differences. Since Beccaria himself was an acknowledged student of Montesquieu, the next chapter of the book (chapter 3) begins with the crucial modifications to Hobbesian penology made by Montesquieu. Although Montesquieu's influence on Beccaria is well known, there have been no sustained attempts to explicate Montesquieu's own liberal theory of punishment as presented in his *Spirit of the Laws*. This chapter argues that Montesquieu's insights into the malleability of human nature and the effects of commerce led him to conclude that the administration of punishment in modern societies can become considerably milder than Hobbes had anticipated. It discusses Montesquieu's view of the beneficial political consequences of the decriminalization of offences against religion and mores, and of the attenuation of penal severity. The chapter ends by examining Beccaria's elaboration of Montesquieu's liberalizing principles of criminal law.

Modern punishment theory from Hobbes up to Beccaria never completely succeeded in expunging the appeal of retribution. I argue that it was left up to Kant to try to reintroduce this principle into criminal justice theory. However, he attempted to justify it on the new basis of modern individual natural right rather than on that of classical politics. Thus I argue (in chapter 4) that one positive accomplishment of Kant's teaching on punishment was to show that retribution remains a serious concern from the point of view of ordinary moral experience, even when that experience has been reshaped historically by the Bible and by the idea of modern natural right. The central claim of this chapter is that a defining moment in the development of the idea of modern criminal justice occurs in Kant's *Rechtselehre*. In that work, Kant precisely identifies the threat posed to individual dignity and autonomy by modern criminal justice (as articulated by Kant's predecessors) and argues that only the principle of retribution can protect the individual from the paternalistic tendencies of utilitarian punishment. Yet Kant's attempt to defend retribution on modern principles was only partly successful, I argue, and thus it left liberal criminal justice theory open to later criticism.

The final chapter (chapter 5) looks back on the development of the idea of modern criminal justice charted in the first four chapters. It does so in the context of a discussion of Foucault's famous (or infamous) critique of the modern penal system in *Discipline and Punish*. I defend Foucault's claim that the modern punishing power is in principle unlimited (which is in agreement with Hobbes's own account of the sovereign's right to punish) and argue that in *Discipline and Punish* the crisis of modern criminal justice finally comes to a head. The chapter goes on to discuss Foucault's critique of the penitentiary, but challenges some of its more radical claims. By taking this historical approach, the present book offers an alternative to the general tendency of punishment scholarship in recent decades – most of which is authored by legal scholars and ethicists – to oversimplify or altogether abstract from the political dimension of criminal justice.

In the concluding chapter, I extend my discussion of the crisis of modern criminal justice into the present by noting certain dysfunctional features of actual public debates about crime, and end by suggesting how these debates might be improved if they were informed by a better understanding of the influence of the history of political philosophy on the criminal justice policies and practices we have inherited.

The Problem of Punishment and the Limits of Reform in Plato's *Laws*

It is often observed that Western societies have been growing progressively gentler since the dawn of the Enlightenment and the spread of democracy, and this appears to be no less true of attitudes towards crime and punishment. Western societies are more respectful of life, more sympathetic to suffering, and consequently less harsh in punishing offenders today than they have ever been. The matter is, however, more complex. The passion of moral indignation aroused in any community by crime – especially violent crime – is still a common enough occurrence; yet it is tempered in its effects. It seems that we allow and even encourage ourselves to feel indignation towards offenders. Indeed, it would be a rare person who did not feel even a little indignation in response to the victimization of a fellow citizen, to say nothing of closer relations. This follows naturally from the fact that we feel responsible for (and to) our fellow citizens, neighbours, and loved ones, and therefore cannot help but take on some of their feelings of outrage when they have been victimized. Accordingly, daily experience confirms that we demand consolation for victims and assurances of the future safety of our community; at least as emphatically, we demand "justice" for the offenders, by which we mean some fitting and unpleasant punishment. Yet after our initial expression of sympathy and outrage on behalf of victims, when it comes time to put "justice" into effect, we begin to rein in our punitive passions and qualify our demands. We scruple about judging the offender before the due process of a legal trial; about exaggerating his guilt in the heat of the moment; about the harsh treatment he might suffer at the hands of criminal justice authorities; and so on.

Provisionally, we might explain this complex response to crime in the following way: on the one hand, our membership in a self-governing political community impels us to punitive indignation; on the other, our humanity – our sense of ourselves as independent individuals with private needs and fears (rather than as duty-bound citizens) – tends to relax our demand for "justice" and to focus our attention instead on repairing the damage done by crime and providing for future security.

The connection, however rudimentary, that thus appears between punishment and republicanism is echoed in the work of a prominent contemporary advocate of the "restorative justice" movement, John Braithwaite. A chief concern of the restorative justice movement is to promote the reconciliation of the offending and offended parties and the reconstitution of disrupted community bonds. Braithwaite and co-author Philip Pettit ground this objective in republican political theory.[1] They, like most other advocates of restorative justice, explicitly reject retribution, among other traditional forms of punishment. Nevertheless, they recognize some validity in the phenomenon of moral indignation, as evidenced by their interest in victim satisfaction ("victims' rights") and in what Braithwaite calls "reintegrative shaming."[2] In order to restore community solidarity, restorative justice makes use of community conferences, during which offenders are confronted with their victims and with representatives of the community. As Braithwaite has shown, this sort of confrontation shames offenders and brings them to express genuine remorse for their actions. This process reintegrates offenders and victims into a single community. Many would recognize in this pattern of shaming, remorse, and reconciliation an important aim of retributive punishment, as ordinary people would understand it. Braithwaite and Pettit's republican approach to criminal justice sets out to satisfy a core goal of retributive punishment even while departing from its traditional methods.

What is important for our purposes here is to consider this connection between republicanism and punishment, and to see whether republican political theory might have something to offer our understanding of punishment that would allow us to improve on the shortcomings of the reigning liberal punishment theory (cf. Introduction, 9–12). In the same work, Braithwaite and Pettit echo some of the now common objections to liberal punishment theory – especially its paternalistic tendency – and the republican alternative they adopt is in part a reaction to liberalism's failure in this regard. According to their position, "republican liberty" cannot be conceived separately from civic membership in a political community. Hence the republican interpretation of liberty "equates freedom not with being left alone [as liberalism does], but with being given equal protection before a suitable law" (57–8). For Braithwaite and Pettit, this definition of liberty serves as the foundation for such penal policies and practices (community conferences, reintegrative shaming) as best advance genuine community; at the same time, it avoids the paternalistic excesses of liberal consequentialism (such as punishment of the innocent and indeterminate sentencing).[3]

Yet serious questions may be raised about the passage taken by Braithwaite and Pettit's argument from the "republican idea" to the institutional reforms they recommend. The authors connect the idea of equality before the law to the long republican tradition stretching back to the classical republics, such as ancient Rome.[4] This connection with the tradition of the austere ancient republics, and with those republics' commitment to legislating public morality, makes sense when the authors endorse shaming and even legal "moralizing" as a core feature of republican criminal justice (88). But one begins to wonder why, unlike the historical republics, the authors stop short of imposing harsh penalties to match the community's harsh denunciation of the worst criminals. If a body of citizens can denounce – and according to Braithwaite and Pettit *ought* to denounce – a murderer as having committed the ultimate wrong against a fellow citizen, towards whom he owed a duty of loyalty, then are we really to be surprised when those citizens demand more than mere public shaming of the murderer as the condition of restoration of community solidarity?[5] The authors themselves concede that this is a potential problem in their account and suggest that the maximum penalties established in republican law might have to be quite severe. Yet they maintain that those harsh penalties would never have to be used in practice – according to them, merely legislating harsh penalties without using them "may achieve the symbolic reprobative functions of the criminal law while toning down [its] excesses" (176). But should we assume that an actual republican community, inspired by the republican idea, *can* be satisfied with nothing more than mere denunciation of crime?

Thus, although Braithwaite and Pettit make the intriguing connection between republican principles and punishment as a moral phenomenon, I believe they have not thoroughly weighed the qualities of the republican spirit that would predominate in the kind of society whose principles they articulate so well. As my exegesis of Plato's understanding of republican life in its full complexity will show, Braithwaite and Pettit are mistaken in assuming that republican citizens would tend to be mild in their views on punishment. It is easy for us, living in a cosmopolitan, "Western" world informed by liberalism and Enlightenment rationalism, to fall into this error, because we easily forget that our own societies are not purely republican. It cannot be assumed, therefore, that our own comparatively mild attitudes towards criminality would also be those of more purely republican societies. Nevertheless, despite our different social, cultural, and historical contexts, we admire and to some extent still strive to affirm republican principles, and this, as the argument of the present study will suggest, makes us at least partly receptive to the republican attitude towards punishment – much more receptive than Braithwaite and Pettit believe. The re-examination of the question of punishment in the context of *classical* republicanism is, therefore, not merely of antiquarian value. It is of interest to us primarily because the problems of punishment are treated as acute moral-political problems by classical republican thought, and these same problems are implicated in our own debates about the rights of criminals and victims and the purpose of punishment. In classical republican thought, these problems are raised more urgently and radically (as I hope to show), and in this it may still be of great use to us.

Although Plato wrote dialogues on a wide range of subjects, he never wrote a dialogue with punishment as its unifying theme. The most extensive treatment of punishment in Plato occurs in a dialogue, the *Laws*, whose unifying theme is legislation – or, more precisely, the legislative art required for founding a small, participatory republic. The implication seems to be that the subject of criminal justice cannot be understood except in light of the broader issue of law and republican rule. Before we turn to Plato's treatment of punishment, therefore, we must first consider this larger context. This will require some extensive exegesis, some of which may be challenging to readers who are not students of the history of political thought. Readers unfamiliar with Plato in particular may be surprised at the amount of attention paid to dramatic elements in the dialogue, as distinguished from straightforward analysis of the Stranger's "theoretical" arguments. This, however, is unavoidable given the dialogue form, in which the drama provides essential clues for correctly understanding the theoretical arguments.

The *Laws* takes as its theme not politics as a whole, but a certain *kind* of politics – republican politics. It is taken for granted in a republic that not men, but laws, must rule. This sharply sets off the *Laws* from Plato's other two political dialogues, the *Republic* and *Statesman*, both of which culminate in the praise of the rule of the wise, who ought not (it is argued) to be restricted by any fixed laws.[6] It is not surprising, then, that there is little occasion in those two dialogues for any discussion of penal law, whereas in the *Laws* such a discussion takes up nearly one-quarter of the entire conversation about the institutions of a well-ordered republic.[7] The unique perspective of the *Laws*, as distinguished from the *Republic* and the *Statesman*, reflects its essentially civic and legalist view of political life (as distinguished from the fully philosophical one that might be encountered in most of the other Platonic dialogues). It is essential to this view that it accepts as fundamental a respect for the law and for its authority.[8] So we are not surprised that two of the three characters in this dialogue are prominent citizens of the oldest and most famous republics of ancient Greece – Kleinias the Cretan and Megillus the Spartan.

This is *not* to say that the *Laws* is simply conventional. It is perhaps better to say that the fundamental attitude of respect for law is one that admits of being either more or less reflective. For example, respect for law is common to Kantian rational autonomy and to the beliefs of the rustic citizens of Magnesia (the city-state described in the *Laws*), although it goes without saying that there is a sea of difference between the two in terms of their critical sophistication. Similarly, while the third interlocutor in the *Laws* – the nameless Athenian "Stranger" – expresses a respect for the ancient laws of Greece, he does not do so blindly, and in the course of the discussion we find him raising far-reaching philosophical questions about the wisdom and origins of those laws. Yet unlike Socrates (who needles the public authorities with his sceptical questions), the Stranger proceeds cautiously, initially deferring to the most ancient beliefs of the Greeks (even when these appear quite childish), until the comparative political advantages of accepting or rejecting them can be carefully weighed. In keeping with his public-spirited mission – the framing of a complete code of laws for a city-state of Greek colonists – the Stranger never allows his philosophical interests to take centre stage; rather, he accepts the ends of republican life, while reflecting on those ends and promoting enlightened reform whenever possible.[9]

The preceding observations on the tone of the dialogue and its characters are necessary for understanding the principles of the Stranger's legislative art, to which we now turn. A discussion of these principles will set the stage for our account of the Stranger's penal law.

The ends of republican politics, which the Stranger initially acknowledges and allows to inform his early discussion of legislation, include order and security. In the simplest sense, a city cannot be said to be well governed if it is not stable, self-sufficient, strong in defence against its neighbours, and united (626c–627c). Since the "unjust" (*adikoi*) members of the city cannot be allowed to prevail, only three possible alternatives remain, according to the Stranger: the unjust must be completely destroyed, or they must be enslaved to the just and law-abiding citizens, or the unjust and the just should be reconciled and made friends (*philous*) through laws laid down by a wise judge or legislator (627e–628a). Kleinias, to whom the choice of these alternatives is addressed, picks the last option, apparently opting for the most politically practicable course of action (as either killing or enslaving a potentially large number of citizens would involve great difficulties; see 628a and cf. 625c–626b).[10]

Although the Stranger begins by accepting as fundamental the city's right to preserve itself against external and internal threats, he quickly convinces his two Dorian companions that virtue is the highest concern of the city and that therefore, mere security cannot be the city's sole preoccupation. This must be true precisely from the city's own point of view, since the city's highest laws and institutions aim explicitly at the virtue of its citizens (628c–e). Virtue, in turn, can be understood not simply as subordinate to the preservation of the city – as a mere set of habits of heart and mind that render individual citizens serviceable to the whole – but as an end in itself: as human excellence. The Stranger appeals to his companions' own sensibilities when he argues that defensive war and domestic order are not ends in themselves, but rather must be regarded as being in the service of peace and the peaceful exercise of the virtues for their own sake. Thus the martial virtues and the virtue of loyalty to one's regime must be regarded as only the lowest part of virtue as a whole (cf. 628c–e with 631b–d). In short, in seeking to reconcile the just and unjust, the law must also try to reconcile the two distinct ends of legislation – order and human virtue.

This important introductory exchange between the Stranger and his Dorian companions sets the tone for the remainder of the dialogue in setting up, as a kind of methodological requirement, that enacted law must be able to persuade rather than merely command and coerce. Accordingly, the commandments of the law must be accompanied by preambles that communicate to citizens the wise purpose of the laws and encourage them to obey willingly (719e–720a, 722c–723b). The Stranger adheres to this standard throughout the dialogue, artfully weaving together argument, exhortation, and command (although this has the effect of making the legal preambles somewhat complex in their structure). By examining the preambles specifically bearing on criminal justice, we can hope to gain insight into what the Stranger understands to be the proper civic view of the purpose and measure of punishment.

Two legal preambles address criminal justice. Before beginning to legislate, the Stranger delivers a formal speech as if all the citizens of the future colony were present (715e–734e), and this speech serves as a general preamble to the laws as a whole. Among the topics taken up by the general preamble is criminal justice (at 728b–d and 730d–732b). The Stranger later returns to criminal justice in Book 9, where he elaborates a special preamble to the penal laws. We will look at these two preambles in order.

The Penology of the General Preamble

The Stranger's Rationalist Penological Principle

The section of the general preamble containing the discussion of wrong-doing and punishment is nested within a longer section whose subject is the right treatment of one's soul, body, and wealth, respectively – the three major categories of one's private property, as distinguished from what belongs to the gods, parents, or the city (726a–734e; cf. 723e).[11] According to the preamble, the highest and most divine possession is the soul. The goodness of the soul consists not in having its desires fulfilled indiscriminately, but in practising those things the lawgiver praises as noble and abstaining from the things he condemns as base (727b, 727c–d). Lower in rank than the soul is the body (i.e., health and life), and lower still and in last place among one's private possessions is wealth (727d–728a). The preamble goes on to exhort citizens to honour the pronouncements of the lawgiver above their own desires and gives an argument explaining *why* they should do so, stressing human ignorance about the most important things. Those who assume that "everything done in Hades is bad" judge incorrectly, since in fact "one doesn't know whether things aren't just the opposite – it may be that among the gods below are to be found the things that are by nature the greatest goods of all for us" (727d). Therefore, one who "considers survival to be always good" would be misled, since whether one's own life is good for oneself depends on what happens in Hades.

At first glance the preamble seems only to be asserting a pious dogma. In fact, however, while the preamble explicitly states that we do not know with any certainty that the things in Hades are bad for us, it equally implies that we do not know whether the things there are *good* either. Apparently, we must rely on the superior wisdom of the ancient poets, who have praised the just life as good for men in both this life and the next. Yet the veracity or authenticity of ancient reports may reasonably be doubted (cf. 624a–625a with 636d), not to mention that the poets themselves are notorious for their fabrications (cf. 669c–d, 700d–e, 719c). Thus, when we begin to reflect on the preamble's seemingly doctrinaire exhortation, we are surprised to discover that it in fact establishes not a dogma but *reason* as its authority. More precisely, it establishes that (1) what the law commands as good is what is good *for oneself*, and (2) what is good for oneself is to be ascertained by evidence available to the individual reasoning human being. The Stranger even goes so far as to attribute to the ancient legislators, to fathers, and to the gods, alike, the view that the virtuous, law-abiding way of life is preferable to the vicious, because it is more pleasant and more beneficial to the virtuous man himself (660e–663b).[12]

The preamble goes on to draw the conclusion that "what is gravest is to become similar to men who are wicked, and, in becoming similar, to avoid good men and be cut off from good conversation, and instead to attach oneself to the bad by seeking intercourse with them" (728b). The preamble here seems to assume that virtue makes human beings happy and that the laws of the city (at least if they are well ordered) lead to virtue. From these assumptions it would follow that those who disobey the laws are actually harming themselves. Apparently, the philosophically inclined Stranger views exclusion from decent society and good conversation as the worst harm that can come to one's soul as a consequence of injustice, and he makes no mention of shame. Yet perhaps someone else would add that pangs of guilt will forever haunt the criminal, spoiling any future enjoyment he might hope for. At any rate, the harm that injustice does to the unjust person himself is, by this account, a much worse consequence for him than any scourging or imprisonment that may be imposed on him by the city as punishment. In this way, the preamble attempts to provide a rational explanation for the public assertion of the wrongness of crime as such – an explanation that is meant to be convincing even without the threat of punishment. In doing so it taps into, and relies on, the belief of all decent citizens that injustice is somehow bad for us, not merely because it exposes us to the threat of a stiff penalty, but more importantly because unjust actions are ugly and therefore degrading to the soul of the doer of injustice.

The Stranger goes on to argue that this purportedly natural and necessary consequence of crime is not a punishment at all, for what is ordinarily understood as punishment is not justice but "retribution" (*timōria*), "since what is just [*to dikaion*] – including judicial punishment [*dikē*] – is noble" (728c). We might be tempted to call the depraved condition into which the criminal falls as a result of his actions a kind of natural justice, but this would be incorrect, according to the Stranger. Justice makes human beings better, not worse, but "both he who undergoes this [i.e., retribution], and he who escapes it are miserable: one because he does not get cured, the other because he is destroyed in order that many others may be saved" (ibid.).[13]

It is quite surprising that the preamble takes for granted such a sharp distinction between justice (*dikē*) and retribution (*timōria*), considering that to the ancient Greeks retribution meant primarily desert-based punishment deliberately and justly imposed by the political authority. We are thereby further alerted to the radical character of the Stranger's definition of penal justice, and prompted to wonder whether the preamble is correct in proclaiming justice to be always beneficial and never harmful. It is true that when punishment encourages the offender to mend his ways, we welcome this and consider it a benefit to the offender himself. But does it follow from this that punishment can never be called just when it does harm, as the Stranger claims? On the contrary, do we not often harm criminals, believing this (the harm itself) to be what they *justly* deserve? To put it another way, the preamble's claim that retribution is neither just nor noble flies in the face of the seemingly universal experience of punitive indignation. For many – perhaps most – people, getting "payback" against those who have done them wrong is essential to what "punishment" means – and when we punish we do so *because* it harms criminals, not despite this. To be sure, that a moral opinion is popular does not make it true; but it does make it necessary for any contrary opinion, such as the one advanced in the Stranger's preamble, to establish itself on firm grounds. Why, then, does the Stranger simply beg the question regarding the justice of retributive punishment? The reason for his seemingly inadequate approach to the question of retribution begins to emerge in the sequel of the general preamble.

"Every real man must be of the spirited type"

Shortly after its initial statement on justice and retribution, the general preamble speaks about the place of the passion of spiritedness in public life, placing great emphasis on the political necessity of encouraging certain punitive attitudes towards crime. According to the preamble, citizens who merely refrain from doing injustice themselves are only third in point of honour. They are less honourable than those who actively work to prevent unjust men from doing injustice by willingly cooperating with the magistrates. "Yet the great man in the city, the man who is to be proclaimed perfect and the bearer of victory in virtue, is the one who does what he can to assist the magistrates in inflicting punishment" (730d). "Every real man," the preamble continues, "should be of the spirited type [*thumoeididē*]" (731b). Since this punitive sort of person is likely to be moved to demand retribution (cf. 731d6), it is surprising to find such a type being praised by the preamble, shortly after it has denied that retribution is noble or just. The preamble proceeds to explain that every real man should be of the spirited type because "there is no way to avoid those injustices done by others that are both dangerous and difficult, or even impossible, to cure, except to fight and defend oneself victoriously, in no way easing up on punishment … This every soul is unable to do, if it lacks a high-born spiritedness" (731b). In other words, effective law enforcement in a small republic, where the citizens must act as their own police force *and* judiciary, requires the vigilance and enthusiastic participation of all. This may be difficult to sustain, the preamble seems to suggest, if the citizens are not animated by a punitive spirit, without which few people will want to get personally involved in such dangerous business as crime control if it is possible to leave the job to others. This is apparently why the legislator must promote spiritedness and praise as "perfect" those who harbour a zeal for punishment.[14]

Still, although the Stranger's preamble appears to praise the punitive citizen, it is careful not to call him "just" or to identify as "justice" the punishment he demands.[15] Moreover, what the Stranger actually says is not that the punitive man *is* perfectly virtuous, but that he is *to be proclaimed* perfect. The preamble does not, then, retreat from its earlier definition of just punishment, in light of which carrying out spirited punishment with the intention of doing harm cannot be considered virtuous in the strict sense. The preamble thus appears to acknowledge the political necessity of promoting spirited anger in a small republican city while at the same time (and with some apparent inconsistency) insisting on the lower moral status of retribution in light of some higher standard of justice – although we must remember that we have yet to see a demonstration of the grounds for this higher standard. The preamble's ambivalence towards retribution, and towards punitive anger, is also reflected in its admonition regarding the proper response to two different types of criminals. Although every real man must be of the spirited type, he should be "also as gentle as possible."[16] "In regard to the curable injustices men commit," one must first understand that no unjust man is ever voluntarily unjust. For no one anywhere would ever voluntarily acquire any of the greatest evils – least of all when the evil afflicts his most honored possessions. Now the soul, as we asserted, is truly the most honorable thing for everyone; therefore no one would ever voluntarily take the greatest evil into his most honorable possession and keep it for the rest of his life. So the unjust man, like the man who possesses bad things, is pitiable in every way, and it is permissible to pity such a man when his illness is curable; in this case one can become gentle, by restraining one's spiritedness and not keeping up that bitter, woman's raging. But against the purely evil, perverted man who cannot be corrected, one must let one's anger have free rein. This is why we declare that it is fitting for the good man to be of the spirited type and also gentle, as each occasion arises. (731c–d)

Here, the preamble makes explicit what was only implied or assumed earlier – that injustice somehow harms the soul of the unjust man – and admonishes citizens not to be indignant towards curable offenders but to pity them. Since no one would ever intentionally harm himself, the curably unjust offenders must have committed their wrongs involuntarily.

This passage in the Stranger's preamble recalls an argument made famous by Socrates, who held that all vice is done out of ignorance and therefore involuntarily.[17] Yet unlike Socrates's famous argument, the Stranger's argument does not go far enough, and as a result it falls into an inconsistency: if injustice always harms the soul of the unjust man, then why ought we to pity only the curable criminal but give vent to our anger against the incurable one? Should we not rather pity the incurably unjust man all the more for his condition (if it is more pitiable to be not only sick but also incurable)? Or does the preamble mean to imply that the incurably unjust man somehow manages to act voluntarily, in spite of the fact that he harms himself?[18] One might argue that a sign of the voluntariness of the incurable criminal's injustice is that he does not repent of his crime, even after suffering punishment. But, on the other hand, this incorrigible contempt for justice, by which the incurably unjust man shows his deep ignorance of what is truly good for him, may be a reason to pity him even more than his curable counterpart, since he is even less capable of helping himself and thus seems to act even less voluntarily (if voluntariness admits of degrees). Or, again, is there some other sense in which an action can be voluntary, other than as aiming at the good and avoiding the bad? None of these issues is settled in the general preamble, nor can they be, since in order to settle them a more complete account of the nature of criminality would be needed. That account is postponed until the special preamble that introduces the penal code in Book 9, when the Stranger treats serious crimes and punishments, or, as he puts it, "the greatest matters" among the judicial penalties (*dikai*).[19]

The Penal Preamble

Capital Crimes

The Stranger identifies three capital crimes: temple robbery, the overturning of the laws, and treason. The inclusion of these particular crimes among the greatest offences – two of which are crimes against the city and the other a crime against the gods – reflects the deep religiosity of the Stranger's republic and, at the same time, its intensely political character. All three are to be tried by the same judicial procedure (described by the Stranger at 855c–856a) and punished in the same way where citizens are concerned (856e–857a).[20] A citizen convicted of a capital crime should be punished with death, the Stranger argues, since "the judge should think of this man as already incurable" because the civic education he received under the best laws was not enough to prevent him from committing one of the greatest crimes (854e). The penalty of death should be regarded as a release from his miserable condition and as the least of evils for him. The death penalty is thus a *dikē*, since it benefits the criminal by helping him avoid the greater evil. The Stranger continues in this section to refer to capital punishment as *dikē* and as *timōria* interchangeably, maintaining the ambiguity we first saw in Book 5. Also, as before, we see an effort made in the law to invoke a sense of anger and indignation towards crime. In order to encourage magistrates to do their duty by punishing criminals, the preamble admonishes that if a magistrate "holding one of the highest offices in the city lets these things escape his notice – or, not because they escape his notice, but because of cowardice, fails to wreak retribution (*timōria*) on behalf of his own fatherland – such a citizen must be held to be second in evil" (cf. 856b–c with d). From this we may already conclude that, according to the Stranger, the best republic – which is supplied by the best laws that can be framed by a philosophical legislator – enacts capital punishment and embraces retribution (albeit equivocally).

In contrast to the extensive treatment given to capital crime, the subject of theft, which immediately follows, gets very short shrift. "As to stealing, whether someone steals something great or something small," the Stranger says, "let there be one law and one judicial retribution [*dikēs timōria*] in all cases" (857a): double the value of the stolen item is to be paid as a fine; if the convicted offender does not possess enough property to pay the fine, he is to be imprisoned until he does pay or until he persuades the successful prosecutor (857a–b). In response to this, Kleinias objects to the Stranger's proposal:

> How comes it, stranger, that we're saying it makes no difference to the thief whether he's convicted of stealing something great or something small, whether from sacred or profane places [*ex hieron ē hosion*], or whatever other respects in which a theft can be entirely dissimilar? For crimes that are thus various, is the lawgiver in no way to follow with penalties of a similar variety? (857b)

Kleinias's objection is provoked by the Stranger's attempt to make the penalties for theft proportional strictly to the material value of the stolen goods, regardless of what other significance the stolen goods may possess, such as their religious value. By putting special emphasis on the difference between the sacred and the profane, Kleinias seems to be indicating that he thinks the significance of crime is not reducible to its material value. He wants thieves guilty of ordinary theft, and those guilty of sacrilege, to be punished in proportion to what seems to him to be the different degrees of their injustice. In other words, Kleinias's objection presupposes an understanding of criminal culpability as indexed to some implicit scale of injustice, whose degrees of gravity can be related to the circumstances of each crime, which include, but are not limited to, its material value.

Kleinias's notion of a scale of injustices, and their corresponding punishments, *seems* intuitive. It is worth noting that many retributivists point to this sort of intuitive sense that injustices have moral degrees as evidence favouring their position. In response, the Stranger now welcomes Kleinias's objection, telling him that it has somehow "reminded" him of something important (857c). Could it be that Kleinias has reminded the Stranger of the self-evident truth of the existence of a scale of proportional crimes and punishments differing in kind (and not only in degree)? This seems impossible, however, in light of the Stranger's earlier discussion of penal justice (in the general preamble in Book 5), where justice was said to look to beneficial consequences and to nothing else. The Stranger's simple rule regarding the punishment of theft, which overlooks the distinction between sacred and profane, seems all the more surprising when we consider that the Stranger himself had included temple robbery among the greatest crimes. Could it be rather that the Stranger has deliberately provoked Kleinias's objection?[21]

As becomes clear in the sequel, the Stranger has been "reminded" not of the truth of our intuitive sense of the need for the sort of proportionality of crimes and punishments alluded to by Kleinias, but of something very different and much more strange. He now says that Kleinias's objection reminded him that "what pertains to the laying down of laws has never been worked out correctly in any way, as in fact can be said on the basis of what has cropped up now" (857c). Recalling his earlier argument about the need for laws to be accompanied by preambles (cf. 719c–723d), the Stranger goes on to assert that human beings living under all existing legislation resemble slaves being doctored by other slaves. Slave doctors, the Stranger explains, practise medicine on the basis of experience rather than knowledge, and prescribe treatments without persuasion or explanation, whereas free doctors practise their art by engaging in dialogue with their free patients, using arguments "that come close to philosophizing, grasping the disease from its source, and going back up to the whole nature of bodies" (857c–d).[22] The Stranger now claims that if one of the slave doctors should come across the free doctor with his patient, he would burst out laughing and declare, "Idiot! You're not doctoring the sick man, you're practically educating him, as if what he needed were to become a doctor, rather than healthy!" (857d–e). The Stranger's approval of the educational approach of the free doctor in the context of a discussion of penal laws seems to imply the superiority of a similarly enlightened approach to criminality. If injustice is analogous to disease, then it would seem to follow that the proper response to crime – that is, what criminals deserve – would be some sort of individualized treatment following the medical model, perhaps informed by some scientific art (*technē*). One imagines this art might be concerned with the individual diagnosis of the criminal and his spiritual disorder, and with the means that would be adequate to reform him. Yet it is difficult to see how such a "medical" art of criminal justice could be concerned with the evaluation of moral qualities of offences, which was the central point of Kleinias's objection. Is the Stranger attempting here, once again, to reassert the superiority of the rationalist conception of justice as beneficence in the face of Kleinias's assertion of penal proportionality as a moral fact?

Kleinias, however, resists the Stranger's remarkable claim here by agreeing with the scolding slave doctor (857e). This resistance on Kleinias's part in turn compels the Stranger to change course yet again. Whereas it seemed as if he and Kleinias had just reached an impasse, the Stranger now asserts, contrary to our expectation, that it may be possible to combine education and punishment after all – but that in order to arrive at that solution they would first need to undertake "a precise inquiry" into the nature of "all injustices" (859b–c). This short exchange serves to introduce one of the climaxes of the discussion of punishment (and perhaps of the whole work), which also happens to be the only "Socratic" elenchus, or cross-examination, of an interlocutor's fundamental opinions about justice in the dialogue.

Kleinias's Opinions about Punishment

Having excited Kleinias's interest, the Stranger recommends that they proceed to examine the opinions of the famous Greek legislators about the noble, the good, and the just things.[23] But the Stranger does not quite do this. Instead, he proceeds to examine how the noble and just things stand in the opinion of the interlocutors themselves – that is, "to what extent we now agree, and to what extent we disagree with ourselves" regarding "the noble things and all the just things" (859c–d). Furthermore, since Kleinias does all the answering while the Stranger asks questions, it is really only Kleinias's opinions about the noble, the good, and the just that are subjected to examination.

The Stranger begins to lay bare Kleinias's deepest beliefs about punishment by asking whether "our" opinions about the just and the noble are consistent. He elicits Kleinias's assent to the following:

> With respect to justice as a whole [*dikaiosunēs holōs*] and just human beings, deeds, and actions, we all somehow agree that all these are noble [*kala*]; so if someone would maintain that just human beings, even if they happen to be ugly in their bodies [*aischroi ta sōmata*], were nevertheless entirely beautiful [*pankalous*] people in respect to their very just disposition [*to dikaiotaton ēthos*] considered by itself, in almost no case would the one who speaks thus seem to speak off key. (859d–e)

The Stranger proceeds to argue, again with Kleinias's assent, that if all things are noble which partake of justice, then this would include the things we undergo or suffer just as much as the things we do. But if this is the case, the Stranger goes on, then they have contradicted the penal laws they had established earlier, for "presumably we established that the temple robber should die – justly – and the same for the enemy of well-made laws … and that while they were the most just of all sufferings, they were also the most shameful [*aischista*]" (860b). In this way, the just things and the noble things appear "to us" at one time to be all the same, and at another time opposed (ibid.). The Stranger adds that this inconsistency or confusion exists not only among "us," the legislators, but also among "the many," who, in view of these things, "proclaim without consonance that the noble things and the just things are separate" (860c).

It is not clear why the Stranger proceeds in this way, or in particular why he wishes to focus on what is sound and unsound in Kleinias's opinions about the noble things and the just things. Perhaps the Stranger means to imply that Kleinias's opinions about these matters will be representative of the opinions of the ancient legislators. Even if this interpretation of the Stranger's way of proceeding here is correct, it leaves us to wonder about its relevance to his purported aim of combining penal law with education. The Stranger had stated that he thinks nothing that pertains to laying down laws had been correctly worked out in any way, which would mean that the most that could be hoped for from a critical examination of the opinions of past or present legislators is greater awareness of their errors. Does the Stranger believe that knowledge of the nature of justice and injustice in the soul – the matter that would be most important in guiding the educational (therapeutic) "punishment" of criminals – can somehow be gleaned from knowledge of the errors of the legislators and the many, alike, regarding the noble, the good, and the just things?

Kleinias admits that he is guilty of the contradiction imputed to him (860c). But was this contradiction unavoidable?[24] In the first place, is it really necessary to define justice, and thus also penal justice, as something that is entirely noble, or could it not rather be the case that some things are just without also being noble? For example, the law commands some things because they are noble and choiceworthy for their own sake (e.g., education), but it also commands other things merely because they are necessary (e.g., war). In this way, while all of the things commanded by the law would be just (in the sense that the city has a right to command them), not all would be noble. Would it not, then, be possible to understand punishment as one of the things that are just but not noble? Furthermore, the Stranger had just distinguished between the beauty of the soul and that of the body. Thus, even if punishment of criminals damaged their bodies, making them appear physically ugly as a result of their suffering, it might still be argued that such suffering affects their souls in the opposite way: by undergoing just punishment, their souls may become better (as the Stranger's preamble earlier suggested) and therefore more beautiful or noble in this more important respect. The reader is left wondering why Kleinias did not avail himself of any of these possible arguments. At the very least he could have argued, as the Stranger had done earlier, that in the case of the incurably unjust man, death would be the lesser evil for him, and therefore executing him would be a noble thing.

The fact that Kleinias does not take refuge in any of these arguments is of the highest significance, on my reading of the dialogue. It seems likely that Kleinias refused to accept the premise that punishment can be both just and noble, and then did not try to avoid open self-contradiction, because he believes that punishment *ought* to be essentially *harmful* to the criminal (and thus in no way noble).[25] In other words, Kleinias seems to believe that punishment is just precisely when it is retributive – that is, when it harms criminals for the sake of harming them, since that is what they deserve, according to Kleinias. But why is Kleinias so strongly attached to this view in the first place, even at the cost of embarrassing self-contradiction? It is true that deterrence, as distinguished from retribution, also requires punishments to be harmful, so one might be tempted to think that Kleinias is not a retributivist at all, but that he merely prefers tough penalties because they deter most effectively. This, however, would be to misunderstand Kleinias. For deterrence presupposes only that punishments must appear *to criminals* to be bad for them (not noble), while nothing prevents more virtuous citizens – who value living justly more highly even than the comfort and liberty of the body – from regarding the same punishment as being corrective and thus in the truer sense beneficial. Yet as we saw, Kleinias denies precisely this; he therefore cannot be said to be concerned with deterrence alone. It appears that Kleinias is firmly convinced of the justice of retribution. It is doubtful that he is himself fully aware of the confused state of his own opinions regarding the relation of punishment to justice and nobility, or of the reasons behind his attachment to retribution – although as we have seen, he does seem to express some perplexity regarding his self-contradiction. As readers of the dialogue, however, we have leisure to reflect on the deeper psychological reasons for this attachment. As we will see shortly, those reasons will prove to be significant for our understanding of the problem of punishment in the republican context.

It is important to keep in mind that throughout the whole discussion between the Stranger and Kleinias, it has been assumed (on the authority of the ancient legislators) that justice is the health and goodness of the soul. This is what had allowed the Stranger to make the argument that just punishment makes men good, since it makes them more law-abiding and therefore more just. Up to now, we have not had any strong reason to doubt this traditional moral assumption about justice (i.e., beyond our general scepticism of the hearsay by which traditional wisdom is passed down). Now, however, Kleinias's insistence that punishment ought to be harmful and shameful for the unjust man, even if it makes him more law-abiding – a view that he expresses as a legislator and on behalf of all legislators (see, again, 858e–859d) – forces us to question that traditional assumption. In other words, Kleinias's perplexity about punishment raises the more fundamental question of how, or whether, justice as law-abidingness is indeed good for the soul.

It bears repeating that Kleinias does indeed believe that justice is the health of the soul. When questioned by the Stranger regarding justice in general, he agreed that regardless of a man's physical condition, he is noble to the extent that his soul is just. If he did not believe this genuinely, he would have had no trouble rejecting this premise of the Stranger's argument, thus avoiding contradiction. Yet while Kleinias believes, and wants to believe, that justice is the health of the soul, he does not *know* it for a fact. Introducing preambles that attempt to explain, using rational argument, the purpose of the penal laws was the Stranger's idea, to which Kleinias showed initial reluctance when he sided with the "slave doctor," who commanded patients for the sake of their health, and against the "free doctor," who philosophized with them. Kleinias appeared to believe that just as knowledge of medicine is unnecessary for making bodies healthy, knowledge of justice is unnecessary for making souls healthy, since following the laws and cultivating the habit of law-abidingness is sufficient. From the point of view of a republican citizen, the virtue of justice is nothing more than the habit of lawfulness.

It seems at first that this applies to Kleinias's own case, since he has lived a life of public service in obedience to the Cretans and their laws, and believed this to be noble and good for him, without ever having examined his way of life until prompted to do so by the Stranger (see 625c–627c). In fact, however, the habitual practice of justice combined with a mere belief in its goodness are *not* sufficient for Kleinias. At the very opening of the dialogue, when the Stranger first asked Kleinias about the purpose of the ancient Cretan lawgiver, Kleinias openly admitted that the truth the lawgiver had divined was that, on every level, there exists a war of all against all, a condition in which true goodness consists in advancing one's own interest even at the expense of the interest of others (626b–d). According to Kleinias's explanation at that time, it follows from this truth that as it would be in accordance with nature for cities to dominate other cities rather than to treat them justly, so it would be equally in accordance with nature for individuals to exploit one another by force or fraud. This, according to Kleinias, is where "the argument" (*ton logon*) leads when it is "correctly followed … up to its source [*archēn*]" (626d). According to this argument, justice would at best be a conditional (and thus fragile) pact, or social contract, among individuals to refrain from mutual depredations – or, as Kleinias expresses this thought, "what most humans call peace [the lawgiver] held to be only a name" (626a). At worst, justice in this sense would be a kind of fraud that some men practise on others in order to make them more willing to serve others' interests while neglecting their own. Despite avowing this doctrine of selfishness, it is clear that Kleinias does not fully believe it himself, for if he did, he could not have lived his whole life according to the laws of the Cretans. Therefore, as that earlier exchange between Kleinias and the Stranger had implied, and as the later cross-examination of Kleinias's opinions regarding punishment and justice has more clearly shown, Kleinias is fundamentally confused about the goodness of justice as law-abidingness as a human virtue, and this confusion is a source of great perplexity for him.

Kleinias has now been shown to be divided between the two sides of his self-contradiction: he both believes *and* doubts, at one and the same time, that justice is the good condition of his soul.[26] It goes without saying that both of these things cannot be true, and this causes him to waver regarding the goodness of justice (see, again, 859d–860b and cf. 625c–627c). Kleinias's doubt about the goodness of justice, as revealed through his opinions about the goodness of punishment, is one instance of a psychological phenomenon that is a principal theme in all of Plato's thought.[27]

With this understanding of Kleinias's self-contradiction regarding the goodness of justice in mind, we can now better explain his indignation towards criminality and therefore his attachment to retributive punishment. Insofar as we are in doubt regarding the goodness of justice for the just person (i.e., whether or not he is better off obeying the law), we also equivocate regarding the badness of injustice in the soul of the criminal. We recall that earlier, in the general preamble to the laws of Magnesia, the Stranger had argued that the criminal does harm to himself by becoming like the unjust and by being deprived of the company of the just. This assumed that justice in the soul is good for the just person – a belief that Kleinias holds only ambivalently. Because of this ambivalence, Kleinias must also be less certain than the Stranger that the unjust person harms his soul by pursuing illicit gain. On the contrary, insofar as Kleinias believes that justice is a mere convention or habit of law-abidingness, and that it restrains human beings from seeking their own advantage at others' expense, he must think that the unjust have gotten away with a gain (whether in the form of property, or pleasure, or some power) and thus have gotten an advantage over the self-denying just men.[28] Indeed, we often speak of the criminal who escapes punishment as having "gotten away with it" – that is, gotten away with something *good*. As much as a republican community (even the best-ordered republic conceived by the Stranger) might cultivate the love of justice, most of its citizens will always find it easier to appreciate the goodness of external goods – wealth, power, and security – than the goodness of justice in the soul, even while affirming the higher status of the latter. As we have seen, when criminals are apprehended in Magnesia, the republic exacts punishments that sometimes impose deprivation or suffering exceeding what is required for compensation or deterrence, in a way that makes those punishments more "fitting" or "proportional" in kind to their crimes. These terms may have been opaque before, but we are now in a position to suggest that they are meant to express a reciprocity by which the balance of external goods is restored after it has been disrupted by an illicit gain. This would also explain why retributive punishment is essentially retrospective, since a "settling of accounts" depends on knowing how much is "owed."

Similarly, Aristotle in the *Nicomachean Ethics* affirms that justice is a human virtue, and he goes on to explain an error whereby "reciprocity is held by some people to be the just unqualifiedly … For either people seek to reciprocate harm for harm – if they do not, that is held to be slavish – or they seek to reciprocate good for good."[29] While Aristotle denies that reciprocity (*antipeponthos*) is justice unqualifiedly, he concedes that it is justice in a certain sense, since it helps preserve the city, which cannot exist without mutual exchange. Plato's Stranger and later Aristotle both teach, therefore, that the psychology behind retributive punishment involves the political concern with negating the perceived illicit gains of the crime, through reciprocal or retributive punishment, in order to prevent the unjust from having (whereas, from the philosophical perspective, they merely appear to have) more than the just. Without this restoration of the just distribution of external goods, the dignity of justice must suffer in the eyes of republican citizens, for it would seem to put the just person at a disadvantage vis-à-vis the unjust, contrary to the public doctrine that justice is good for the just. If the foregoing interpretation of Kleinias's opinions about justice and punishment is correct, then Kleinias's attachment to retributive punishment is ultimately founded on an error or confusion regarding the meaning of justice.

Having uncovered the fundamental confusion in Kleinias's opinions regarding justice and punishment, the Stranger might have gone on to complete the refutation. But unlike Plato's Socrates (who takes every opportunity to challenge his interlocutors' ignorance), the Stranger takes a more politic approach.

Voluntary and Involuntary Injustice

Kleinias being unable to find a way out of his perplexity, the Stranger comes to his rescue. He proposes that they look together to see how "they" (the legislators), as distinguished from "the many," hold a view of the just and the noble that is in fact harmonious, despite their apparent confusion (860c). When Kleinias agrees, the Stranger goes on to state a view – which he claims to have expressed earlier – "that the bad are all bad involuntarily in every respect" (860d):

> The unjust man is presumably bad, but the bad man is involuntarily so. Now it never makes sense that the voluntary is done involuntarily. Hence the man who does injustice appears involuntarily unjust to the one who sets down injustice as something involuntary. This is what I must agree to now. For I agree that everyone does injustice involuntarily. And if someone, out of love of victory or love of honor, asserts that the unjust are indeed involuntarily so, but that many voluntarily do injustice, my argument, at any rate, remains the former and not the latter. (860d–e)

We may recall that the Stranger had indeed already stated a modified version of this ("Socratic") thesis in the general preamble in Book 5. While, there, he had qualified his thesis to apply to curable injustices only (without offering any reasons for the qualification), he now presents that thesis in its unqualified form.

The Stranger does not take the time to share his deeper reasons for believing that all injustice is involuntary;[30] rather, he simply affirms his view because, as he says, he believes it to be true, and because it would not be pious or according to custom for him to lie (861d). Does the intervening examination of Kleinias's opinions about punishment somehow supply the insights necessary to substantiate the Stranger's claim here? The most important thing we have learned from that examination is that the civic view (shared by legislators and citizens alike) is divided not only regarding the question of the nobility of punishment but also regarding the more fundamental question of the goodness for the individual of the virtue of justice. Someone in doubt about the goodness of justice vacillates, thinking at some times that justice is better, at other times that injustice is preferable, but never having any settled knowledge of how the matter really stands. Now doubting something would seem to be the same as being in ignorance about it, and if that is so, is it not also the case that those who act in ignorance act involuntarily (if to make a free choice is to make it with full knowledge of what one is doing)?[31] Contrary to the general preamble's message that the incurable and "thoroughly evil" are appropriate objects of anger, no one who acts unjustly in fact desires injustice knowingly or voluntarily as long as he is in doubt about the goodness of justice. The Stranger seems to believe that such deep-seated doubt regarding the goodness of justice is much more widespread than we might care to believe (we may recall that it afflicts the legislators and "the many," alike), and this is the most profound psychological insight that Plato intends to teach through his treatment of punishment.[32] Such vacillating doubt may be discerned (in the right conversational setting) even in the most public-spirited model citizens, such as Kleinias himself. The same doubt may also be discerned in those who are on the opposite extreme: those who seem to be most dismissive or contemptuous of justice. It is striking that even the most cynical among us will still grow angry when he believes he has suffered wrong, thereby revealing a deeper concern for justice.[33] If this is right, then it follows that all injustice is involuntary in the strict or truest sense.

The most radical political consequences of the Stranger's view of crime and punishment can no longer be ignored. The Stranger's view destroys the distinction between voluntary and involuntary injustice, which was a core feature of all ancient legal traditions, according to the Stranger (861b), and which, perhaps, would be essential to any workable law code. Upon this distinction depend all laws pertaining to the mitigation of criminal liability, such as those recognizing conditions of duress, provocation, incompetence, and so on. (Indeed, it is such mitigation that gives our own, liberal criminal law its character of fairness and relative mildness.) In addition, the Stranger's thesis shakes our confidence in the therapeutic potential of punishment. We tend to treat first-time offenders more leniently than repeat offenders, in the belief that the former's injustice has more of the quality of error in it and is somehow less reflective of the offender's "true character." Thus we believe that the curable criminal is one who knows sufficiently well that injustice is harmful to his soul, and merely forgets temporarily or is swayed by powerful passions. A gentle penalty would be all that is required, as a reminder, to "cure" the first-time offender and to "set him straight." On the Stranger's view, however, the conventional forms of punishment – such as fines, threats, imprisonment, and physical suffering – could not be curative in the strict sense if all injustice is, as the Stranger claims, perpetrated in the context of the fundamental confusion regarding the goodness of justice for the just man. For deterrence of the first-time offender cannot cure him of his ignorance but can only induce him – conditionally and for a certain time – to refrain from injustice. He is not cured, because the deepest cause of his injustice – his ignorance – is not removed; indeed, it *cannot* be removed in this way. (To expect that such ignorance can be removed by punishment in any form would be to believe that punishment can be more educational than educational institutions!)

More radically still, the Stranger's thesis destroys the distinction between justice and injustice with respect to individual character. If each of us is compelled by our nature to do what he or she believes to be best, then just and unjust actions differ only in the sense that the former are carried out under the unstable belief that justice is better for us, whereas the latter are carried out under the opposite belief. It cannot be said that the just and the unjust differ in the character of their beliefs fundamentally, because, according to the Stranger's view, the vast bulk of human beings (the many and the legislators alike) vacillate, in doubt, between the opinion that justice is the health of the soul and the opinion that it is merely a useful habit of obedience. In the most fundamental sense, these are only two sides of the same state of soul: its ignorance regarding the goodness of justice (or, more broadly, of virtue).

It goes without saying that criminal law is unimaginable without distinctions between voluntary and involuntary and between culpable knowledge and inculpable ignorance. Clearly, the Stranger is fully aware of these radical implications, for he now explicitly raises the question of how the thesis he has just uttered will affect their ability to frame a penal code. Will they have to distinguish involuntary injustices from voluntary ones? Will they then have to enact greater penalties for voluntary crimes than for involuntary ones (legislating "in defiance of the difficulty")? Or will there have to be equal penalties for all on the grounds that there *are* no voluntary injustices (860e–861a)? The first alternative has been ruled out by the Stranger's thesis, while the second is politically impracticable (cf. 861b). The Stranger now claims that it may be possible to escape their difficulty if they can show how "these things are two [i.e., the voluntary and involuntary], and what the other difference is [i.e., between them], so that whenever someone imposes the judicial penalty on either of them, everyone may follow the things that are being said and may be able to judge, somehow or other, what is fittingly laid down and what is not" (861c). The Stranger signals thereby that what follows may be a more politically salutary doctrine than the view he has been developing up to this point. The alternative, "political" account of the psychological causes of crime that follows attempts to accommodate the punitive civic outlook, while at the same time gently moving that outlook as much as possible in the direction of the Stranger's enlightened understanding of the involuntariness of all injustice.

Actions and Motivations

The Stranger begins by asserting that some harms committed by citizens against one another in their associations have the character of the voluntary (*hekousion*), while others have the character of the involuntary (*akousion*). A harm done to another is not necessarily an injustice, whether great or small, nor is a benefit justice. Rather, "when a benefit comes to pass that is not correct [*ouk orthēn*], the one responsible for the benefit is committing an injustice" (862a–b). Generally speaking, "if someone gives something to somebody, or, on the contrary takes something away, such a thing shouldn't thus be called simply just or unjust, but what the lawgiver should observe is whether someone employs a just disposition and character in doing some benefit or injury to somebody" (862b). The lawgiver should concern himself with both injustice and harm, but he should keep the distinction between them straight when framing his criminal laws. Whenever some harm has been done, the laws should redress the injury by "preserving what may be destroyed, setting upright again what has fallen, and making sound what has been killed or wounded – and once compensation has made atonement for each of the injuries, he should always try through the laws to create friendship in place of discord between the doers and sufferers" (862b–c).

The Stranger's concern here with compensation and rehabilitation is consistent with the rationalist penological principle he has established. But what of the brief mention of friendship as a second and distinct aim of penal law, especially considering that the text implies that compensation paid to victims may in some cases be insufficient to restore friendship between the "doers" and "sufferers"?[34] We are left to wonder what more the legislator can be expected to do to satisfy the victims. Does the Stranger have in mind the legal provision for solemn ceremonies of reconciliation – perhaps involving symbolic sacrifices to substitute for the retributive punishment of the criminal? Or does he imagine a kind of conference, in which victims air grievances and remorseful offenders express their shame? Perhaps this is what the Stranger wishes for. Yet once we consider what we have already learned from the Stranger himself about the qualities of the republican character, and about the public attitude of the laws towards criminality, we cannot expect such mild measures to be sufficient to effect the necessary reconciliation. The Stranger does not mention retribution explicitly here, but it is likely that he would expect citizens and magistrates in his best republic to seek "reconciliation" (effectively, the mollification of the law-abiding and indignant majority) after crimes committed by punishing retributively, in addition to whatever would be required by way of compensation and assurance of future security. If this is what the Stranger believes would happen in practice, in spite of his own best wishes as legislator, then we can conclude that he has acquiesced in the practice of retribution as politically unavoidable, even (or especially) in a well-ordered republic.[35]

So much should be done by the legislator about the harms inflicted and suffered in the city. With respect to injustices, however, as distinguished from harms, the legislator's approach should be entirely therapeutic, according to the Stranger. When harms or benefits are done unjustly – that is, when they proceed from an unjust character – as many of these injustices as are curable, "being regarded as diseases in the soul," should be cured in the following way. "Whatever injustice, great or small, someone might commit," the legislator should "teach and compel" the unjust man "either never again to dare voluntarily [*hekonta*] to do such a thing or to do it very much less" (862c–d). To accomplish this, the legislator should employ deeds or words, pleasures or pains, honours or dishonours, and even fines or gifts. By these means he should try to "bring about hatred of injustice and desire, or lack of hatred, for the nature of the just" (862d–e). As for the offender whom the lawgiver perceives to be incurable, he should institute a "just penalty" (*dikēn*) of death, because he knows, "presumably," that it is worse for him to go on living. Such capital punishment confers a "double benefit" by releasing the offender from the greater evil of injustice and by emptying the city of bad men and setting an example for would-be criminals (862e).

The thrust of the passage we have just summarized is to separate conceptually the inner motivations of our actions from their external effects (i.e., harms or benefits), as well as to define once again the scope of penal justice proper (*dikē* – as distinguished from compensation on the one hand, and retribution on the other) as limited to the rehabilitation and improvement of the individual offender.

One important implication of the conceptual framework for penal legislation being developed by the Stranger here is the radical innovation of committing to individualized punishment. For the purpose of meting out an appropriate penalty, every actual criminal law code has recourse to one or another general classification scheme for the different types of crime according to their effects (e.g., murder vs assault, robbery vs burglary, etc.). This allows the classification of individual crimes as well as their ranking in terms of severity – the implicit assumption being that the greater the harm done, the worse (morally) was the psychological disposition of the perpetrator. Thus, even after we account for extenuating and aggravating circumstances for each particular crime we may still maintain that, all other things being equal, a murderer is more culpable (and therefore liable to a more severe punishment) than a pickpocket. A corresponding classification scheme of mandatory penalties (or ranges of permissible penalties) allows each crime to be indexed to its appropriate penalty. Yet there seems to be no inherent connection between the effect of a deed and the particular psychological state under which it was committed – and this is part of what the Stranger's sharp distinction between injustice and harm is meant to draw to our attention.[36] Nothing prevents the most heinous, misanthropic person imaginable from scrupulously obeying the law out of a concern for his own safety, just as nothing prevents an admirable character from tragically falling prey to an impulse (perhaps even a noble impulse) that in the circumstances leads to a great crime (consider the crime of Prometheus).[37] The Stranger's radical separation of injustice from harm would therefore preclude any attempt at general classification of crimes and punishments, and would require all punishment to be individualized. Every criminal would have to be examined by the judge, on a case-by-case basis and without the aid of legal equivalencies determined in advance, as to his psychological disposition, regardless of the harm done by his crime. Although the Stranger does not here explicitly draw out the implications – which are completely lost on Kleinias and Megillus – of his radical conceptual innovation, we must keep them in mind as we proceed.

So much is clear regarding the task of the legislator in his approach to crime, but how the Stranger's distinction bears on the question of "the voluntary" is not. We seem to be invited to conclude that the two forms of the voluntary correspond somehow to actions and motivations, respectively – but exactly what this means remains mysterious. Earlier, the Stranger had asserted that "the bad are all bad involuntarily in every respect" – or, to put it differently, human beings always and by nature pursue what they believe to be their greatest good. It is difficult to see how this general principle can admit of any meaningful *moral* distinction between actions and motivations.[38] If we always intend what is best for us then every action we choose, whether harmful or useful to society, is done for the sake of our greatest good, and since the voluntary is always directed at our own good in this way, there would seem to be no room left for speaking of the "voluntary" in other senses, unless based on distinctions that are incidental.[39]

Most commentators, however, understand the Stranger to be introducing a concept of voluntary action in a "legal" as distinguished from a philosophical sense. According to this view, the voluntariness of a crime in the legal sense would only be used to determine criminal liability, but not its injustice, which is always involuntary.[40] This legal concept of voluntary action allows the traditional distinction between voluntary and involuntary crimes to stand, but it does so only tendentiously. That is because the physical aspect of crime (i.e., the harm), as the Stranger has defined it here, would strictly no longer have any relation to guilt or desert in the ordinary sense (the sense in which the ancient lawgivers and cities have understood it). Unlike the Stranger, actual societies distinguish voluntary from involuntary crime so that they can separate those who deserve punishment (the "unjust") from those who do not deserve it (the "just"). This is exactly how the citizens of Magnesia will understand the pronouncements of their penal law: when that law enjoins that voluntary crimes should be punished more harshly than involuntary ones (cf., for example, 864c ff.), Magnesians will believe that such crimes deserve harsher punishments for retrospective considerations,[41] whereas according to the Stranger they would "deserve" this because the greater corruption of the voluntary criminal's soul requires stronger cure.[42] In short, while the Stranger's solution works on a political level, it fails to resolve Kleinias's moral dilemma.[43] At any rate, for Kleinias, the Stranger's thought here remains opaque, prompting him to ask for clarification.

Justice and Injustice in the Soul

The Stranger obliges Kleinias by offering an account of the parts of the soul responsible for criminality. This account apparently has its origins in common opinion – in what "you say and hear from one another … about the soul" (863b).[44] According to this popular view, there are three things in the soul that can cause wrongs or faults (*hamartēmata*):[45] spiritedness, pleasure, and ignorance (cf. *Republic* 436b–441c). Ignorance is itself further divided into two parts or kinds: the "simple" version resembles Socratic ignorance in that it is aware of itself (it is consciousness of knowing what one does not know), while the "double" version "occurs when someone lacks understanding because he partakes not only of ignorance but also of the opinion that he is wise" (863c). The Stranger assumes that only the presumptuous kind of ignorance will ever be responsible for grave wrongs (with respect to the extent of the injury, and to the degree of injustice from which it flows), and directs the lawgiver to punish it severely (presumably because reform of such a person would require more extensive correction). Crimes stemming from the simple kind of ignorance, on the other hand, are to be forgiven or dismissed with light penalties (863d). In this way, the Stranger's scheme for punishing ignorance conveniently reconciles the demands of deterrence (in punishing the more dangerous crime more severely) with those of justice (in dispensing the right kind of reformative penalty to each kind of criminal). It would even satisfy the demands of just deserts (by punishing the arrogant, and thus apparently more unjust, criminal more severely than the humble one) – *if*, that is, the Stranger's immediate effort to establish theoretically the voluntariness of some crimes should ultimately prove successful.[46]

All three of these forces or parts in the soul, the Stranger continues, "often turn each man in directions opposite to that toward which his intention … draws him" (863e). In the face of spiritedness or pleasure, "we … say" that we might be "stronger" or "weaker" – that is, we might be able to conquer our passion and avoid doing wrong, or conversely we might succumb and be conquered by it. In the case of ignorance, however, "we've never heard that one of us is 'stronger,' while another is 'weaker'" (863d). The Stranger gives little by way of explanation of the foregoing account, evidently because he expects it to be already familiar to his audience, Kleinias and Megillus. To be sure, there is little need to describe how pleasure, spiritedness (*thumos*, which primarily refers to anger or aggression), or ignorance can lead to wrongdoing. It is also fairly evident what the Stranger means by our being either "weaker" or "stronger" in the face of these influences. We have all had experiences of struggling with strong passions. Sometimes we struggle successfully, but other times we seem to surrender to, and even welcome, the illicit passion, although at the same time we say we somehow "know" that what we do is wrong. This is the very experience we point to when we speak of some wrongs as being voluntary, since it seems that it is "up to us" whether we continue to struggle against our illicit passions or surrender to them. On the other hand, we recognize circumstances in which a passion is so strong that resistance is altogether impossible; but perhaps these latter cases are less common, so that for the most part our experience with intemperate passions gives us the sense that, however hard it might be to resist temptation, we are ultimately in control and thus accountable.[47] Lastly, we know that when it comes to ignorance, as distinguished from passion, there is no way to struggle against it, which is why we tend to think that ignorance extenuates culpability.

In a kind of addendum or corollary to this popular psychology of criminality, the Stranger further elaborates the meaning of justice and injustice. "I would clearly define for you," the Stranger now says to his companions, "what I say is the just and the unjust, without complication" (863e). Up to now, justice was conceived to be lawful conduct and the habitual disposition to such conduct, while injustice was understood as criminal action and a criminal disposition. The Stranger now elaborates on that earlier conception by defining injustice as "the tyranny in the soul of spiritedness, fear, pleasure, pain, feelings of envy, and desires, whether it does some injury or not." "When, on the other hand, the opinion about what is best (however a city or certain private individuals may believe this will be) holds sway in souls and brings order to every man, then, even if it is in some way mistaken, what is done through this, and the part of each man that becomes obedient to such a rule, must be declared to be entirely just and best for the whole of human life" (863e–864a). The first part of the Stranger's claim – that the tyranny of the passions is injustice in the soul – has a certain plausibility. Yet it is startling to hear the second part of the Stranger's pronouncement, that justice in the soul is adherence to an opinion about what is best *however a city or certain private individuals may define it* – even if that opinion is mistaken. This has been described by one commentator as the "good conscience" view of justice.[48] Everyone (even the staunchest libertarian) would rightly be alarmed by such a public doctrine, since it would justify even the most destructive and misanthropic ways of life, so long as they were led consistently, in accordance with some principle.[49] One consideration goes part of the way to assuage the reader's alarm: in the Stranger's republic there will be strict regulation of moral opinion through extensive educational laws (see especially Books 6–7), and heavy penalties will be imposed for heresy (see Book 10). This effectively means that the opinion about what is best that will predominate shall be the opinion of the law, which in the present context we may assume to be wise. At the same time, it is necessary to mention that while the foregoing may be sufficient for the ordinary citizen, there remains the question of what the legislator himself – whether as founder or as one of the constituted "guardians of the law" (see 752d ff.) – will look to for guidance as his standard of what is best. Presumably, the true legislator must ultimately look to reason and nature itself for guidance regarding what is best, or to the gods (see 645b and context).[50]

With this account, the Stranger appears to have fulfilled his appointed task of vindicating the traditional distinction, fundamental to all criminal law, between voluntary and involuntary wrongdoing, despite his own earlier assertion that anyone who does wrong does it involuntarily. Kleinias, at any rate, expresses his satisfaction. To repeat, it now appears to have come to light that crime is voluntary, and thus culpable, in those cases in which the wrongdoing individual has declined to struggle against his illicit passions as he ought to have done (and, presumably, could have done). The Stranger, for his part, seems satisfied as well, as he does not now repeat his earlier objection to the law's distinction between voluntary and involuntary injustices. Perhaps it is enough for him that the new distinction between the voluntary and the involuntary has the advantage of echoing and legally reaffirming the common civic understanding. Yet it goes without saying that the political utility – even necessity – of the legal definition of the voluntary hardly suffices for a proof. The Stranger's silence and apparent acquiescence in this matter leaves many questions unanswered. As we have seen, the Stranger had previously gone out of his way to distinguish his own view from the conventional opinion shared by Kleinias, Megillus, and the city as a whole, which leads us to suspect that the Stranger ultimately regards the legal distinction he has elaborated, between voluntary and involuntary crime, as spurious. It should come as no surprise that the author of the *Republic* would be willing to accommodate a certain degree of ignorance in political life that he (or his Stranger) may regard as ineradicable. Although the Stranger had earlier said that it would not have been pious or lawful for him to conceal the truth (cf. 861d), it is precisely the requirements of lawfulness and piety that now compel him to silence his philosophical objections.[51]

The Stranger ends his long discussion of the voluntary by repeating or summarizing his threefold psychological scheme – ostensibly so that it may be "still more firmly fixed in the memory" – but with an alteration that proves to be significant. In the "repetition," "the striving for expectations and true opinion concerning what is best" replaces ignorance as one of the three causes of crime (864a–b). The Stranger does not explain this substitution and appears to regard the repetition as identical to the original (perhaps because the striving for true opinion may be supposed to imply ignorance about what is best). Yet the Stranger's casual manner of speaking cannot silence our sense of the disproportion between the repetition and his first statement that the rule in the soul of the "opinion about what is best" is nothing other than justice itself. Apparently, a republican society will continue to look up to reason and the gods as its highest authorities, even as in practice it acts to suppress anyone who strives to ascend from the confused and incomplete public dogmas to the truth about what is best – an uneasy tension, which may explain both Socrates's popularity in Athens and his eventual condemnation and execution under its laws. This tension or opposition receives its fullest expression in the *Laws* in what proves to be the peak of the whole dialogue: the theological justification of the law against impiety in Book 10 (a discussion of which is beyond the scope of the present study).

What makes this opposition all the more remarkable is that the Stranger calls the city of Magnesia, founded by the Stranger himself, the best practicable regime (albeit only second-best in point of virtue; see 739a–e). This may imply, among other things, that Plato believed that the fundamental tension between political power and knowledge – a tension that becomes fully palpable in the course of the attempt to elaborate a truly just penal law – may be endemic to politics, as such, and not merely to the city of Magnesia. It may also imply that the public doctrine of criminal justice in a republic (and perhaps in any political society?) is especially vulnerable to rational critique and thus constitutes a sort of Achilles's heel of the whole moral order underpinning the political order. This, finally, would suggest that the justification of criminal law deserves the special attention of philosophical legislators and statesmen everywhere.

Completion of the Penal Code

Having completed his disquisition on the theoretical principles of punishment, the Stranger proceeds to the task of framing Magnesia's penal laws. This task occupies him for the remainder of Books 9 and 10 and sections of Book 11. Plato scholars have remarked on the sharp contrast between the radically innovative character of the Stranger's theoretical principles and the traditionalism of his penal code – which in many ways (albeit with certain striking exceptions) follows Athenian practice.[52] In the first place, the penal code addresses crime using largely traditional categories, apparently in order of descending gravity: murder and homicide (864d–874e); violent assault (874e–884a); insolent things done by the young (884a–913a); infractions in business and commerce (913a–922a); abuse of inheritances and orphans (922a–930e); neglect of parents (930e–932d); a miscellany of other crimes (932e–942a); and military offences (942a–945b). While this approach may seem intuitive at first glance, it is questionable from the point of view of the Stranger's focus on the individual offender's soul and character, as distinguished from the physical damage caused by his crime. It is true that we tend to regard the extent of the harm as a sign of the degree of injustice in the soul – for example, we assume that a murderer is more morally corrupt than a petty thief. Yet the Stranger has argued that injustice in the strict sense is the rule of passion in the soul *whether or not it does any damage* (or even if it confers some benefit). As we have seen, if applied consistently this definition would require an extensive overhaul of traditional evaluations of crime and of sentencing practices, in favour of an individualized approach in which the focus shifts from actions to psychological states. As a further result of this fundamental shift in approach, since the particularity and wide variety of psychological states would be difficult to reduce to broad categories, crime would elude its codification into law – which, in turn, would frustrate the cause of republican government, which crucially depends on the rule of law. This, along with the other difficulties we have had occasion to consider, amply accounts for the Stranger's decision to rein in his reformist project.

Second, and more obviously, several legal provisions in the Stranger's penal code would, by any sophisticated standard, be considered simpleminded and even crude. There is an abundance of provisions concerning pollution and purification, omens, curses pronounced by dying victims, exorcisms, and other such superstitions, which one would be at pains to fit into the Stranger's philosophical treatment of crime and punishment.[53] For example, the Stranger legislates that if a man should be killed by an animal or an inanimate object (unless it's a lightning bolt "or another missile from god"), that animal or object should be formally accused and tried by a judge and then, if found guilty, cast out beyond the city's borders (873e–874a). It is clear from all this just how far the Stranger goes to accommodate the prejudices of the Magnesian republic – the "matter" upon which the Stranger's legislative art must work, and to which it must be adapted, lest he lose his whole labour (cf. 707e– 709a). There is, therefore, less need to pay attention to the fine detail of the Stranger's penal code than to his penological arguments.[54]

Yet the conservative features of the Stranger's penal code cannot be allowed to obscure its radical innovations. The most remarkable of these innovations is the Stranger's dispensation for the punishment of young heretics in Book 10. Since this constitutes a very long section of the dialogue, a summary must suffice for our purposes. The Stranger (on his own initiative) raises certain critical objections to conventional piety that would have disastrous consequences for the moral order that undergirds the political regime of Magnesia – namely, critical doubts about the existence of providential and just gods. The Stranger attributes these sceptical objections to a few precocious youths among the citizens, whom he conjures up for the occasion. Instead of dealing with these young sceptics harshly, he sympathizes with their perplexities and grants their opinions a kind of formal hearing in the form of a dialogue among intellectual equals carried out on a highly sophisticated level. The core of the views of these young sceptics turns out to consist of the materialist doctrines of the pre-Socratic natural philosophers, and the ensuing discussion culminates in a refutation of these doctrines and a provisional vindication of the theological opinions of the city.[55] Following this vindication of the law against impiety, the Stranger proceeds to lay down a law against anyone who is nevertheless convicted in court on charges of heresy. The heretic is to be judged first as to whether his crime is truly motivated by his desire to know and to resolve his theoretical perplexity or by an unrestrained desire to live lawlessly (i.e., by his unjust character). Depending on this determination, the heretic is sentenced to one of two prisons. The restrained heretics are sent to a prison called a Moderation Tank (*sōphronisterion*) for no less than five years, where they are to be individually reformed, apparently through educational means, by high-ranking magistrates of the so-called Nocturnal Council. The members of this Nocturnal Council, we later learn, are an elite magistracy, a sort of conclave of philosophic statesmen (961a–b, 964d–965a, 968a). The unrestrained heretics, on the other hand, are to be sent to a separate prison in a wild and secluded part of the territory to live out their lives there as incurably unjust and dangerous individuals (907d–909d).

The Stranger's reluctance to treat the perplexed heretics as most traditional societies and legislators would treat them – namely, to punish them severely without further ado – and the great lengths to which he goes to educate them, and even to argue with them as intellectual equals, truly gives practical expression to the Stranger's radical definition of criminal justice.[56] It seems possible that the five years spent by each perplexed heretic in the Moderation Tank will be an opportunity for him to receive an uninterrupted quasi-philosophic education from the best-educated and most competent elders in the city – an education modelled after the Stranger's own dialogue with the fictitious young objectors. Such a "penalty" would fully meet the high standard of justice subscribed to by the Stranger himself. This is the only set of provisions in Magnesia's entire penal code that *does* depart from traditional criminal law's focus on external acts in favour of an individualized approach that looks to reason or science, rather than to law, as its guide.

The very limited scope the Stranger allows for the sort of innovations that would be dictated by his radical principles forces us to draw a very sobering and even somewhat disappointing lesson. Genuine moral reform of an offender, according to the Stranger, must involve either effective rational persuasion of the superior choiceworthiness of justice over injustice, or the restraint of immoderate desire, or possibly both. In all three cases, such reform must be carried out on an individualized basis, by someone with comprehensive knowledge of the human good and of the nature of the soul and the various workings of its drives, and on a subject who is receptive to it. Therefore, as we can see for ourselves, and as the Stranger's curtailment of individualized criminal justice in his penal code confirms, the conditions required for genuine moral reform – a young and agile mind with a respect for justice, on the one hand, and a wise and patient educator wielding political authority, on the other – would be all too rare.[57] This implies that in most cases, penal "rehabilitation" will really amount to one or another form of deterrence, using threats, inducements, or shame to prevent the criminal from reoffending, but falling short of true moral improvement.[58] Moreover, the life of a law-revering, economically equal, and stable republic dedicated to the cultivation of virtue must, to a significant extent, sacrifice scientific enlightenment (cf. 818a), artistic innovation (cf. 657b), and the cultivation of the humane or "quiet" virtues that have become predominant in modern ethical and political thought. These conditions limit the possibility of humanizing reform even further, beyond the intrinsic difficulties of using punishment to effect moral education.[59]

Conclusion

As we have seen in this chapter, the character of Plato's theory of punishment is in crucial respects informed by his understanding of republican politics. For citizens of the well-ordered republic of the *Laws*, punishment – particularly its proportionality to the crime – is a very serious moral concern, much more serious than it is, for example, to the guardian class of the *Republic* or to the statesman of the *Statesman*. In a republic, citizens must govern themselves according to their best understanding of justice and its requirements. As Plato's Stranger shows, however, that understanding of justice is necessarily imperfect. Most importantly, republican citizens, on the Stranger's account, are prone to a peculiar confusion regarding the goodness of justice as a human virtue. On the one hand, the rigours and responsibilities of republican life demand an intense love of, and belief in, justice as the highest virtue leading human beings to happiness. Yet this love of justice is haunted by a profound doubt – a nagging suspicion that it is, in fact, the unjust man who truly pursues his own good, not allowing the restraints of law and justice to stand in his way. Through the Stranger's complex psychological analysis, Plato is able to show how this central feature of the civic outlook powerfully contributes to the moral appeal of retributive punishment, for insofar as citizens doubt the goodness of justice and envy the criminal, they will believe that a harm proportional to his offence must be exacted to negate the "benefit" of the crime. This punitiveness is an ugly fact about republican life, yet it must not be confused with mere irrational or animal vengefulness. One sign of this is that this punitive spirit is amenable to some degree of refinement, providing the legislator (in this case, the Stranger himself) with opportunities to moderate the practice of retributive punishment.

In a political community ruled by laws rather than by enlightened experts, the correction of offenders must come under legal regulation no less than any other facet of social life. This means, among other things, that a republican society must develop workable legal doctrines of "voluntariness," "desert," "guilt," and "proportionality," without which the practice of criminal justice according to laws would be difficult if not inconceivable. These legal concepts may not be theoretically transparent, and they may in fact not even be consistent in the strictest sense with enlightened principles of justice – as the Stranger's discussion reveals. Nevertheless, a republic must make efforts to reconcile somehow these useful legal doctrines with justice understood in the truest sense, and it must learn to do so through a legislative art like the one practised by the Stranger – at once philosophic and practical. The Stranger's approach may serve as a model for republican attempts to address the thorny moral problems of punishment, especially because of his unwillingness either to sacrifice open-minded reflection for the sake of order, or to abandon political prudence for the empty triumph of an abstract ideal. Most importantly, the Stranger helps us understand that the characteristic civic outlook on punishment is intimately linked to its deepest moral convictions, and that the former cannot be radically uprooted without also profoundly shaking the latter. The Stranger's own understanding of human virtue, as choiceworthy for its own sake and as constitutive of happiness, leads him to radical conclusions – including the conclusion that truly just punishment would have to meet a very high standard indeed: that of morally improving the offender himself by teaching him the true value of living a just life. Understanding this high standard to be all but impossible to achieve in political life, the Stranger moderates his reformist zeal.

Whatever we think of Plato's view of republican politics in the *Laws*, and of how that view influences his teaching on punishment, an obvious question now looms: If a highly traditionalist approach to punishment is best suited for a small, isolated, and thoroughly Greek republic, is it reasonable to assume that it would be equally suitable to our own, modern, scientifically enlightened, liberal democracies? It goes without saying that Plato had no experience with modern liberal democracy and so, arguably, could not have raised such a question for himself. Only once the social, economic, and political conditions that would make liberal democracy possible began to appear did serious minds begin to consider the possibility of unprecedented, wholesale penal reform. The remainder of the present study examines the theories of the greatest of these philosophical reformers and the consequences of their ambitious reform project. Once we have completed that investigation, we will have occasion to re-evaluate Plato's approach.

Chapter 2

Modern Natural Right and Punishment in Hobbes's *Leviathan*

Punishment becomes an especially important topic in modern political thought because the limits of the government's right to punish serve to define the boundary separating arbitrary violence from legitimate political authority over naturally free individuals. This creates the need for a normative theory of punishment that is able to reliably trace these limits and ground them theoretically. Hobbes is generally recognized as a foundational political thinker in the modern tradition; he was also the first to attempt a systematic normative theory of punishment consistent with modern natural right – the basic principle of modern politics.

To appreciate the need for a normative theory of punishment in the modern context, we might consider Machiavelli's advice to princes and republics regarding "cruelty well-used." According to Machiavelli, the stability of any political order requires the occasional show of overwhelming force by the governing authority – veiled, whenever possible, under a pretext of avenging justice. To have their desired effect of subduing or pacifying a tumultuous populace, these "punishments" must be excessive and bloody.[1] Hobbes, too, would later conclude that the primary role of the sovereign is to instill fear in his subjects by an overwhelming power: an irresistible "Leviathan"-state, according to the Hobbesian analysis, is the only way to restrain the politically destabilizing irrational passions to which human nature is prone. Thus, from the outset, modern politics' aim has been peace and security, and its means, fear. The problem with this political principle, however, as Hobbes himself recognized, was that its most extreme implications – peacetime curfews and detention camps, kangaroo courts, mass executions, and so forth – although not likely to occur with any frequency in practice, would excessively alarm most law-abiding people. As a result, the principle itself might be popularly regarded (rightly or wrongly) as much too threatening and too degrading to human dignity to be accepted. Hobbes saw that, for the new political principle to gain acceptance, it would be necessary to locate somewhere within the theory of absolute sovereign power minimal normative limitations on the use of that power.

Thus, Hobbes has gained a reputation as *the* modern theorist of absolute sovereignty, but he is also the author of the first normative theory of punishment in the modern tradition.[2] That theory of punishment, articulated in the *Leviathan*, contains several serious inconsistencies or tensions and, as we will see, ultimately fails. That failure is instructive and will help us greatly to understand the enduring problems of punishment in the modern context and the subsequent historical development of punishment theory. As we will see, Hobbes would use two distinct strategies – each with its own difficulties – to attempt to overcome the dilemma of having to find limitations on a sovereign power that is absolute. His first strategy was to argue that while the sovereign may not be limited by any *other* power, he remains bound by the "laws of nature" – that is, by precepts of reason forbidding a sovereign to punish his subjects except under specified conditions. The second strategy relied on Hobbes's concept of "authorization" and attempted to demonstrate that a criminal who is punished by his sovereign has actually authorized (and therefore consented to) his own punishment, since as a subject he authorizes all of the actions of his sovereign. The analysis in this chapter will show where these strategies – and Hobbes's theory of punishment as a whole – fail, and why they cannot succeed. This ultimate failure notwithstanding, Hobbes's theory of punishment contains a radical critique of traditional criminal justice concepts – a theme that the present chapter will also develop.

In Hobbes's teaching on punishment, the most obvious and perhaps most significant innovation is its unequivocal rejection of retribution. Classical political thinkers had raised searching questions regarding the justice of retribution, yet they refrained from pursuing those questions too far and generally sought to accommodate retribution in their most political works. In contrast to Plato's and Aristotle's cautious and accommodating treatments of retribution, however, Hobbes spells out with the utmost clarity the furthest implications of a thoroughly rationalist approach to criminal justice. Such an approach implies the rejection of retributive punishment and, with it, many of the traditional concepts of criminal justice.

Punishment and the Natural Law against Revenge

To see how the more general assumptions of Hobbes's political thought prepare the ground for his theory of criminal justice, we may begin by considering his denial of a universal standard of goodness, or *summum bonum* (*Leviathan* 11.1).[3] Absent an objective standard of goodness – which Hobbes denies exists on the basis of his subjectivist psychology – our judgments of others (i.e., of their personal merit or depravity) must be regarded as merely partial or subjective (10.16). For what we think we are doing when we judge others as praiseworthy or blameworthy, meritorious or morally culpable, is comparing their actions, and their characters as reflected in their actions, to some natural and universal standard of human goodness. Accordingly, Hobbes argues that in the state of nature, no imputation of merit (or demerit) can carry with it any moral consequences; rather, it can have moral consequences only when it is agreed to by convention and where this agreement can be enforced by a constituted sovereign authority (cf. 6.7 and 6.59 with 10.54). In the state of nature, there is neither justice nor injustice, and therefore there is no such thing as punishment, let alone normative principles for its regulation.

But once civil society is constituted by the recognition of a sovereign power, the sovereign has not only a right but also a duty to define what is good and bad, base and noble, for the regulation of his subjects' relations with one another, with a view to their peaceful and prosperous coexistence. After these artificial standards of goodness and wickedness have been established, would their enforcement by the sovereign then have to take the form of traditional criminal laws and punishments? Hobbes argues that it would not. While it is within the scope of the sovereign's authority to impose a standard of human goodness akin to the classical or Christian models – comprising all the virtues of a perfect human being – there is no need for this. On the contrary, in opposition to the reigning tradition, Hobbes denies that human beings are perfected through political community and maintains that politics need look no further than the preservation of peace.[4] Furthermore, Hobbes's observation of human beings led him to conclude that legislating a morally demanding doctrine of virtue not only does not promote peace but in fact has the opposite effect. According to Hobbes, the powerful passions invoked by any notion of human goodness involving great self-sacrifice are hard to control – even by threats of physical harm – and are therefore dangerous to political unity and peace. This has important implications for criminal law. To enforce a demanding standard of moral virtue in the commonwealth would require sanctions against a host of activities that in no way endanger anyone's security or material well-being. What is more, when traditional criminal law took its sights by a standard of human perfection, it invoked the indignation of the public against those who might fail to live up to that standard. This rendered traditional punishment retributive and harsher than it needed to be for purposes of deterrence alone: when criminals are considered to be not only dangerous but also base, wicked, and impious, the attitude of the public may be expected to be more severe. On the other hand, were the sights of politics to be lowered, as they ought to be in the Hobbesian view, all the severity of traditional punishment would become unnecessary. Accordingly, Hobbes's seventh law of nature is:

> *That in revenges* [i.e., retribution of evil for evil] *men look not at the greatness of the evil past, but the greatness of the good to follow.* Whereby we are forbidden to inflict punishment with any other design than for correction of the offender, or direction of others. For this law is consequent to the next before it [i.e., the sixth law], that commandeth pardon upon security of the future time. Besides, revenge without respect to the example and profit to come is a triumph, or glorying, in the hurt of another, tending to no end (for the end is always somewhat to come); and glorying to no end is vainglory, and contrary to reason; and to hurt without reason tendeth to the introduction of war, which is against the law of nature, and is commonly styled by the name of *cruelty*. (15.19; emphases in original)

According to this passage, some acts of "retribution" or "revenge" would be appropriate under the law of nature, so it appears as if Hobbes is here affirming the rightness of retribution rightly understood. That is, rightful retribution would aim at correction and rehabilitation of the offender, or incapacitation, or general deterrence (punishing the criminal to set an example for others), or restitution (compensation of victims), or any combination of these (and perhaps other) beneficial effects. But it is clear that in this context Hobbes is giving retribution a wholly unconventional meaning, since – as ordinary experience abundantly shows and as more careful analysis confirms (see the preceding chapter) – retribution looks principally to the past and only incidentally to the future. In other words, Hobbes here is simply ignoring the whole problem of backward-looking punishment. Whereas traditional penal thought had been concerned with two distinct ends – the just deserts of the criminal *and* the utility of the penalty – Hobbes's teaching decisively narrows the scope of penal justice to include only the latter.

In his comment on the natural law against backward-looking retribution, Hobbes argues primarily from the more fundamental principle of utility. But he also alludes to another feature of the natural law against retribution – which might well be described as its humane and humanizing spirit – by characterizing backward-looking retribution not merely as imprudent or ineffective but also as "cruel" and "vain."

There is some debate among scholars about whether Hobbes's political teaching has a moral grounding or merely proceeds from his materialist psychology.[5] This question has some bearing on the issue of Hobbes's penal theory. A commonly raised objection to utilitarian penal theory – whose principle is the "greatest happiness of the greatest number"[6] – is that its attempt to justify the harming of a minority (i.e., the punishment of criminals) in the name of the interest of the majority cannot succeed. The crux of this objection is that when two interests are opposed to each other, the majority has no greater moral claim than the minority simply because of its greater number. For punishment to be truly justified (i.e., for it to count as *moral*), it would have to be shown that the criminal somehow deserved his punishment; or that the punishment was in the common interest (the criminal's as well as society's); or that the sovereign authority had some other ground for imposing the penalty that was not reducible to partial interest. A penal theory based solely on the materialist psychology laid out in Part I of the *Leviathan* ("Of Man") would have to be utilitarian and thus would remain open to the objection just now raised.[7]

In fact, Hobbes never intended for his political teaching to rest solely on his mechanistic account of human behaviour as fundamentally selfish.[8] He makes this clear in several ways. In the Preface to the *De Cive*, Hobbes writes that according to the scientific (resolutive–compositive) method, political science would follow philosophy and physics and would have its principles derived from those more fundamental branches of science. But Hobbes also says there that he was able to complete his political treatise independently, before completing his works of more abstract philosophy, because he "saw that it did not need the preceding parts, since it rests upon its own principles known by reason."[9] This is confirmed in the Introduction to the *Leviathan*, where he says that the principles of political science derive not from abstract reasoning but rather from careful reflection on the ordinary experiences of other human beings and on our own passions – "for this kind of doctrine admitteth no other demonstration."[10] Nevertheless, these statements leave open the possibility that careful reflection on our experience of human beings may still lead us to the conclusion that men have always behaved selfishly – and indeed Hobbes does believe this to be true. Yet Hobbes cannot simply leave it at this, since such an account of human beings as simple self-seekers would remain incapable of solving the problem of vainglory, as Strauss has shown.[11] The passion of vainglory (or pride) poses a special problem because, although vainglory makes men in society into aggressors, threatening to return them to the violent state of nature, this fact alone is not enough to allow Hobbes to reject the pursuit of glory and domination as irrational. That is because, holding a subjectivist conception of the good as he does, he must conclude that the enjoyment derived from contemplating one's own power ("glorying") is no less rational an object of our desire (and thus no less good) than any other pleasure – even when the power we delight in is imaginary, not real (11.6). A moral basis for politics thus comes into sight as necessary in order to adjudicate between the destructive selfish passion of vainglory, on the one hand, and the politically edifying but still selfish passion of the fear of violent death, on the other. Hobbes solves this problem by introducing the concept of a natural right to self-preservation that is universal (not merely grounded in the subjective desire for self-preservation). When one's life is in danger, even the use of force and fraud in self-defence is "generally allowed" – that is, acknowledged by reason as morally permissible, and not merely as a brute fact of human behaviour (13.4).[12] This moral insight (moral because grounded in universal or "right" reason) becomes the foundation for Hobbes's political teaching and by extension for his theory of punishment.

True, this remains a peculiar kind of moral foundation. For in Hobbes's account, the natural right to self-preservation is essentially selfish: it neither confers on the right-bearer an entitlement to the active assistance of others nor imposes a natural duty on others to provide such assistance. Nonetheless, this radically original moral insight – albeit a low-aiming one – encouraged Hobbes to develop what might fairly be called a humanizing normative theory of punishment, in the sense that it is compatible with the "humane" treatment of offenders, rather than merely serving as prudential counsel to the sovereign authority as to the most effective means for preserving security.

The humanizing dimension of Hobbes's political teaching can be seen in his argument that human beings in civil society ought to acknowledge their natural equality (15.21). It is true that this natural equality is derived by Hobbes from the fact that, in the state of nature, no man is so superior as to be able to secure himself against being killed by the weakest. Yet although this necessity to acknowledge others as our natural equals is selfish in origin, Hobbes allows for the doctrine of natural equality to take on a morally edifying, humanizing tone. The pleasure of vainglory not only makes men into aggressors but also obscures in them any awareness of their fundamental vulnerability as individuals, and hence their equality – indeed, the passion of vainglory necessarily presupposes the forgetting of one's vulnerability. In the *De Cive*, Hobbes states that, although in the state of nature "there is in all men a will to do harm," they do not will or intend this "for the same reason or with equal culpability." For, he explains, the one who acts only in self-defence acknowledges natural equality and is therefore "a modest man," whereas the man who "suppose[es] himself superior to others" and "wants to be allowed everything" is also blameworthy.[13] According to Hobbes, a very common manifestation of vainglory is punitive anger. Recall that retribution and the punitive indignation that fuels it aim to secure no material benefit, but only what is thought to be distributive justice: the restoration of a certain equilibrium in the distribution of possessions, liberties, and other goods, such that the unjust do not enjoy greater well-being than the just. By their own admission, angry victims and victims' rights advocates are concerned with restoring the dignity of victims by depriving offenders of the equal dignity they no longer "deserve" (e.g., by shaming them). From a Hobbesian point of view, however, this becomes nothing more than the desire for a pointless (albeit pleasurable) "triumph" (cf. 15.19), when considered in light of the fundamental truth of our vulnerability as individuals. Since our demand for retribution ultimately cannot be sustained upon the only moral basis recognized by all human beings, this "moral" need turns out in fact to be nothing other than a desire for a particularly intense (and for this reason deceptive) pleasure.

Criminals are indeed *legally* culpable, on Hobbes's account, since they pose a threat to peace – but this only makes them liable to punishment that would provide "caution [i.e., security] of the future time" (15.18). Nothing that the criminal has done in the past can ever alter the fundamental fact of his moral equality with every member of the law-abiding majority. The retributivist's desire for a triumph over criminal offenders is vain, on Hobbes's view, and thus also cruel (because pointless) and not merely imprudent. Put another way, it is cruel because it implies an almost wilful ignorance about what makes us all human: our equal vulnerability to death and suffering. In this way, the natural law against retribution comes into sight not only as a counsel of prudence but also as an expression of enlightened humanity. A good Hobbesian, although motivated by nothing other than enlightened self-interest, would still be revolted by the barbarism implicit in retributive punishment.

It is worth emphasizing that the foregoing analysis should not be taken to mean that Hobbes's natural law against retribution imposes any kind of absolute duty on the sovereign authority to refrain from all that may be thought to be "cruel" in punishments. This does not follow for the basic reason that, for Hobbes, the laws of nature, as such, are not proper laws, but actually "convenient articles of peace" automatically informing any enlightened reason (ch. 13, end). Nevertheless, it is important not to overlook Hobbes's optimism about the capacity of human beings – selfish though they naturally are – to transform themselves morally on the basis of that very selfishness, rightly understood.[14] Hobbes's brief but arresting statements on the natural law against retribution exemplify this optimism and give evidence of his prescience regarding the character of what would become the modern moral attitude – the attitude of "humanity" that would become an explicit theme of liberal political thought after Montesquieu.

Hobbes continues to develop his enlightened and humanizing understanding of criminal justice in the chapter "Of Crimes, Excuses, and Extenuations." The guiding question of this chapter pertains to the nature of crime, and the novelty of Hobbes's answer to that question can best be appreciated if we first recall the classical republican conception of law. According to Plato's Athenian Stranger, the laws of the city must encompass all aspects of human life, and most importantly, they must aim at the greatest good: human virtue and happiness. Consequent to this view of law, criminal law must be compatible with the overall aim of improving (or at least not harming) the souls of citizens, including of course offenders. Since the main burden of improving the souls of citizens falls on the educational laws, criminal law functions in the supportive role of enforcing morality as well as rehabilitating offenders (for whom the educational laws were not sufficient). Another function of the criminal law in the classical republic is to deter that relatively small number of citizens who are not voluntarily law-abiding. In Hobbes, by contrast, this deterrent function becomes the primary and sole aim of criminal law and punishment (and, indeed, of all law). The traditional function of enforcing morality through criminal law can no longer be sustained: since all private ends, including the pursuit of happiness, are beyond the law's scope, individual subjects may remain at liberty to pursue happiness as they understand it (see ch. 21). From this it follows that "where law ceaseth, sin ceaseth" (27.3).[15] Since in a Hobbesian commonwealth the laws will not be paternalistic, the scope of the criminal code will necessarily be much more limited. Hobbes's gloss on the Sermon on the Mount in this chapter illustrates this momentous change of orientation. According to Jesus, we are guilty of sin (and liable to punishment) not just when we offend against the law in deed, but even when we merely contemplate the offence. Conversely, Hobbes goes very far in the opposite direction: "The consideration of this has made me think them too severe, both to themselves and others, that maintain that the first motions of the mind (though checked with the fear of God) be sins" (27.1).

The humanizing implications of the Hobbesian conception of criminal law are further revealed in subsequent discussions of ignorance, the power of the passions, and the possible complicity of the criminal law itself in the propagation of crime. In these discussions, Hobbes goes much farther than the Socratic philosophers ever dared go in openly drawing out the implications of a thoroughly rationalist approach to criminal justice.

Hobbes's explicit view that "the source of every crime is some defect of the understanding, or some error in reasoning, or some sudden force of the passions" (27.4) is in perfect harmony with the private view of Plato's philosophic Stranger (although the latter was forced to qualify his view in his public statements as legislator and teacher of legislators).[16] Plato and the other Socratics had cautiously indicated that the confines of our moral knowledge (and hence, of our competence for responsible action) and of our capacity for self-restraint in the face of powerful passions are actually much narrower than most people believe.[17] Nevertheless, Plato's Stranger encouraged lawgivers and magistrates to try to rehabilitate offenders through measures designed to chasten their passions, increase their capacity for self-restraint, and instil in them a love for justice. Hobbes, by contrast, unambiguously maintains that human nature is largely unchangeable or incorrigible. "As for the passions of hate, lust, ambition, and covetousness, what crimes they are apt to produce is so obvious to every man's experience and understanding, as there needeth nothing to be said of them, saving that they are infirmities so annexed to the nature, both of man and all other living creatures, as that their effects cannot be hindered but by extraordinary use of reason, or a constant severity in punishing them" (27.18; cf. 27.1). Thus, according to Hobbes, law must not try to transform human nature, but must try to accept it and keep it within acceptable bounds by constructing institutions that will be able to work *with* the passions rather than directly against them. So it is futile for the commonwealth to attempt to eradicate the causes of crime in man's naturally selfish drives. Nor would it be wise to rely on human reason alone to teach men that their own truest interests lie in upholding the laws. Rather, the commonwealth must try to hinder the harmful effects of the passions by relying on another powerful passion – fear – to keep men in check.

This is certainly a much less flattering picture of human nature than the one taught by the ancients, for it implies that almost none of us is strong enough to resist committing injustice without the threat of punishment to restrain us: "whensoever the hope of impunity appears, their effects proceed" (27.18). Yet this view of human nature also makes possible the lowering of the demands we make on our criminal justice institutions, thereby improving our chances of achieving the remaining (much more attainable) demand for security. Since the self-regarding passions are natural and ineradicable (and thus should not be condemned as "base"), and since punishment no longer needs to concern itself with the moral rehabilitation of criminals, the framing of criminal codes with a view to deterrence can be done much more simply and systematically (without the need to weave together contradictory elements, as Plato's Stranger attempted to do in his own penal legislation). According to the classical view, injustice in the soul has little relation to the harm caused by the crime (see above, chapter 1, 39–41). Since the nature of the particular injustice in the soul varies for each individual, as does the type of punishment necessary to correct it, it is difficult to predict – and thus difficult to codify – what punishments will be suitable for what crimes. But while this individualized approach to injustice may be appropriate for the purpose of rehabilitation (at least on the Platonic–Aristotelian assumptions), it is not quite suitable for the purpose of deterrence. That is because deterrence depends entirely on the predictability or certainty of the punishment (a point on which Hobbes expands in the following chapter), which means it depends on it being known that there is no way to escape it or to lessen its severity by appealing to the discretion or partiality of judges or assemblies. Thus the wide discretion of judges that is implied by the rehabilitative approach to crime actually works at cross-purposes with the requirements of deterrence. The narrowing of the scope of Hobbesian criminal law, on the other hand, allows for the restriction of judicial discretion and the further refinement of legal categorizations of crime.[18] This increase in the formal sophistication of criminal law would be advantageous both for its effectiveness – since deterrence requires predictability – and for its fairness – since defining a crime in the law in advance takes away from the appearance of arbitrariness in a judicial ruling.[19] This advantage of Hobbesian criminal law is distinct from, and compatible with, the advantage already discussed of affording greater freedom from coercion for private thoughts and feelings.

Finally, we may mention another advantage of Hobbes's novel conception of crime, as it emerges from his analysis. While classical republican theory was openly hostile to the nakedly self-regarding desires for physical pleasure, gain, and personal safety, since these desires were thought to undermine the public-spiritedness of citizens and the unity of the city, it was more hospitable towards the passion of anger. As we saw in the previous chapter, the laws of Plato's Magnesia were deliberately ambiguous towards anger – at times even praising it outright – since Plato's Stranger understood this passion to be capable of opposing the selfish desires and becoming allied to the public interest. Hobbes inverts this relationship, clearing the selfish desire for comfortable self-preservation of all opprobrium while reassessing the public function of anger and judging it more harmful than useful. Hobbes thus dispenses with the complicated and precarious rhetorical approach towards the vengeful passions employed by Plato and Aristotle. By accommodating anger in the interest of public unity, the republican tradition was in fact allowing a powerful cause of crime – for "there are few crimes that may not be produced by anger" (27.17) – to become entrenched in the commonwealth. Hobbes's security strategy liberates political theory and practice from this troublesome inconsistency.

In the spirit of this rationalist attitude towards crime, Hobbes shows how the sovereign authority ought to moderate its criminal code (both for the advantage of its own power and as a reflection of its humanity) in a section on "excuse" and "extenuation" (27.21 ff.). "Where a man is captive or in the power of the enemy (and he is then in the power of the enemy, when his person, or his means of living, is so) if it be without his own fault, the obligation of the law ceaseth, because he must obey the enemy or die; and consequently such obedience is no crime." An enlightened understanding of the weakness of human beings and of their natural self-regard liberates us from the kind of indignation that demands that individuals remain loyal to their country even when they, or their goods, are under the control of enemies. We may observe that this forgiving policy extends even to offenders who break the law out of concern for their property (their "means of living"). This holds true also for any man who breaks the law when "destitute of food or other things necessary for his life … as if in a great famine he take the food by force or stealth [possibly from another, equally hungry man]," for then he is "totally excused."

This accommodation of human weakness also leads Hobbes to excuse or extenuate injustices that may have been encouraged by failures of the sovereign authority itself:

> The same fact, if it have been constantly punished in other men, is a greater crime than if there have been many precedent examples of impunity. For those examples are so many hopes of impunity given by the sovereign himself; and because he which furnishes a man with such a hope and presumption of mercy as encourageth him to offend hath his part in the offence, he cannot reasonably charge the offender with the whole. (27.32)[20]

Similarly, "those facts which the law expressly condemneth, but the lawmaker by other manifest signs of his will tacitly approveth, are less crimes than the same facts condemned by both the laws and the lawmaker." Here Hobbes gives the example of duelling – condemned by law throughout Europe, but sanctioned by well-bred custom as an honourable way of defending one's name. In these and many other ways, Hobbes demonstrates what has since become a truism in modern criminology: that a significant cause of crime in traditional societies had been inconsistency in the criminal laws themselves, and in their enforcement. In an interesting inversion of priorities, we are made to see that what is needed is not the reform of individual offenders – as per republican theory – but the reform of the criminal justice system itself.

On the other hand, in contrast to much of contemporary criminology, which locates responsibility for crime not in individuals but in their social environment (that is, in poverty, broken families, poor educational opportunities, etc.), Hobbes is much more hopeful about the capacity of individuals to respond rationally to credible threats from the civil authority. Notwithstanding his view of the power of the passions and the weakness of human reason, Hobbes assumes throughout that deterrence *can* be effective (a proposition contested by some of today's criminologists and psychologists), for "there is no suddenness of passion sufficient for a total excuse; for all the time between the first knowing of the law and the commission of the fact shall be taken for a time of deliberation, because [the would-be criminal] ought, by meditation of the law, to rectify the irregularity of his passions continually" (27.33). This expectation of self-control should not, however, be confused with the sort of self-denying virtue praised by classical thought, since Hobbes is not relying on reason to rule the passions, but on certain selfish passions (viz., fear of punishment) to oppose the others with the aid of reason.[21]

Hobbes's discussion of crime ends with a consideration of the subjective – or what we might call cultural – component of any criminal code. The logic of Hobbes's political teaching implies that only attacks on property, or on individual or collective security, ought to be criminalized by the commonwealth (the latter because they endanger life, the former because they make life onerous). But in actuality, most political communities criminalize all sorts of activities that have little to do with security. In some countries, public indecency (e.g., public nudity or profanity), adultery, and polygamy are criminal offences, although it is not clear how such activities would endanger either life or property. In others, atheism is criminalized, while in still others certain public expressions of religion are illegal (such as the French law against face-covering). While the logic of Hobbes's analysis of crime would seem to favour the decriminalization of all such activities by commonwealths, he understood that even enlightened societies would likely remain attached to traditional institutions like the family, and to some traditional virtues, and that their criminal laws might have to be made to reflect that attachment.[22] Accordingly, Hobbes distinguishes crimes against the commonwealth (i.e., against its peace, order, and authority) from crimes against private individuals. It is clear that some offences against individuals, especially violent and property offences, also imply a danger to the public (cf. 27.54), but there are others – such as the ones just mentioned – that do not. The question is how an enlightened society ought to treat such merely perceived offences against some of its members, when the natural law is silent regarding any matter that does not somehow affect comfortable self-preservation.

Hobbes's answer to this question is simply that the sovereign should consider the sentiments of his subjects and seek to accommodate them as much as is possible within the bounds of the natural law by enacting criminal laws (or tolerating existing criminal laws) that reflect those sentiments. Thus, when comparing crimes, the greater crime "is that where the damage, in the common opinion of men, is most sensible" (27.41; cf. 27.49). Therefore, "mutilation of a limb" (aggravated assault) can be counted as a greater crime "than the spoiling of a man of his goods" (theft), since the former seems to most people to be a more serious offence than the latter (when in fact it is quite possible that certain thefts can be more damaging to one's future well-being than non-fatal bodily injuries). Similarly, Hobbes argues that it might be popularly considered more offensive to kill one's parent than to kill a non-relation; to commit a crime "in the time or place appointed for devotion" than in any other time or place; to rape a married woman than a non-married one (27.48, 51, 52). In the last case, however, we may observe that most contemporary Western societies have advanced beyond even Hobbes's expectations, since our criminal laws now consider rape equally bad whether the victim is married or not, and Hobbes would certainly have applauded such an enlightened and egalitarian development.[23]

We have now arrived at the second crucial moment in the development, in the Western rationalist tradition, of the idea of criminal justice since the original classical formulation. In our earlier discussion of punishment in the context of classical republican theory, we observed that the gentle and self-contented (one might even say aloof) outlook on crime embodied by Plato's Athenian Stranger, which inclines towards feelings of pity for the criminal on account of his confused and disordered soul, cannot be a model for republican citizens, who must always remain vigilant and adhere to a selfless conception of virtue. By fundamentally rethinking what it would mean to live in a well-ordered society, and by abandoning the classical republican ideal, Hobbes made it possible for rational penal reform to escape the limitations of classical republican life. The society envisioned by Hobbes would encourage private self-interest and rely less on the cultivation of selfless virtue with all of its accompanying harshness. This vision allows Hobbes to take the first steps towards a thoroughly modern theory of punishment.

The Aim and Limits of Punishment

The *Leviathan* begins the second of its two chapters devoted to criminal justice, "Of Punishments and Rewards," by defining punishment as "an evil inflicted by public authority on him that hath done or omitted that which is judged by the same authority to be a transgression of the law, to the end that the will of men may thereby the better be disposed to obedience" (28.1).[24] This definition of punishment derives directly from Hobbes's earlier discussion of the natural law against retribution and clearly restricts the aim of punishment to deterrence alone. Although we have already discussed several features of Hobbes's penal theory that align with enlightened humanity, there is no doubt that the sword of justice in a well-ordered commonwealth will appear repressive. In a way, this is unavoidable, since in order for punishment to be effective it must control the powerful passions in all men through fear, and this requires that it be sufficiently severe: the aim of punishment is "terror" (28.10). This may conjure up an apprehension that such a system of punishment would be tyrannical, arbitrary, or "Machiavellian." Anticipating this fear, Hobbes attempts to show that a rational penal system would be circumscribed within certain reliable limits.

Hobbes begins his elaboration of the proper limits of the punishing power by clarifying the origin of the right to punish:

> Before I infer anything from this definition, there is a question to be answered of much importance, which is: by what door the right or authority of punishing in any case came in? For by that which has been said before, no man is supposed bound by covenant not to resist violence; and consequently, it cannot be intended that he gave any right to another to lay violent hands upon his person. In the making of a commonwealth, every man giveth away the right of defending another, but not of defending himself. Also, he obligeth himself to assist him that hath the sovereignty in the punishing of another, but of himself not … It is manifest therefore that the right which the commonwealth (that is, he or they that represent it) hath to punish is not grounded on any concession or gift of the subjects.
>
> But I have also showed formerly that before the institution of commonwealth, every man had a right to everything, and to do whatsoever he thought necessary to his own preservation, subduing, hurting, or killing any man in order thereunto. And this is the foundation of that right of punishing which is exercised in every commonwealth. For the subjects did not give the sovereign that right, but only (in laying down theirs) strengthened him to use his own as he should think fit, for the preservation of them all; so that it was not given, but left to him, and to him only, and (excepting the limits set him by natural law) as entire as in the condition of mere nature, and of war of every one against his neighbor. (28.2)

Since the natural right to defend one's life and limb is prior to, and the foundation of, all obligations, it is inconceivable that anyone could grant another the right to do him physical harm for any reason. Consequently, the sovereign's authority to punish subjects must be grounded not in the consent of the subject but in the absolute freedom of the state of nature, which the sovereign retains undiminished even in civil society, as he is not a party to the social contract (17.13).[25] Yet despite this straightforward deduction of the right to punish from the unlimited right of nature, Hobbes seems to wish to avoid unequivocally drawing the conclusion that the sovereign's right to punish is equally unlimited. Everything depends on what is meant by Hobbes when he says that the sovereign's right to punish is absolute "excepting the limits set him by natural law." Hobbes repeats the idea that the natural law forbids all punishment "which is inflicted without intention or possibility of disposing the delinquent (or by his example, other men) to obey the laws." According to Hobbes, any punishment that does not do so is no punishment at all, "but an act of hostility" (28.7). But is it quite appropriate to call this reason for refraining from imposing certain kinds of punishment a true *limitation* on the sovereign? Assuming that Hobbes is right to claim that fear of violent death and the desire for comfortable self-preservation can be reckoned on to preserve political order (cf. 13.14, 14.3), and assuming that the prudent sovereign wishes for nothing more than to enjoy stable rule, Hobbes's admonition to the sovereign not to violate the natural law against excessive punishments is not a restraint, but a counsel to do what is in his own best interest – and no limitations whatsoever are said to restrict him in the pursuit of that interest.

Hobbes next draws a series of inferences from his definition of punishment and his conception of its origin in right. One of these is that a penalty should not exceed the amount of harm stipulated in the positive laws of the commonwealth. "For seeing the aim of punishment is not a revenge, but terror, and the terror of a great punishment unknown is taken away by the declaration of a less, the unexpected addition is no part of the punishment" (28.10). Penalties that are not announced in advance are not advantageous for the sovereign, for the simple reason that they cannot deter. In fact, by their very unpredictability, extralegal punishments may even undermine respect for law by making punishment seem wilful, while allowing would-be criminals to hope to avoid the harshest penalties by appealing to the sovereign's mercy (cf. 27.32).[26] Another inference from Hobbes's definition of punishment is that offenders have a right to public trial before they can be punished (28.5; cf. 23.9). Any punishment that is not preceded by a public conviction has no ability to deter, since no one (besides the sovereign and his ministers) could know what the punishment is for. For similar reasons, the law of nature forbids inflicting punishment for an action that was criminalized *ex post facto* (28.11). Where no law exists prohibiting an action, punishment cannot be anticipated and thus can have no deterrent power. Similarly, Hobbes denies that pre-trial incarceration can be considered punishment, since no harm imposed before culpability has been determined can have any deterrent effect (28.20).

There is a danger that modern readers (who may already agree with Hobbes that deterrence ought to be the sole purpose of punishment) may underestimate the provocative import of Hobbes's arguments. In what we have seen so far, Hobbes's arguments lay out in general terms what policies would serve the sovereign's interest in maintaining his rule, and he allows his readers to suppose that such policies would converge with individual subjects' concerns about fairness, justice, and their own protection under the law. This convergence cannot be assumed *a priori*, however. On the contrary, it becomes clear that Hobbes is begging some very important questions in this regard when he eventually undertakes to show that, for all practical purposes, the natural law would forbid the punishment of innocents.

Punishment, according to Hobbes, can only be "for transgression of the law … and therefore there can be no punishment of the innocent" (28.22). Yet the derivation of the right to punish has left open the logical possibility that the harming of subjects may sometimes be justified by the requirement of general security even when no law has been broken. Hobbes's commitment to an unlimited right of nature prevents him from invoking any prior norms or duties that might restrict sovereign authority.[27] And since he cannot argue against harming the innocent in principle, he is reduced to arguing against this on grounds of political utility. According to Hobbes, the natural law forbids harming the innocent because "there can arrive no good to the commonwealth." But, again, this merely assumes that harming the innocent can never be politically expedient, whereas in fact it is possible to imagine a scenario in which it is. When an angry and riotous mob believes some innocent man to be responsible for a very serious crime he did not in fact commit, the prudent sovereign may have to execute the unfortunate man under a false pretext of justice, if this is the only available means for placating the violent mob. Could Hobbes really have failed to imagine such a possibility? In fact, Hobbes openly admits elsewhere that if the sovereign does violence to an innocent subject, he does so without injustice, as the Biblical David did to Uriah and as Jephtha did to his daughter (21.7).

Some contemporary utilitarian punishment theorists might be inclined to defend Hobbes here by resorting to the "definitional stop." According to this argument, harming the innocent may perhaps sometimes be justified by political expediency, but it can never be justified *as punishment*, since, as Hobbes says, punishment is only "for transgression of the law." Yet this argument fails because it assumes that the stated aim of punishment – "correction of the offender, or direction of others" – is logically dependent on an actual transgression of the law, whereas in fact there is no reason why it should be, as can be seen from the hypothetical example I have sketched. Once Hobbes made the decision to abandon the connection between punishment and the commonsense notion of desert, he could no longer recur to this notion as a way of establishing a binding limit on the punishing power. Moreover, as we have seen, Hobbes *cannot avoid* abandoning the commonsense notion of desert because this is one of the premises of his wholesale rejection of backward-looking retribution. To put it more positively, Hobbes intended to liberate punishment from its irrational origins in ordinary political opinion by limiting its scope to the rational aim of security – an objective state of affairs that, according to him, has no relation to our speculative opinions about inner "worth," "desert," "guilt," or "innocence." Yet the price of rationalizing punishment in this way is that one must also accept its radical moral implications. Normally, when we say that the innocent ought not to be punished, we do not mean that "nothing useful would be accomplished by punishing such individuals." Rather, we mean that if we punished them, this would somehow upset the scales of justice, or it would conflict with our sense that good things should happen to good people and bad things only to bad people, according to some rough proportion, which we may have difficulty defining precisely, but which we apprehend when it is violated. If these are indeed the thoughts behind the ordinary objection to punishment of the innocent, then the objection cannot be maintained within a Hobbesian framework, from which the principle of retribution has been expunged.[28]

Perhaps it is because he was aware of the morally extreme implications of his principles that Hobbes still tried his best to argue against punishment of the innocent on commonsense, non-utilitarian grounds – although this would make such arguments merely rhetorical. In the same chapter, Hobbes claims that in addition to being imprudent, punishment of the innocent is also forbidden by the natural law commanding gratitude (rendering good for good) and by the natural law commanding equity (equal distribution of justice). Punishing innocents amounts to rendering evil for good, which is ingratitude, and it amounts to a violation of equity, since it imposes harm on some innocents but not on all (28.22). We can see just how misleading these arguments are if we try to relate them to Hobbes's theoretical framework. In an earlier part of the *Leviathan*, Hobbes had established gratitude as being due to benefactors because "no man giveth but with intention of good to himself," since when that intention is frustrated "there will be no beginning of benevolence or trust; nor, consequently, of mutual help, nor of reconciliation of one man to another; and therefore they are to remain still in the condition of war, which is contrary to the first and fundamental law of nature, which commandeth men to *seek peace*" (15.16; emphasis in original). The natural law commanding gratitude is, therefore, itself justified as a consequence of the fundamental right to self-preservation. Similarly, "equity" is defended with a view to the consideration that, without impartial treatment of persons, "the controversies of men cannot be determined but by war" (15.23).

The preceding does not, however, mean that we should dismiss Hobbes's suggestion that a deterrence-based criminal justice system would be more humane on the whole (in the sense that it would be milder than the alternative). For it seems plausible that a criminal justice system informed by Hobbesian principles would dispense with many punishments (all of those that in no way contribute to security or that are purely retributive) and that it would be receptive to adopting the mildest possible modes of punishment, so long as they are effective (since suffering is no longer itself the end of punishment). To anticipate later chapters of the present study, it is fair to say that the impressive accomplishments achieved by the modern criminal justice system were first made possible by Hobbes's unleashing of the punishing power from its traditional moral restraints. This has led to the transformation of criminology into a technical science, which in turn has vastly increased the sophistication of modern criminal justice policy analysis. Nor can we overstate the significance of Hobbes's new conception of criminal justice for the many modern innovations in criminal procedure (in investigation, trial, appeal, etc.), all of which have minimized the miscarriage of justice due to human partiality. Having said this, we should not be too quick to attribute these happy developments to a corresponding improvement in the moral understanding of criminal justice. The extent to which Hobbes's theory of punishment succeeds in convincing us of the justice and nobility of the kind of criminal justice system he proposed can only be judged after we have traced further historical developments in the practice and theory of modern criminal justice.

Punishing the Guilty and the Doctrine of Authorization

The preceding analysis has shown that Hobbes's theory of punishment implies that it is permissible to punish the innocent in certain circumstances, in conformity with natural law. This, in turn, led us to observe that in Hobbes's framework, words like "innocence" and "guilt" lose their ordinary meaning. Admittedly, for reasons stated by Hobbes, eventualities such as punishing the innocent would be exceedingly rare for practical purposes. We are inclined simply to ignore (as merely "academic") the thorny moral problem of justifying such a step should it ever come to pass, and this is just what Hobbes himself does by concealing the problem under rhetorical obfuscations. Yet the same problem re-emerges in another context in which it cannot be ignored: the much more common case of punishing the guilty.

The requirement of justifying punishment of the guilty is itself often ignored. While we have immediate and strong reservations about punishing the innocent, we have no such objections to punishing the guilty. On the contrary, when the guilty suffer punishment, we say they had it coming without thinking to ask why we believe this to be true. Thus when we were confronted with the difficult case of punishing the innocent in a political emergency, we demanded justification, but there does not seem to be the same urgency to look for a justification for punishing convicted criminals. Rather, the controversy surrounding punishment of criminals is commonly about *how much* and *what kind* of punishment they should receive. The need to justify the punishment of criminals cannot, however, be escaped in the context of Hobbes's thought,[29] where we find him once again trying to soften the shock of the paradoxical implications of his political rationalism.

There is nothing inconsistent in Hobbes's claim that the sovereign has the right to punish convicted offenders even while the offender has an equal right to resist. It is true that the criminal, as Hobbes understands him, is completely guiltless in the strict sense (he is no more morally blameworthy than any other human being, since we are all motivated by the same desires that are beyond our control) – yet this does not make the criminal immune from punishment. What is more, the criminal is entirely justified in resisting his punishment, as his right to defend himself from harm is the first and most fundamental right (cf. 14.8, 29). The subject's obligation to his sovereign becomes void as soon as his life or means of existence become threatened, which is the case when he is sentenced to punishment (21.12).[30] None of this poses any theoretical difficulty for the punishment of criminals: when the criminal's obligation to his sovereign becomes void, he returns to the state of nature, in which nothing can be just or unjust (since "notions of right and wrong, justice and injustice, have there no place" – 13.13), from which it follows that, just as the criminal has a right to defend his life and limb, the commonwealth has a right to restrain or kill the dangerous criminal as an enemy in the state of nature. Thus, there exists a clash of rights in the conflict between the criminal and civil society without any injustice being committed on either side. This is because, for Hobbes, a right is essentially a liberty – nothing more or less (14.3) – and as such it does not impose on the sovereign the obligation to respect the subject's right to resist (just as in the state of nature no one is obliged to respect any other's right to preserve himself).[31]

Despite the unimpeachable consistency of Hobbes's arguments in defence of society's right to coerce anyone who poses a danger to it, this doctrine remains extreme from the point of view of ordinary morality. Hobbes himself saw this as a problem to be addressed.[32] One way in which Hobbes shows his awareness of this as a problem is by insisting on characterizing the coercion of criminals by the sovereign as "punishment," explicitly distinguishing this from an act of "hostility." He attempts to substantiate this distinction by arguing that, although the criminal has a right to resist his punishment, that punishment is nevertheless *not* an act of hostility because the criminal himself authorizes his own punishment, just as he authorizes all of his sovereign's actions (28.3 and 6; cf. 18.3). Accordingly, the first and fourth inferences of the natural law regarding punishment state that any evil inflicted by anyone other than the sovereign is an act of hostility "because the acts of power usurped *have not for author the person condemned*," as (it is implied) they ought to have if they are to be considered punishment in the strict sense.

One difficulty with this doctrine of contractarian authorization of punishment is that Hobbes has already shown that the sovereign's right to punish is not a grant and thus does *not* rest on the consent of the punished, but on the right of nature. It might be argued that Hobbes was forced to conclude that the criminal authorizes his own punishment as a consequence of his more basic argument (elaborated earlier in the *Leviathan*) that each subject authorizes all of his sovereign's actions, without exception, by virtue of the nature of the original social contract (17.13, 18.6, 21.10, 14). But this only compels us to ask why the subject must authorize all of his sovereign's actions in the first place. If the end of civil society, and thus of sovereignty, is to secure the safety of each – since this is the condition of the obligation of each to his sovereign – then does it not follow from this that subjects should authorize the sovereign's actions only up to the point that they actually serve this purpose?[33] Hobbes admits, however, that punishments – or at least severe corporal and carceral punishments – seriously threaten the well-being of the criminal and thus cannot reasonably be construed as having the criminal's preservation as their end. Furthermore, how are we to make sense of the strange consequence that the criminal authorizes his own punishment yet at the same time rightfully resists that same punishment, as if he could both will and not will his punishment simultaneously?

Hobbes's most direct attempt to make sense of the latter difficulty runs as follows.

> Again, the consent of a subject to sovereign power is contained in these words *I authorize, or take upon me, all his actions,* in which there is no restriction at all of his own former natural liberty; for by allowing him to kill me, I am not bound to kill myself when he commands me. It is one thing to say *kill me, or my fellow, if you please,* another thing to say *I will kill myself, or my fellow.* (xxi.14; original emphases)

This argument turns on what seems to me to be a specious assumption that the subject can authorize his own death without authorizing the means to it. It is specious because it is hard to imagine how one can truly consent to the end (the punishment) without also consenting to the means to that end (e.g., turning oneself in to the authorities instead of fleeing the country). It seems to me that one must will either the end and the means, or neither. That being so, it would make Hobbes's attempted solution here meaningless, or merely formal.[34] I am consequently inclined to agree with those who regard Hobbes's doctrine of authorization as a rhetorical strategy, since his theoretical framework does not actually depend on this doctrine.[35]

By holding that the criminal authorizes his own punishment, Hobbes makes punishment appear to take place entirely within the civil order, rather than in the state of nature as a conflict between two hostile powers. This conforms better to the commonsense point of view that criminals remain members of civil society despite having offended against its laws, and are still entitled to respect as fellow members of that society. In actual practice, while we condemn criminals as unjust and blameworthy, we still consider them *our* fellows for whom we cannot help caring and to whom we still believe we owe some obligations. It seems impossible to accept that as soon as a citizen has been convicted of a punishable crime, he is immediately expelled from the community. What is more, as Hobbes's new account of criminality points to the fundamental guiltlessness of the criminal's motives, there remains even less reason in modern societies influenced by Hobbes to treat criminals with contempt than there had been in traditional ones informed by the retributive outlook. The rhetorical assertion that the criminal authorizes his own punishment was, then, essential for Hobbes to be able to present his new conception of punishment persuasively, as not only effective but also humane.

Conclusion

Hobbes's theory of punishment was the first moral theory of punishment constructed entirely on modern principles. What makes it remarkable, and what enables it to set the tone for all subsequent modern thought on criminal justice, is its attempt to show that a penal system aiming at deterrence could be not only highly effective but also humane.[36] So it would be a mistake to classify Hobbes as a teacher of a purely utilitarian conception of crime and punishment.

Hobbes also contributed to the improvement of modern punishment by making it possible to increase the effectiveness of deterrence by encouraging the scientific study of crime and by sketching the outlines of a more rational criminal law aimed at deterrence. It is noteworthy that his definition of deterrence – "that the will of men may thereby be better disposed to obedience" – is capacious enough to include rehabilitation (as long as it serves the ultimate goal of crime prevention). This, as we will see, cleared the way for later rehabilitation movements in Western countries (the reform of criminals through prison labour, drug rehabilitation programs, community reintegration programs). Hobbes himself, however, was content to leave men as they were – with their selfish passions largely unchanged – and thus did not feel compelled to stress the state's potential role in dispensing non-punitive preventive care to past offenders who were predisposed to crime by psychological illness, drug addiction, or dysfunctional family settings. But how successful was the Hobbesian marriage between utility and humanity? How persuasive is he when he assures us that the humane treatment of criminals never conflicts with social utility? This question fundamentally informs the subsequent development of modern penal theory.

As we have seen, Hobbes had no qualms about spelling out, in the clearest possible terms, that one particular consequence of his conception of natural right was that retribution could no longer be justified. On Hobbes's principles, the traditional demand for retributive punishment could only be understood as rooted in cruelty and vainglory.

Nevertheless, while his moral psychology had relativized the content of the good, this relativism did not extend to the content of justice. The meaning of justice is not subjective but universal, according to Hobbes's analysis. According to that analysis, making covenants and enforcing them through rationalized punishment is the only means by which human beings can secure their lives and livelihoods, and this remains true despite the diversity and mutability of the objects of men's desires. There is therefore much in Hobbes's thought on crime and punishment that is promising – and, we might even say, morally edifying – but there is also much left to be desired. His argument against retribution is consistent with his fundamental political principles, but from the point of view of ordinary moral sensibilities it merely begs the question by means of a simple consequentialism. This leaves us to wonder: Is it not possible to make some room in the practice of modern criminal justice for a retributive element, even if this should require sacrificing some of its logical coherence? Hobbes's refutations of moral positions he opposes often emphasize the intolerable evil that is the state of nature, and the fragility of civil society, which is always threatened by the anti-social passions of individuals. Yet considering the overwhelming power of the state in comparison to the weakness of the individual in civil society, it would not seem to be excessively dangerous to make some effort to accommodate commonsense notions about what the criminal deserves. Is it not worth considering whether we could not find in retributive punishment the solution to the nagging Hobbesian problem of the ugly conflict between society's right to punish and the natural right of the criminal to self-defence? Is it not possible that corporal and carceral punishment, and perhaps even capital punishment, might be justified as what a criminal might deserve, precisely as a naturally free being and a bearer of rights? This line of argument would eventually be pursued by Kant (and later Hegel), who would go on to reject Hobbesian punishment in order to complete the task Hobbes had set for himself: to articulate a moral theory of punishment grounded in modern principles.

Chapter 3

Liberalizing the Criminal Law:
Montesquieu and Beccaria

Among Montesquieu's many contributions to liberalism is his teaching on criminal law. Nothing indicates more clearly the importance of this subject for Montesquieu than his pronouncement in *The Spirit of the Laws* that "the citizen's liberty depends *principally* on the goodness of the criminal laws."[1] Before Montesquieu, Locke's critique of absolute sovereignty had already made institutional restraint of sovereign power a theme of liberal political thought, but Locke had not specified the proper limits of sovereign power in the sphere of criminal justice in particular. Montesquieu would therefore be the first to take up this project. *The Spirit of the Laws* follows and extends the Lockean argument that the separation of powers is essential to free government, but it teaches also that even in a system of separated powers of government, the liberty of individual citizens will not be secure until it is protected from arbitrary or oppressive criminal laws.[2]

Montesquieu's liberal theory of criminal law follows Hobbes in important ways. Hobbes had taken pains to commend to the sovereign such moderate practices as transparency and publicity in the criminal law, and fairness and regularity in punishment, as well as the limitation of penal severity (which was not to exceed the requirements of deterrence). All of these innovations are echoed and reaffirmed in Montesquieu. Yet Hobbes's principle of absolute sovereignty left his doctrine of criminal justice in a precarious position, since it could not but undermine his efforts to trace moderating limits on the punishing power. In Montesquieu, by contrast, we find no evidence of a doctrine of absolute sovereignty or even of a social contract. Indeed, Montesquieu denounces in no uncertain terms the sort of "justice" dispensed by despotic governments, and for this reason he is celebrated as the father of classical liberal criminal law, in the sense that we now understand it as belonging to a larger theory of limited government and constitutionally protected individual rights.

The teaching on criminal law evolves gradually over the course of several books of *The Spirit of the Laws*, culminating in the explicit proposals for reform in Book 12. Montesquieu departs most markedly from Hobbes by positing that a government whose fundamental purpose is to provide individual security will rely less than any other form of government on the *threat* of punishment itself: a political society committed to individual liberty is the least punitive of all. Concretely, this means that free governments must learn to depend less on instilling fear and more on cultivating mild mores (popular sentiments cultivated by education and civil institutions) as a means to sap those destructive urges that are the common causes of criminality. While Montesquieu's intentions are easily stated in this way, it is not a simple matter to explain the philosophical insights behind them. An adequate understanding of *The Spirit of the Laws*'s teaching on criminal law reform requires some careful reflection about the place of the subject of criminal law in Montesquieu's political teaching as a whole.

Fear, Human Nature, and Despotism

According to Hobbes, the overwhelming and irresistible power of the absolute sovereign is entirely suitable for maintaining order because man is by nature a rationally self-seeking being. Concerned above all with his private good, each individual will be law-abiding and peaceable only as long as he believes that general fear of the sovereign's sword will keep all in check. The principle and task of criminal justice, according to this view, may therefore be straightforwardly reduced to deterrence. This cannot suffice for Montesquieu, however, since he departs from Hobbes's understanding of human beings as by nature rationally selfish. While human beings in the state of nature selfishly seek to satisfy basic needs, they are not rational. Moreover, and perhaps more importantly, Montesquieu denies that the fearfulness, timidity, and crude self-regard that characterize man in the state of nature continue to be his dominant motivations after he has entered into civil society.

Montesquieu's account of human nature introduces the important premise of our essential malleability. Man is "that flexible being who adapts himself in society to the thoughts and impressions of others,

[who] is equally capable of knowing his own nature when it is shown to him, and of losing even the feeling of it when it is concealed from him" ("Preface" [xliv–xlv]).[3] It is this malleability or adaptability that – more than either our rationality or selfishness – explains the character of human beings in society.[4] This insight accounts for the shift of emphasis in Montesquieu's political thought to the amazing variety in the particular circumstances of actual societies, which can have a great deal of influence on passions, beliefs, and institutions. This directly informs Montesquieu's great maxim that the laws and form of government should relate not so much to abstract principles of natural law, or natural right, as to the particular disposition of the people for whom they are established (1.3).

From this new theoretical vantage point, Montesquieu is able to agree with Hobbes's claim that the fear of an overwhelming power could serve as the principle of government, while denying that this is the only possible stable political arrangement. According to Montesquieu's threefold typology of governments, fear is the principle that informs despotism, as distinguished from republics and monarchies (3.9). Fear of violent death can become the dominant passion in society only after a certain way of life debases man's soul and renders it slavish (4.3). Hobbes was right, then, when he argued that in a political society founded on the principle of fear, the criminal laws must be simple and strict (cf. 6.2), but he was wrong to have assumed that every political society must be founded on fear. It is not necessary here to expound the reasons why Montesquieu regarded despotism as an inferior form of government compared to the two "moderate" forms of government – monarchy and republic.[5] For our purposes it is enough to acknowledge that, according to Montesquieu, wherever the particular circumstances of a nation permit liberty and moderate government, this course will be preferred by wise legislators to the alternative of despotism.[6] Therefore, since the criminal laws of each society must agree with the principle of its form of government, it would be a grave mistake for moderate governments to try to simplify their criminal laws, as Hobbes would have them do. For such laws would at best be in permanent contradiction with the spirit of moderate government and at worst would tend to undermine such government, leading it in the direction of despotism.

There is an additional reason, besides its theoretical simplicity, why the argument advanced by Hobbes for a simplified and rationalized criminal law is tempting, and that is that it appeals not only to our concern for security but also in a way to our sense of justice. It is not uncommon for the victim of a crime to feel that, above all, justice must be swift, and this is exactly what a rationalized criminal law promises – for to rationalize law is to simplify it in accordance with a single principle, such as utility (the greatest happiness of the greatest number) or reciprocity (an eye for an eye). We are most struck by the inconvenience of the innumerable formalities and delays that seem to pervade criminal proceedings, and we want these to be lessened as much as possible and brought into conformity with a clear principle of justice. Montesquieu acknowledges the moral appeal of immediacy and simplicity in criminal justice and admits that this is more likely to be found in absolute states. "It is constantly said," he writes, "that justice should be rendered everywhere as it is in Turkey" (6.2). Yet Montesquieu also stresses the unseen dangers of simplifying criminal justice. The delays and formalities of criminal laws – frustrating as they may be from the point of view of our insistent demand for simple and immediate justice – serve as indispensable safeguards of individual liberty, inasmuch as they provide the accused with a range of legal remedies to challenge any suit lodged against them.[7] This is particularly important when a public accusation is serious, when conviction might place the life and household of the accused in mortal danger. Thus Montesquieu (like Locke) was more sensitive than Hobbes to the problem posed by the weakness of the individual in the face of his powerful sovereign. Even if the sovereign should be so enlightened as to avoid unnecessarily oppressing his subjects, to them this would still be much too flimsy a guarantee of their safety. The citizen can feel secure only if he knows that legal protections exist of which he can avail himself – those same innumerable avenues of appeal and delay at all stages of the criminal process that can be so frustrating to victims of injustice. For these reasons, the drive to rationalize the criminal law by removing what appear to be inconvenient and unnecessary formalities can be very dangerous to liberty. Thus from a Montesquieuean perspective, retributivism and utility – two very different theoretical principles – pose the same problem for moderate government if applied systematically to criminal law, since either would lead to the law's oversimplification.

On the other hand, if the legal remedies available to the accused are to be multiplied, just as Montesquieu recommends, would this not make it easier for the innocent and the guilty alike to escape conviction, and would this not thereby encourage crime and vitiate the most basic function of government, namely, the security of the innocent?

Shame, Liberty, and Moderate Government

Montesquieu's emphasis on human malleability enabled him to elaborate an alternative way in which moderate governments might maintain peace without always having to resort to the threat of force. In moderate governments a decent sense of shame becomes a much more effective deterrent against criminality than the fear of death, whereas in despotic states men are so oppressed and miserable that one has little hope of influencing them except by threatening them with very severe punishments. Montesquieu argues that individuals living in moderate states not only enjoy the security of their lives and possessions but also feel the esteem of their fellows and develop a passionate love of their homeland. Consequently, they fear losing these social goods even more than they fear pain and death. Since a bad reputation is enough to cause one to lose one's enjoyment of social goods, in moderate states where "one fears the loss of life more than one dreads death as such ... punishments that merely suppress life are sufficient." In such societies, the wise legislator "will insist less on punishing crimes than on preventing them; he will apply himself more to giving mores than to inflicting punishments" (6.9).[8] Insofar as a criminal conviction in itself carries with it the infamy of the crime, this is sufficient to deter many crimes even if no punishment should follow. Accordingly, in moderate states "the greatest penalty for a bad action will be to be convicted of it" (ibid.). Thus, even though in moderate states the guilty may successfully appeal, delay, or mitigate their deserved punishment, the threat of conviction, with its accompanying opprobrium, could well be expected to prevent crimes just as effectively as the threat of severe penalties does in despotic states. Perhaps even the prospect of being *accused* of a crime would be enough in many cases to check wrongful behaviour. In this way, Montesquieu indicates how the important political problem he has in view might be solved – that is, how it may be possible to maintain conditions in which individual citizens could feel truly secure from arbitrary legal prosecution, without sacrificing public security to the extensive legal protections guaranteed to the accused.

In addition to this argument for decreasing reliance on punishment, as such, as a means of crime prevention, Montesquieu goes on to argue for a decrease of the severity of punishment. According to him, increasing severity in punishment is not just contrary to the spirit of moderate government – it is self-defeating. Once again, Montesquieu's view of the natural adaptability of human beings provides the key to his analysis. "Experience has shown that, in countries where penalties are gentle, the citizen's spirit is struck by them as it is elsewhere by heavy ones" (6.12). Where some law is frequently violated, the simple legislative response is to impose a stiffer penalty, and this does the job for a short time. Yet over the long term "the imagination becomes inured to this heavier penalty as it had to the lesser, and as fear of the lesser penalty diminishes, one is forced to establish the heavier in every case" (ibid.). All that the escalation in penal severity accomplishes is to brutalize citizens by rendering them insensitive to extreme suffering, thus making them harsher towards one another and less (not more) fearful of punishment. Eventually, even capital punishment becomes only a marginally effective deterrent of crime, although once society has reached such a pass, capital punishments become the only possible method of maintaining order. Thus, Montesquieu calls the death penalty "the remedy … for a sick society" (12.4). Such considerations lead Montesquieu to conclude that punitive criminal laws corrupt moderate governments: contrary to Hobbes, moderate government and security can and do go together. But if the escalation of penal severity can corrupt citizens and render them slavish, then perhaps the moderation of punishments through enlightened penal reform can have the opposite effect by instilling gentle mores and encouraging mild sentiments, while improving security and strengthening the institutions of moderate government (6.13).

We must now complicate the simple account of Montesquieu's teaching presented so far. Montesquieu illustrates his thesis about the nature of criminal law in moderate governments with his customary use of detailed historical examples. Yet a careful reading of the chapters on criminal law makes one doubt that Montesquieu's historical examples fully bear out his conclusions. Most dubious is Montesquieu's claims about the mildness of the criminal and penal laws of certain exemplary republics and monarchies of which he speaks. The surface argument about the connection between moderate forms of government and mild criminal laws carries some plausibility: in despotic states subjects are mere possessions of the despot, but in moderate states – that is, monarchies and republics – citizens are endowed with substantial legal rights and are relatively free in their intercourse with one another; as a result, in moderate governments individuals could be expected to be treated with greater respect and consideration, especially when their guilt or innocence is in question in a criminal trial. Yet the historical proof Montesquieu marshals in support of this argument as it applies to actual republics and monarchies is ambiguous at best. Let us take the case of republics first.

Montesquieu gives evidence of some mild penal practices in early Rome, Sparta, and Athens (all of them republics and therefore moderate governments according to Montesquieu's schema). Yet that evidence is elsewhere (and sometimes in the same context) contradicted by descriptions of practices carried out by those same cities that can only be described as harsh and punitive.[9] Montesquieu's extensive discussion of the penal laws established by the Roman republic may serve as our case in point. He concedes that the laws of the Twelve Tables, enacted sixty years after the birth of the republic, were "full of very cruel provisions" – including capital punishment for many crimes as well as "punishment by fire." He attempts to excuse this appearance of republican cruelty by arguing that those severe penal laws were authored by a few individuals – the Decemvirs – empowered with extraordinary authority, whose rule would later become despotic (6.15). Yet Livy, who is Montesquieu's source on this subject, relates the same events somewhat differently. According to Livy's account, the plebs were allowed to review and amend the legislation of the Decemvirs before it was enacted, which seems to suggest that the plebs were largely satisfied with the legislation as proposed by the Decemvirs. Moreover, the criminal laws Montesquieu identifies as cruel remained in force in Rome, according to Livy, even after the tyrannical Decemvirs were deposed.[10] Montesquieu tries to argue further that the gentleness of the republican spirit still shines through in the fact that those remaining harsh provisions of the penal laws in the Twelve Tables were eventually modified or abrogated by the Roman people. Yet he himself makes clear that those changes did not come until very much later – approximately 250 years after the founding of the republic.[11] All of this makes the case in favour of Montesquieu's thesis seem tenuous at best, at least when it comes to the Roman republic.

Even more telling, Montesquieu's thesis – that republican penal justice is moderate – is contradicted by his own theory of the nature of republican government. He repeatedly stresses the unnatural harshness of the republican way of life. That way of life demands so much repression of one's most natural drives in the name of the public good that it renders human beings prone to excessive anger and cruelty (3.3–4, 4.5–6). Thus despite leaving the comforting surface impression that republics are gentle and humane (perhaps in order to avoid disappointing readers with a deep admiration for classical politics), Montesquieu quietly but clearly indicates that this form of government will nearly always tend to cultivate harshness in citizens and in the criminal laws themselves.

In a similar way, Montesquieu deliberately overstates the gentleness of criminal laws in monarchies, the other form of moderate government. The extent of this overstatement would have been quite palpable to thoughtful readers in Montesquieu's time. He claims that in moderate states "the head of even the lowest citizen is esteemed" (6.2), and while this may be true relatively speaking (when compared with despotism), he does not deny that the lowest-ranking individuals in a monarchy are not accorded the same esteem as the highest-ranking. What is more, the highest orders in monarchies are believed to possess honour – that is, to be sensitive to it and to value it above even life itself – whereas no such sensibility is attributed to the common people. This implies that, from the point of view of the higher classes in a monarchy, shame cannot be used as an effective measure to deter criminality in the common people, as it can in the nobility (6.10). Since, according to Montesquieu, honour is prized as the highest good in monarchies, the lack of it among the common people draws upon them the contempt of the nobility and the court, along with all the accompanying cruelty in the administration of justice that may be expected. Contrary to Montesquieu's general claim about criminal law in monarchies, therefore, his arguments actually imply that it would be perfectly natural for monarchical laws to impose corporal punishments on the common people. Indeed, Montesquieu himself later tacitly concedes that punishments imposed in monarchies on the highest orders tend to be significantly milder than those imposed on the lowest.[12] Over the course of his discussion, Montesquieu observes that under the European monarchies, forensic and penal practices included torture (or "the question"); the wheel, and other excruciatingly painful and disfiguring punishments; the death penalty for a wide range of crimes; and corporal punishment of the lower orders.[13]

It is important in this context to add another dimension to Montesquieu's ambiguous treatment of the supposedly gentle criminal laws of republics and monarchies. The European monarchies that Montesquieu had before his eyes were, of course, Christian ones. Elsewhere Montesquieu praises Christianity's moderating effects on mores,[14] yet he says very little about Christianity's influence on criminal laws. Is it possible that Montesquieu maintains a respectful silence about Christianity in this connection because it had not had a moderating effect on criminal law in Europe – and perhaps even the opposite effect? The only mention of Christianity in all of Book 6 (the book treating criminal law thematically) is found in a chapter on the powerlessness of Japanese laws. There, Montesquieu attributes that powerlessness to the harshness of the Japanese manner of punishing offenders. Montesquieu's explanation for why that nation punishes so harshly has recourse to certain opinions peculiar to the Japanese:

> In Japan almost all crimes are punished by death because disobedience to such a great emperor as Japan's is an enormous crime. It is not a question of correcting the guilty man but of avenging the prince. These ideas are drawn from servitude and derive chiefly from the fact that the emperor is the owner of all the goods and so almost all crimes are committed directly against his interests. (6.13)

It is striking how much the idea that the Japanese have about their emperor resembles the idea that the Bible has of its God (cf. 12.4).[15] If the parallel is granted, then could the biblical idea have had a similar effect on criminal law in Christian Europe, rendering it harsher and more punitive (and therefore less effective – see 6.13) than it might otherwise have been?

Therefore, notwithstanding the unreserved praise Montesquieu sometimes flatteringly bestows on criminal law in the so-called "moderate" governments, his fully developed view is much more complex. Paradoxically, the criminal laws of a people will not be moderate simply by virtue of the fact that their government happens to be moderate – that is, monarchic, republican, or Christian. It seems that some additional conditions must exist to allow for moderation in criminal law. What are these conditions? Notwithstanding Montesquieu's allusions to some less than gentle aspects of the criminal justice practised in the European monarchies, it remains true for him that the European states are fertile soil for moderate politics because their laws, institutions, and climate are hospitable to liberty (understood as the security of the citizen and the constitutional separation of powers). The arguments for this thesis – so central to the *Spirit of the Laws* as a whole – are complicated and are developed at length in other parts of the work. One highlight is Montesquieu's presentation, in Books 11 and 19, of his model of liberal society – an idealized England – a nation that, unlike other moderate nations and governments, has liberty as its chief aim. According to that well-known account, England's fortuitous mixture of commercialism, restlessness of spirit, and a certain kind of equality (19.27), when combined with a favourable political system (11.6; Montesquieu was, of course, speaking of England after the Glorious Revolution of 1688), created conditions for an unprecedented pursuit of liberty. Such liberal politics is uniquely hospitable to moderate criminal law reform, because moderation in criminal justice means nothing other than putting the emphasis on protecting the liberty (i.e., security, or the "opinion of ... security") of the citizen – whether he be a defendant or plaintiff, whether an offender or a law-abiding member of society.

The most distinguishing quality of human beings is their ability to adapt to their physical and social circumstances, which includes the capacity to conform to the opinions of the society into which we they are born, taking up its predominant beliefs and practices and regulating their lives in accordance with them. It stands to reason that this quality makes us sensitive to shame, since we are loath to incur a bad reputation with our fellows. Thus, by the same token, we normally avoid wrongdoing not only because we fear a penalty, but also out of a decent sense of shame (12.4 [pp. 190–1]). This decent aversion to injustice may be undermined wherever tyrannical rulers terrorize and brutalize their subjects, but since the chief aim of liberal societies (such as Montesquieu's England) is the protection of life and private property, individuals there are left free to engage in all sorts of voluntary commerce (broadly understood), so that they come to value their membership in their chosen associations. With such positive incentives to social membership, liberal societies are uniquely well suited – better than any other form of moderate government, to say nothing of despotism – to practise non-coercive and indirect methods of law enforcement.[16] Hobbes was correct when he defined the aim of punishment as deterrence, but his view of human nature prevented him from appreciating that effective deterrence in liberal societies should be sought in the celerity, regularity, and ignominy of punishments, not in their severity. One could even go so far as to say that, up to a point, in liberal states the severity of punishments is inversely proportional to their effectiveness.

Although it is true that not all eighteenth-century European states were as committed to liberty as Montesquieu's England (and perhaps not even England itself),[17] they possessed most of the elements discussed by Montesquieu as being crucial for liberalism, and therefore they had at least the potential of successfully carrying out liberalizing reforms, including the important reform of criminal law. This set of historical circumstances provided Montesquieu with the opportunity to outline the principles that such reform might follow if it was to achieve its full potential.

Montesquieu on the Idea of Criminal Justice

There remains, however, a further difficulty with the picture we have painted so far. Montesquieu teaches that laws in general flow from, and are informed by, the structure and nature of the established government. This would lead one to expect English criminal law in particular to be milder and more humane than the more traditional criminal codes of other European nations, in proportion to the degree to which the English constitution is more liberal than the other national constitutions. Yet Montesquieu mentions English forensic practices only to criticize them (such as the English Parliament's practice of issuing bills of attainder).[18] In fact, the English criminal law of this period (the "Bloody Code," as it is referred to now) embodied many punitive ideas and enacted many harsh practices – a fact that could scarcely have escaped Montesquieu's notice. According to Blackstone, writing in 1769, English law recognized no fewer than 160 capital crimes.[19] Contrary to what Montesquieu has prepared us to expect, eighteenth-century England was very far from achieving enlightened criminal law reform; indeed, it was no better off in this respect than the other European monarchies. But how could this be if the structure of the English constitution was exceedingly hospitable to liberty?

Montesquieu could not explain the severe character of England's criminal code by reference to its constitution, nor does he ever suggest that this penal severity was merely the product of inept legislation or that it was an artefact of the imperfect state of the technical sciences of criminology and penal administration. Rather, he indicates that these excesses were the result of incorrect *ideas* about punishment – in particular, traditional notions about the scope of wrongdoing to which punishment properly applies.[20]

Montesquieu apparently follows the classical and Christian traditions in affirming that punishment is by its nature retributive or desert-based: "punishments" rightly understood are "a kind of retaliation, which causes the society to refuse to give security to a citizen who has deprived or has wanted to deprive another of it" (12.4 [p. 191]). Montesquieu appears to draw this view of punishment from his understanding of natural law or justice broadly conceived, as presented earlier in *The Spirit of the Laws*. According to that earlier presentation, natural laws are certain necessary relations in the nature of things, which, as such, do not owe their being to human convention. In particular, natural justice dictates that "if there were intelligent beings that had received some kindness from another being, they ought to be grateful for it," and, conversely, "that one intelligent being who has done harm to another intelligent being deserves the same harm in return" (1.1). We are surprised to find Montesquieu expressing this endorsement of the traditional concept of reciprocity and desert in punishment, especially considering how much he follows Hobbes in other respects.

It seems that Montesquieu finds fault not with the traditional idea of retribution as such but rather with the scope of its application. Traditionally, punishments were held to apply to all sorts of wrongdoing, which Montesquieu groups into four categories of crime: crimes against mores; those against religion; those against public tranquility; and, finally, those against security. According to Montesquieu, however, punishments (*supplices*) – as distinguished from penalties in the broader sense (*peines*) – ought properly to apply only to this last class. Thus, it would be in accordance with natural justice for society to express its anger and indignation against those citizens whose violence threatens public security and to punish them with a reciprocal harm, as they deserve. But this would not be appropriate in the case of other sorts of crimes. Montesquieu thus implies that criminal justice in traditional societies – including biblical Israel and the ancient republics, to say nothing of despotic regimes – violated natural justice.[21]

Montesquieu supports this view of a more limited scope for retributive punishment for the following reason. Retribution or vengeance may apply to crimes of the other three classes, but it is not the place of the *civil* authority to punish them. Since the ultimate purpose of civil society is or ought to be security, only crimes against security are crimes against civil society, which may and ought to avenge itself by natural right. A crime against religion, on the other hand, is a crime against God and should be left for God himself to avenge.[22] It follows more generally that each penalty should be drawn "from the particular nature of the crime" – that is, from the sphere of activity in which the crime was committed (12.4 [p. 189]). Montesquieu seems to regard collective religious practice, and the collective practice of moral virtue, as the sphere of what Locke had called "voluntary associations." Such associations (as Locke had understood them)[23] are often useful to civil society as sources of moral and civic education, and as such, they can safely be tolerated and even encouraged by it. But insofar as these associations have eternal salvation as their goal – a goal that is beyond the scope of political life – they lie outside of the civil authority's jurisdiction in all matters that do not affect security. This means both that the state should not attempt to regulate the spiritual beliefs of religious or moral associations on the one hand, and on the other that it is absolved of any responsibility for enforcing the doctrine of any particular faith.

Montesquieu does not deny that civil society may have a legitimate interest in maintaining and regulating religion, mores, and public tranquility, since all of these can have an effect on security. But in this regard, legislation need only correct; it need not punish. The chief mode that correction of breaches of religion, mores, and public decency should take in a liberal polity is loss of reputation and social standing – as Montesquieu had previously suggested and as he now repeats in Book 12. Sacrilege may be sufficiently corrected (i.e., either deterred or negated in its consequences) by expulsion from the congregation of the faithful. Breaches of "public or individual continence" – that is, offences against the virtue of moderation – should be curbed by public infamy, but fines might also be imposed (perhaps because someone willing to offend against common decency might not be deterred by shame). Finally, breaches of public tranquility or order may be corrected by exile or by "penalties that restore men's troubled spirits and return them to the established order" (12.4). It would appear that many of these corrective measures could be carried out by society itself (as distinguished from its public officials), especially in cases of offences against religion or mores. When an individual insults what is held sacred by his fellows or offends their accepted standards of decorum, no one is in a better position than that community itself to censure or, if necessary, cast out the offender – all without having to resort to coercive measures, which are usually reserved for the civil authority.

Montesquieu's conception of liberal criminal justice thus appears to combine political goods that had been irreconcilable in traditional societies. It seems that the happy circumstances of liberal societies allow for mildness in the penal laws; for effective deterrence without a dangerous centralization of power; and for retribution to be adequate to the principles of natural justice without having a brutalizing effect on society.[24]

But liberal criminal justice, as outlined by Montesquieu, faces two problems. First, as we have seen, Montesquieu fundamentally follows Hobbes in making individual security the primary goal of politics; but Hobbes had shown that the fundamental natural right to self-preservation, if consistently followed in its political implications, is incompatible with the traditional concepts of moral responsibility, desert, and punishment. Montesquieu affirms that retribution is in accord with natural justice, but nowhere does he prove this. On the contrary, he himself had argued that retributive punishment is at home in despotic regimes, which are an inferior form of government.[25] Perhaps something led Montesquieu to believe that the concern for reciprocity is connected to a human phenomenon that transcends even the differences among the three types of government – namely, the family. After all, do we not initially learn reciprocity in the context of the family – namely, in the debt of gratitude we believe we owe our parents?[26] Contrary to both Hobbes and Rousseau, Montesquieu regarded the family as in some sense natural and thus believed that the part of morality originating in the family must be accommodated by wise legislation.[27] Furthermore, according to Montesquieu the decency of a society depends on the maintenance of its mores – even in liberal polities, where mores may be somewhat less pure.[28] For all of these reasons it may be politically desirable for the laws to express in an attenuated way – to echo, as it were – certain core elements of purer mores, including righteous indignation, when this can be done without compromising the liberty of the citizen. For example, since the severe punishment of violent crimes is in accord with liberalism's emphasis on security, the criminal law would not be in contradiction with the spirit of liberty if it were to impose the death penalty on very serious violent crimes such as murder, for that punishment would simultaneously be in conformity with the spirit of retribution. Having said all this, however, we must add that such political considerations do not amount to a *proof* of the justice of retribution.

The second problem confronting Montesquieu's liberal conception of criminal justice runs in the opposite direction. If we grant that the concern to return harm for harm must be accommodated politically, we might go on to wonder whether the scheme of criminal law sketched by Montesquieu would be sufficient for this purpose. We might wonder whether the restriction of punishment to crimes against security, and whether the relatively mild modes of correction proposed for offences against mores and religion, would fully satisfy justice as reciprocity, especially in the case of what are considered to be the most egregious wrongs against "mores." Would it be enough merely to enact deterrent penalties against horrendous crimes such as rape, sadism, and pedophilia, and then to allow society informally to censure rapists, sadists, and pedophiles? Or would such penalties fall short of what retributive justice, as ordinarily understood, would demand?

These difficulties arise in the context of Montesquieu's discussion in Book 12. He names rape and kidnapping as two crimes that attack security and mores at the same time; he then argues that punishments, in the strict sense, rightly apply to such crimes *only* as offences against *security* (12.4 [p. 191]). He does not mention exactly what punishment he believes rapists deserve, although we know well enough that the criminal laws of most actual governments impose very serious penalties against this crime with the intention of expressing society's moral outrage. In fact, it could be argued that the seriousness of this crime has more to do with its violation of morality or mores than it does with the physical harm it causes.[29] That is because rape seems to be a serious crime in our eyes not only because it damages the victim's body (damage which may in some cases be minimal) but also because it damages her dignity.

We might question in yet another way Montesquieu's grounds for narrowing the range of punishable crimes to crimes against security alone. While some basis may be found for this in the Christian distinction between the spiritual and the temporal, it is not so clear that Christian political thinkers always drew the same conclusions for criminal justice as Montesquieu has done. According to both Calvin and Augustine, the ultimate authority to punish is God's alone, yet God can and does delegate this authority to his human representatives and especially to the civil authority.[30] According to these authors it follows that, since God punishes all injustices (and not merely crimes against public security), the civil authority may well take it upon itself to punish moral wrongs, especially those that offend public decency, modesty, and the family. It seems unlikely that Montesquieu – who was well aware of the enduring human phenomenon of righteous indignation – would have favoured the erosion of the legal expression of society's anger towards morally serious crimes like rape: such a thing would fly in the face of any decent society's most deeply cherished beliefs. Rather, he seems to have anticipated a gradual decline in the absolute (but not the relative) severity of penalties imposed on morally egregious crimes, as the severity of punishments prescribed by liberal penal codes gradually declined overall.[31]

As we have seen, Montesquieu's endorsement of retributive punishment was qualified by his commitment to liberty and by his appreciation of the affinity between retribution and despotic government. Consequently, he seems to have attempted to continue Hobbes's rhetorical project of transforming the popular idea of punishment by contriving to limit the scope or application of the principle of retribution as much as practicable. Whereas in the classical and biblical traditions the principle of retribution had applied to all wrongdoing, in Montesquieu's teaching righteous anger and retribution are (to repeat) reserved for crimes against security alone. Other moral wrongs were to be attributed merely to human frailty and, as such, pitied. By elaborating a set of programmatic principles for criminal reform (while blurring most of the difficult and radical moral–theoretical questions they raised), Montesquieu seems to have intended to contribute to the vast cultural project of political Enlightenment that was already well under way. For this large-scale project, the transformation of popular ideas about criminal justice would be crucial because its effect would be to decrease, over time, society's serious concern for the reciprocal return of harm – a major obstacle to the softening of mores that Montesquieu viewed as necessary for the spread of commerce, liberal institutions, and scientific enlightenment.

Montesquieu's Legacy and Beccaria's Treatise

Montesquieu's new ideas about criminal law reform in liberal societies were astonishingly successful in Europe and North America, although much of that success had to wait for his ideas to be popularized by the Italian *philosophe* Cesare Beccaria, in the latter's short treatise *On Crimes and Punishments* (1764). This was perhaps to be expected, for the daunting size and complex structure of Montesquieu's work must have made it less accessible to the wider reading public. Beccaria himself did not hide the debt his work owed to the "immortal President de Montesquieu." Not long after Beccaria's treatise was published, enthusiasm for penal reform spread throughout Europe and the United States. Instantly, criminal law became a favourite subject of political pamphlets as well as legal and philosophical treatises. Beccaria's admirers included other theoreticians, such as Voltaire, D'Alembert, Blackstone, and Bentham, as well as influential sovereigns and statesmen like Catherine II of Russia, Maria Theresa of Austria, and Thomas Jefferson.[32]

Beccaria's work is perhaps best known for its opposition to capital punishment, but in this he followed in the footsteps of Montesquieu, who had argued that the death penalty was the remedy resorted to by a "sick society." Actually, Beccaria's most significant theoretical contribution was his attempt to ground the right to punish in the social contract of liberal theory.[33] In this he departed from both Hobbes and Montesquieu, who found the origin of the right to punish in nature rather than in human convention. Beccaria's argument is as follows:

> It was necessity ... that constrained men to give up part of their personal liberty; hence, it is certain that each man wanted to put only the least

possible portion into the public deposit, only as much as necessary to induce others to defend it. The aggregate of these smallest possible portions of individual liberty constitutes the right to punish; everything beyond that is an abuse and not justice, a fact but scarcely a right. (ch. 2)

On this liberal-contractarian basis, Beccaria proceeds to argue against capital punishment:

By what right can men presume to slaughter their fellows? Certainly not that right which is the foundation of sovereignty and the laws. For these are nothing but the sum of the smallest portions of each man's own freedom; they represent the general will which is the aggregate of the individual wills. Who has ever willingly given up to others the authority to kill him? How on earth can the minimum sacrifice of each individual's freedom involve handing over the greatest of all goods, life itself? ... Thus, the death penalty is not a matter of *right*, as I have just shown, but is an act of war on the part of society against the citizen that comes about when it is deemed necessary or useful to destroy his existence. (ch. 28)

Beccaria's argument in this passage invokes the Hobbesian authorization thesis in order to reject it. This is perfectly reasonable, for we have already seen that Hobbes had failed, despite his best efforts, to square the circle, as it were, of showing how the criminal might retain his right of self-preservation while at the same time authorizing his sovereign (by way of the social contract) to put him to death.

Beccaria's refutation of the state's right to impose capital punishment is misleading, however, because the absence of a right to punish does not, in Beccaria's own view, constitute an absolute moral prohibition against executions. On the contrary, the death penalty would continue to be appropriate in two cases, according to Beccaria. First, if a criminal threatens the very existence of civil society itself – because "he still has sufficient connections and such power that he can threaten the security of the nation even though he be deprived of his liberty" – then "his death is required" (ch. 28). Second, even when there is no imminent catastrophic threat to the existence of the civil order, the execution of a criminal would still be necessary "if his death were the one and only deterrent to dissuade others from committing crimes." Beccaria goes so far as to call this last use of capital punishment "just and necessary." In order to soften the jarring effect of this apparently self-contradictory concession, Beccaria suggests that in "the experience of all ages ... the ultimate punishment has never deterred men who were determined to harm society." In other words, although it is theoretically possible that the death penalty might be justifiable in some circumstances, in practice, according to Beccaria, it is such an ineffective deterrent that it may safely be retired as an obsolete form of punishment. But *is* this claim about the uselessness of the death penalty in fact true? It may be that Beccaria does not really mean that the death penalty has no ability to deter, but rather that it is not the *only* effective means of deterrence. While the death penalty is a better deterrent than no punishment at all, it is, according to Beccaria, a weaker deterrent than milder but more enduring punishments; it is in this sense that the death penalty can be said to be useless. The claim that mild but long-lasting punishments are the most effective depends on a psychology that emphasizes the strength of habit and the weakness of reason's control over the passions. Thus, Beccaria argues that "it is not the severity of punishment that has the greatest impact on the human mind, but rather its duration, for our sensibility is more easily and surely stimulated by tiny repeated impressions than by a strong but temporary movement. The rule of habit is universal over every sentient being, and, as man talks and walks and tends to his needs with the aid of habit, so moral ideas are fixed in his mind only by lasting and repeated blows" (ch. 27). By this view, hard labour and imprisonment would be better punishments than the death penalty, since their effects are more continuous. Beccaria further argues (drawing on Montesquieu) that whatever effectiveness the death penalty may possess when it is first instituted eventually decays over time; indeed, it may even indirectly contribute to crime as people become accustomed to the sight of violence and suffering inflicted by human beings. "To the degree that punishments become more cruel, men's souls become hardened, just as fluids always seek the level of surrounding objects" (ch. 27).[34]

Beccaria's argument that the death penalty is ineffective as a deterrent in most – but not all – practical circumstances still leaves those rare cases to be accounted for, in which harsh punishment presents itself as the only expedient. Punishment in such cases must also be accounted for as right or just, if we are to have a fully satisfying moral theory of punishment. This, of course, is precisely the problem that Hobbes had faced, a problem that he attempted to solve by recourse to contractarian authorization – which, as we have seen, Beccaria rejects. Although in the final analysis, the social contract is incapable of authorizing capital punishment, this failure is not fatal to Hobbes's theory of punishment, as we saw, because Hobbes located the origin of the right to punish in the state of nature (i.e., in the natural right of self-preservation). Beccaria, on the other hand, makes no room for such a right, and this puts his theory of punishment in jeopardy.

Perhaps for this reason Beccaria elevates general utility to the status of a moral principle. To be precise, while Beccaria argues that the social contract is the *origin* of the right to punish, he makes general utility – the "greatest happiness shared among the greatest number" – the purpose and measure of punishments, and indeed of all laws and public policies generally (see "Introduction"). We learn from Beccaria, however, that general utility is "just" in a sense that is not distinguishable from the force and advantage of the majority. "Note that the word 'right' is not a contradiction of the word 'force'; the former is, rather, a modification of the latter – namely, the modification most useful to the greatest number … By 'justice,' moreover, I do not mean anything but the bond necessary to hold private interests together" (ch. 2). But what makes the advantage of the majority just or right from the point of view of the criminal? Certainly not any duty to sacrifice his own interest to that of civil society, since Beccaria explicitly denies the existence of any such duty (see ibid.).[35] At least in the Hobbesian picture the criminal would have to acknowledge that the sovereign was proceeding against him with the same right of nature as he himself claimed. Thus, general utility does not prove to be any more successful than contractarian authorization in avoiding the morally problematic implications of the modern punishing power.[36]

Perhaps Beccaria believed that the unresolved theoretical difficulties in his treatise would not prevent its practical proposals from gaining a popular audience; perhaps, that is, he anticipated that his resounding condemnation of severity in punishment in the name of humanity would appeal to popular sensibilities that had been softened by the influence of liberalism. Thus, in the context of his claim that capital punishment is a poor deterrent, he writes that "if [the argument] does not persuade men, who always suspect the voice of reason and heed the voice of authority, then one needs only to consult human nature in order to feel the truth of my assertion." Similarly, his treatise occasionally appeals to a certain kind of benevolence stemming from "kindly virtues born of an enlightened reason" (ch. 3). He seems to be suggesting that even when we have some reason to doubt that mild penalties would be as effective as severe ones, we might still listen to our hearts and opt for humane (although somewhat less effective) measures, regardless of what reason may tell us. The problem of the unaccounted-for case of the sovereign treating the criminal as a mortal enemy in the state of nature may be forgotten by those of us who have confidence in the goodness of our hearts.[37]

The generation of penal reformers that followed Beccaria in Europe and the United States agreed almost unanimously on theoretical principles.[38] What remained was to start putting these principles into practice by drawing up large-scale programs for modernizing criminal justice institutions in light of the discoveries of modern medicine and the burgeoning fields of psychology and criminology. Above all, the reformers began expressing enthusiasm for the newest technical innovation: the penitentiary.[39] Credit for this innovation is to be given especially to the American penal reformers at the time of the founding and in the early nineteenth century. The penitentiary movement began in Philadelphia, where it was supported in equal measure by the Quakers, who abhorred all forms of violence, and by the Enlightenment rationalists. Montesquieu and Beccaria had shown the world how punishments could become milder without losing their effectiveness; the American reformers then followed this principle to its end: incarceration is the ideal punishment, since it is the least physically painful and degrading (or so it was thought) while still being sufficiently threatening to serve as a deterrent. What is more, varying the length of prison terms would modulate their severity, and this would allow incarceration to replace virtually all other forms of punishment.

If these advantages were not enough to recommend it, penitentiary punishment offered a further benefit: it promised to rehabilitate prisoners, who could engage in useful trades and educational programs while serving their time. This would prepare them to lead more productive, independent lives upon their reintroduction to society. Some of the more pious reformers even believed that the penitentiary would provide an opportunity for inmates to meditate on their past actions, to repent of their crimes, and perhaps even to embrace religious salvation. (Indeed, this supposed aspect of modern carceral punishment is what gave prisons their popular name: "penitentiaries.") When he visited the United States in 1831, the French statesman and political philosopher Alexis de Tocqueville's official business was to investigate the American penitentiary system on behalf of the French government. In the course of their travels, he and his friend Beaumont expressed reservations about the prospects for genuine moral and religious reform of prisoners in the new penal institutions; indeed, Tocqueville described Americans' preoccupation with penal reform as a kind of "monomania."[40] Nevertheless, both men spoke highly of the institutions themselves as forming the core of a humane and effective new system of punishment.

The influence of Montesquieu's criminological and penological ideas on the religious understanding of these matters can be seen in the writings of some of the more pious penal reformers, such as Benjamin Rush, who established the Philadelphia Prison Society during the founding era. Rush published two influential essays on punishment in which he championed the new, scientific approach to crime advocated by the European philosophers, while seeking to justify that approach in the light of scripture. According to Rush, the Christian obligations of forgiveness and universal benevolence – which included the promotion of repentance for the salvation of men's souls – were binding on individual Christians as well as on state governments. The penitentiary, he argued, served the ends of the Christian faith beautifully.[41] By contrast, there was no religious duty to impose the death penalty; in fact, a duty *not* to impose it was incumbent on all Christians and their governments. Following a Montesquieuan strategy of apologetics, Rush argued that only God can take life, since he alone gives it (15).

Rush's scriptural arguments can be characterized (and not unfairly) as somewhat tendentious, and they are worth restating here as evidence of the extent to which the Montesquieuan–Beccarian influence on penal thought went unquestioned. Rush admits that some might object to his appeal to the authority of scripture, observing that there are passages in the Bible in which God directly commands the Israelites to punish murder with death. In response to this objection, he provides three arguments (21). First, he claims that nothing in scripture is *against* reason, although some things in it are *above* reason. Since capital punishment is against reason, it cannot possibly be the will of God. Second, the "order and happiness of society" is agreeable to the will of God, and since capital punishment destroys the order and happiness of society, it must again be contrary to the will of God. One might wonder, though, whether Rush is not avoiding the real question here, since nowhere in the Gospels or in the Hebrew Bible does it say that the will of God cannot be contrary to reason, or that the "order and happiness of society" must be understood in terms of rational utility, as Rush seems to understand them. Rush cites two well-known Biblical passages on punishment: the first from Leviticus, in which God utters that "he that killeth a man shall surely be put to death"; and the second from Genesis, addressed to Noah, in which He says that "whoso sheddeth man's blood, by man shall his blood be shed."[42] Rush claims that in both these passages the divine utterance is not a command or precept, but rather a statement of fact about the habitual practice of human beings – namely, that societies tend to punish murder with death, whether or not this is in accordance with God's will (14–15, 21–2). Yet one might wonder at Rush's confidence in his interpretation, for the context of each of these utterances seems to indicate that they are commands from God to his subjects (the Israelites and Noah, respectively) to execute a particular guilty party. In both cases God appears to be delegating the punishment of the guilty to a human agent. One wonders whether Rush is not intentionally misrepresenting these passages.

Rush's third argument against capital punishment on scriptural grounds is more persuasive. He argues that the laws and commandments given by God to the Jews were only suitable to them and that the retributive penal laws of the Jews ought not to be binding on Christian societies. Appealing to the authority of Paul, he argues that the imperfection and severity of the divine dispensation for the Israelites was intended to provide a contrast to the mildness of Jesus, who presented his own teaching as to some extent eclipsing the Mosaic law (8, 22). This does not, however, affect the commands given by God to Noah, which are understood to apply to all survivors of the Flood. This is as far as Rush goes in his scriptural arguments – which is to say that he does not go very far in addressing the many difficulties posed by scriptural exegesis on this subject. Instead, Rush seems to take the reasonableness and moral uprightness of the penal reformers' principles for granted – as evident to all – and devotes the bulk of his discussion to showing the expediency of penitentiary incarceration and the ineffectiveness of capital punishment.[43]

Conclusion

Montesquieu accepted Hobbes's basic political teaching on the primacy of individual security, but he also undertook to correct Hobbes's prescriptions for criminal justice practices in light of his own insights into the nature and conditions of actual liberal societies. Much more clearly than Hobbes, the French philosopher recognized liberalism's potential for softening mores and moderating passions, and he concluded that criminal laws should gradually accommodate this salutary change, and reinforce it by lessening the severity of criminal justice and by relying more on the positive incentives of social membership than on naked threats. In accordance with this greater emphasis on the role of the historical change in popular passions in humanizing Western criminal justice practices, Montesquieu did not make it his priority to develop a systematic theoretical defence of the right to punish based on modern natural right; instead, he turned his attention to the task of outlining a long-term program for liberal criminal law reform. Montesquieu thus ignored, without ever resolving, the troubling perplexities that had plagued Hobbes's efforts to justify punishment on modern principles.

Beccaria followed Montesquieu in many respects, while popularizing and drawing out the practical implications of the latter's reformism. But whereas Montesquieu had a statesmanlike appreciation for the limits of rational reform – which included a willingness to accommodate some vestiges of the popular attachment to retribution – Beccaria's little treatise attempted to synthesize the rationalist zeal of Hobbes (including the latter's psychological reductionism and contractarianism) with a lofty appeal to the nobler sentiments of his age. This synthesis was as popular as it was incoherent. Thus, an unsatisfactory utilitarianism quickly came to dominate criminological and penological thought in the West, and that utilitarianism would soon come under attack by Kant.

Retribution and Individual Autonomy in Kant's *Rechtslehre*

From its beginnings, and on through its various transformations up until the end of the eighteenth century, modern rationalist penal theory had justified punishment exclusively as a means of preventing crime. All other benefits of punishment – such as to rehabilitate offenders, or to placate popular indignation – were viewed as ancillary to this primary one. Since the purpose of retribution, as commonly understood, was essentially backward looking, it could in no way be admitted as an aim of punishment, whether primary or ancillary. As noted earlier in this book, Hobbes's seventh law of nature commanded that "*in revenges* (that is, retribution of evil for evil) *men look not at the greatness of the evil past, but the greatness of the good to follow.*"[1] Kant was the first modern thinker to oppose this movement in punishment theory, regarding it as undue lowering of the sights of criminal justice. Because there has been considerable scholarly dispute about the extent to which Kant actually championed retribution – and about the extent to which he was willing to qualify his support for retribution in order to accommodate competing political concerns such as expediency, necessity, or honour[2] – we must allow the scholarly debates to intrude on the development of our argument more than has been the case in preceding chapters. While I will make some concessions to the objectors in what follows, I will show that Kant remains *the* modern champion of retribution.

Kant argued that retribution is primarily what we mean by punishment, and that contrary to earlier modern thought on this subject, it is possible to think through and make sense of retribution as the primary aim and justification of punishment. According to Kant, the true meaning of retribution is accessible through notions already familiar to us from everyday usage. Yet while the notions of "fit" and "proportionality," "debt" and "desert," are recognizable to ordinary moral experience, they are still far from being theoretically transparent. Accordingly, Kant set out to explicate these common notions (primarily in his *Rechtslehre*) and to show how they are connected to practical principles of reason, while also showing why a purely utilitarian (or deterrence-based) conception of punishment is inadequate. According to Kant, it is precisely our reason – as distinguished from the mere passion for revenge – that requires retribution in appropriate circumstances.

Retribution as a Moral Duty of the State

Kant follows Hobbes in constructing civil society and government out of a lawless state of nature, via a social contract.[3] Since the civil order is our sole bulwark against a return to the state of nature, and the fundamental condition of all right, the first duty of the constituted state is to preserve itself and its subjects. On this basis, it would seem that the principle of punishment would have to be deterrence. It thus comes as a great surprise to readers of the *Rechtslehre* that when Kant turns to discuss punishment, he denies that deterrence – or any other material benefit – can be its primary concern: "*Punishment by a court ... can never be inflicted merely as a means to promote some other good for the criminal himself or for civil society*" (*MM* 6:331 [105]; emphasis in original). The essence of punishment is not deterrence but retribution, for "only the *law of retribution* ... can specify definitely the quality and the quantity of punishment; all other principles are fluctuating and unsuited for a sentence of pure and strict justice" (ibid., 6:332 [105–6]; emphasis in original). And what exactly is the principle of retribution, as dictated by strict justice? "None other than the principle of equality (in the position of the needle on the scale of justice), to incline no more to one side than to the other ... whatever undeserved evil you inflict upon another within the people, that you inflict upon yourself; if you steal from him, you steal from yourself; if you strike him, you strike yourself; if you kill him, you kill yourself" (ibid., 6:332 [105]). Punishment, then,

> must be inflicted upon [the criminal] only *because he has committed a crime*, for a man can never be treated merely as a means to the purposes of another or be put among the objects of rights to things: His innate personality protects him from this, even though he can be condemned to lose his civil personality. He must previously have been found *punishable* before any thought can be given to drawing from his punishment something of use for himself or his fellow citizens. The principle of punishment is a categorical imperative. (Ibid., 6:331 [104–5]; emphases in original)

As this passage indicates, Kant's view is that retributive punishment is a requirement of the categorical imperative – the foundational principle of all morality. The criminal, by virtue of his status as an end in itself, is immune from any punishment based on a purely utilitarian (or consequentialist) calculus, since such a punishment would amount to his being treated not as a person, but as a thing; not as an end, but as a mere means.[4]

We must begin by briefly reviewing what the categorical imperative is and why it requires human beings to be treated as ends in themselves. Kant's famous "Copernican" revolution precipitated a parallel revolution in moral philosophy. The crucial transformation was in the status of physical security (or of material goods more generally). Earlier modern thought held that civil society came into being in order to safeguard individual well-being, but according to Kant, subjective individual goods can be good only conditionally; for without a good will even happiness itself becomes only an empty enjoyment. Through his critical philosophy Kant claims to have shown that the goodness of any enjoyment that human beings can experience depends upon some unconditional good, and that that good can only be the good will, which performs duty for duty's sake (*Gr* 4:393 [61]). Since every person, as a rational being, possesses such a will, each must be treated as an ultimate end in itself. Accordingly, one of Kant's formulations of the categorical imperative is: "act in such a way that you always treat humanity, whether in your own person or in the person of any other, never simply as a means, but always at the same time as an end" (ibid., 4:429 [96], second illustration). Treating others as ends in themselves means, more specifically, acting towards them in such a way that our actions are always compatible with others' choices, and thus with their ends, whether the content of those ends is laudable or deplorable.[5] Since each individual is an autonomous being, I must treat my fellow not as a mere passive object of my benevolence, but rather as an end "in all his actions" as well, by making his ends "as far as possible *my* ends" (ibid., 4:428, 430 [95, 98]).

In light of this new vision of human goodness and dignity, Kant finds the principles of punishment formulated by Hobbes and Beccaria inadequate, because they are incapable of respecting the humanity inherent in each criminal – a humanity that must be respected no matter how heinous the crime. It is not just that those earlier thinkers had failed to draw the proper conclusions for criminal justice from the social contract. Rather, the social contract itself is insufficient to ground any moral theory of punishment. For that, one must begin from different premises, namely, from the categorical imperative.

Unfortunately, Kant did not leave a clear argument deducing the principle of retribution from the categorical imperative, so we must construct such an argument for ourselves based on Kant's indications. Whenever he speaks about punishment (including his discussion in the *Rechstslehre*), Kant appeals to what might be called enlightened popular moral opinion, taking his premises from that authority rather than deriving them from first principles. While critical philosophy is crucial for elucidating the rational grounds of morality, it is not always necessary for deciding every practical question. That is because, according to Kant, critical philosophy is in harmony with ordinary moral opinion – so long as it is enlightened, for having cast off ignorance and prejudice in the age of Enlightenment, modern societies have arrived at a correct understanding of man's duties, although very few people actually call themselves philosophers.[6] Thus, instead of recapitulating the derivation of the categorical imperative, the introduction to the *Rechtslehre* ("Preliminary Concepts of the Metaphysics of Morals") presents a kind of glossary of basic terminology from everyday use, including notions such as "person," "choice," and, indeed, "crime."[7] In this summary of the basic terms of enlightened popular morality, Kant defines a person as someone whose actions, as well as their consequences, can be imputed to him as their author (*MM* 6:223 [16]). Thus we say that someone is responsible not only for his ill behaviour (e.g., throwing a tantrum), but also for its consequences (e.g., damaging the property of others while so enraged). Yet Kant goes further than this to argue that the consequences of one's actions include their due reward or punishment.[8] If this is true, then respecting the autonomous choices of others involves punishing them whenever they should transgress the law.

The notion that punishment is a form of respect for persons may sound odd. Kant does not deny that as a selfish ("natural" or "empirical") being, the criminal does *not* wish to be punished. But he nevertheless insists that we are not merely selfish beings, but also at the same time moral and rational agents whose concerns transcend our private interests – and in this he purports to echo ordinary moral experience. When viewed as a moral and rational agent, the criminal necessarily wills his deed along with all of the effects it entails, including any punishment due for voluntary wrongdoing.[9] To repeat, as a selfish being he will surely resist his punishment; but as a rational being – and for his own sake we must assume that he has not irretrievably lost his rationality – the criminal necessarily accepts that punishment must follow crime, in his own case no less than in another's, as a dictate of universal law. Thus, where Hobbes's doctrine of authorization failed to show why a criminal should accept his own punishment as just, Kant's distinction between the empirical self and the rational-autonomous self manages to do just that (assuming we accept the premises). Moreover, Kant does not introduce any principle of authority other than rational autonomy: in having a duty to undergo punishment, the offender is obligated to sacrifice his private interests, but he is thereby obligated to no higher authority than his own rational agency.

In this sense, to punish a criminal would be to pay him the highest compliment, whereas to let him off the hook would be to condemn him as childish, irresponsible, and something less than a full human being.[10] Rewards and punishments, then, are imputable effects of our deeds just as much as are any of the other effects of our actions, which is to say that we are the authors of our own punishments and rewards. According to Kant, only retribution satisfies the moral requirement of treating criminals as autonomous agents, since only it, as distinguished from utilitarian punishment, defines the imputable rightful effect of the criminal's action. Utilitarian penalties have nothing to do with the grounds of a criminal's choice, since they look only to future conditions, such as security or well-being. Retribution, on the other hand, establishes a proportionality or likeness, in both quantity and quality – according to the principle of "like for like" or *lex talionis* – between the offender's action (i.e., the crime) and its rightful effect (i.e., his punishment). In this way, retribution respects and fulfils the offender's autonomous choice.[11] It is for these reasons that Kant presents the right to punish in the *Rechtslehre* as civil society's moral duty to its criminals (what we would call a "positive" right). Kant illustrates the strictness of this obligation when he comments on the hypothetical example of a society about to dissolve itself by the consent of its members – at which point punishments will no longer have a deterrent effect at all. In such circumstances even the last murderer remaining in prison, according to Kant, must still be executed "so that each has done to him what his deeds deserve" (ibid., 6:333 [106–7]).[12]

Kant concluded from the failures of Hobbes and Beccaria that any theory of punishment simply cannot be made coherent if punishment is understood as being concerned exclusively with deterrence. Yet insofar as those earlier thinkers were aware of this insoluble difficulty, they still refused to resort to commonsense moral opinions about desert and retribution as a possible solution to their quandary, for that would have amounted to reintroducing the harsh, politically destabilizing passions that modern political philosophy had worked so hard to temper. Kant certainly did not wish to return to a pre-modern conception of punishment. Nonetheless, he saw a new possibility: the violent passion for revenge that Hobbes had denounced as a species of vanity and a vestige of an older, less enlightened political tradition was, Kant believed, distinct from the concern with the dignity of the criminal that had inspired a retributivist like Kant himself. Whereas the former was the product of ignorance, selfishness, and violent habits, the latter was born of an impartial concern with fair relations among equal human beings under a universal law. In other words, Kant (in agreement with Montesquieu) believed that commerce and liberal institutions had exerted a historical humanizing effect on popular sensibilities and were continuing to do so,[13] and he deduced from this observation that whatever concern with retribution remained in post-Enlightenment popular opinion must have its origin in practical reason itself. Kant could now invoke popular notions about punishment as his authority because public opinion had, for the first time, ceased to be vengeful.

There is, however, a serious problem with the account I have provided so far – one that has led some Kant scholars to reject his view of punishment as incoherent.[14] The difficulty stems from the fact that morality and right are not identical for Kant; rather, the latter is understood to be contained within the former. Moral laws, as such, are the unconditional dictates of pure practical reason, which are in turn divided into two kinds, juridical and ethical, according to the manner of their incentives. Juridical laws, or laws of right, can have external incentives, meaning that conformity with these laws can be coerced; whereas ethical laws must serve as their own incentives, in the sense that conformity with them requires that we obey them for their own sake.[15] From the point of view of juridical legislation it does not matter what motivates us to act lawfully – whether it be a noble respect for the moral law or a base desire for profit. Thus, for example, I may fulfil a contract merely because I hope to engage in profitable commercial dealings in the future. Although it cannot be said that I have thereby acted ethically, I nevertheless have done all that is required of me by juridical law. For its part, the state can do everything necessary to constrain me to obey my contractual obligations, but it has no right to inquire into my motivations for complying. But if this is the case, then if I should actually break the law, what business does the state have in punishing me for my "inner wickedness," as Kant would have it? How can criminals be punished for their immoral motives if juridical legislation is indifferent to inner motivation?[16] There is, in addition, the problem related to the fact that

Kant says elsewhere that while God can see into our souls and know our true motivations, human beings have no such insight.[17] How, then, can the state punish a criminal retributively "in proportion to his inner wickedness" if it cannot know his true motivations?

I will address the second difficulty first. There is one passage in the *Rechtslehre* that wrestles with the tension between the moral requirement to punish criminals as they deserve and the difficulty we have discerning one another's true motivations. There Kant advances a tentative (and perhaps not completely satisfactory) solution. He tries to show that in the case of capital crimes, the "fitting of punishment to the crime" will *always* occur by "imposing the death sentence in accordance with the strict law of retribution," since "only by this is a sentence of death pronounced on every criminal in proportion to his *inner wickedness*" (*MM* 6:333 ff. [106 ff.]). To explain his point by way of illustration, Kant gives the example of two rebels: one who acts from the honourable (though ultimately mistaken) motive of wishing to depose a government he regards as illegitimate, and another who acts only for the sake of his private gain. Kant argues that both would receive what they deserve if they were sentenced to die. "Since the man of honor is undeniably less deserving of punishment than the other, both would be punished quite proportionately if all alike were sentenced to death; the man of honor would be punished mildly in terms of his sensibilities [i.e., valuing honour more than life] and the scoundrel severely in terms of his [i.e., valuing life more than honour]" (ibid., 6:334 [107]). Thus there would be no need for the state to inquire into the two criminals' actual motivations; whatever their motivations happened to be, a sentence of death (as dictated by the principle of retribution) is the fitting punishment!

This would indeed be an ingenious solution to the problem were it to hold generally in all cases of possible crimes and motivations. Unfortunately, it is doubtful that it *would* hold in all cases, and thus Kant's solution is partial at best. Nevertheless, what is important is that this passage shows that Kant refused to abandon his position that punishment must requite deeds in terms of what gives them their moral worth – namely, their motivations.[18] Perhaps Kant believed that, ultimately, we have to accept a certain amount of uncertainty in judging the motives of others, given the morally undesirable alternative. For Kant (as later for Hegel), not punishing for fear of making a mistaken judgment about motivations or circumstances would have morally worse consequences than abolishing retribution, since a mistaken judgment causes undue (and admittedly regrettable) physical harm to the criminal, without touching his inner dignity, while abolishing retribution entirely would amount to denying to all criminals their rationality, thus dehumanizing them.[19]

In order to address the first difficulty – that juridical legislation's indifference to incentives of action seems to rule out retribution – we must first specify more precisely what Kant meant by "right" as this concept is developed in the *Rechtslehre*. Because of his status as an end in itself, man is the highest being in nature. In relation to the rest of nature, man is an absolute master who possesses an unlimited right to use, transform, and even destroy non-rational beings according to his will.[20] In actuality, however, there are many rational beings coexisting at the same time in a finite physical environment, each with an equally rightful claim to unlimited external freedom. This inevitably brings human beings into conflict over external possessions. As a result of the equality of all rational beings, men are required to observe the law of external reciprocity, according to which any action is right as long as it can coexist with everyone else's equal external freedom.[21] Reason authorizes enforcement of this law, since this can be done without impinging on anyone's freedom: any asymmetrical coercion of another is a hindrance to equal freedom, and thus the enforcement of the law of reciprocity can be justified "as a hindering of a hindrance to freedom" (ibid., 6:231 [25]). This universal authorization of reciprocal coercion then becomes the source of all rightful or juridical – that is to say, external – legislation. In civil society, the entire authority to enforce the law of reciprocal coercion belongs to the state, by virtue of which it can arbitrate conflicts and compel those who defy the authoritative arbitration to submit to it by force.[22]

We must also keep in mind that while our juridical obligations may be externally coerced, they are also at the same time morally incumbent upon us, since duties of right are also necessarily duties of ethics.[23] As such, they ought to be obeyed even without external compulsion. This implies that when I disobey a juridical law I not only disrupt the equilibrium of an external system of reciprocal rights, but also act immorally and thus incur moral guilt. As we have already seen, Kant understands punishment essentially not as the enforcement of laws, but as recompense for moral guilt, since punishment is the categorically (rather than conditionally) necessary consequence of wrong. As such, punishment does not derive from the state's authority to enforce the system of equal external freedom – that is, from right – but rather from the categorical imperative that enjoins us to treat others as ends by respecting their autonomous choices – that is, from the moral law in a more fundamental sense.

We can now see how Kant could have conceived of punishment as essentially retributive without contradicting his distinction between juridical and ethical lawgiving. In this we have a prime example of how, in Kant, morality not only coexists with but also in certain cases qualifies and restricts the administration of right. While the principle of right requires deterrence as a means of enforcing equal external freedom, the administration of punishment cannot be purely deterrent (i.e., deterrence cannot be its only justification), because that would violate the moral requirement that we treat human beings as ends. Deterrence can be a rightful aim of punishment, but only on the condition that it has met the requirements of the principle of retribution.

Some commentators have tried to bring Kant back in line with classical liberalism by challenging, on his own grounds, his conclusion that retribution is a strict duty of the state. Most recently, Thomas Hill has claimed that Kant's "crucial thesis concerns our liability to suffer in the recognition of our own misdeeds, not our right or duty to make others suffer for theirs."[24] Hill believes that according to Kant there is no duty, but only an authorization, to punish the guilty, for his "retributive policies" are "not based on ... intrinsic desert; nor do they stand as fundamental moral requirements ... Rather, they are best understood as derivative features of a practice that requires independent justification."[25] On Hill's reading, Kant's fundamental justification for punishment is deterrence, which Hill takes to be implicit in the state's function as the enforcer of civil society's laws. Those passages in the *Rechtslehre* in which Kant appears to endorse a retributivist position of the sort I have laid out above should, according to Hill, be interpreted in light of the purely deterrence-based justification of the institution of punishment as a whole. Retribution, therefore, serves only as a necessary condition – but not a sufficient one – of punishing the guilty; rather than being a strict duty, it is only a restraint on the state's enforcement power keeping it from punishing the innocent and from punishing the guilty disproportionately.[26] In short, there is no moral imperative to punish the guilty when no beneficial consequences can be expected to follow.[27]

Tunick has attempted to defend a similar reading of Kant.[28] He points to two passages in the *Rechstlehre* where examples are given of justifiable exceptions to the law of retribution. He reads these as providing evidence that, for Kant, punishment is fundamentally consequentialist. In one passage Kant relates a hypothetical case in which a shipwrecked and drowning man saves himself by pushing another shipwrecked man off a plank, thus keeping himself from drowning.[29] Kant says about this case that a court should not punish the first man for murder, and the reason he gives is that "the punishment threatened by the law could not be greater than the loss of his own life" by drowning. Tunick interprets Kant as implying that, since there would be no point in having a penal law in this instance, for it could have no deterrent effect, the purpose of penal laws as such must be deterrence.[30] Tunick attributes the same meaning to two more examples, in which Kant says that a soldier who kills his opponent in a duel and a mother who kills her illegitimate child ought to be exempted from capital punishment (as required by the principle of retribution), because in both cases the law against murder conflicts with an overriding incentive of honour (of a brave soldier in the one case, of a chaste woman in the other), albeit one created by a "barbarous and undeveloped" custom.[31]

I believe that Hill's conclusion goes too far. As I have tried to show in my analysis of Kant's statements on punishment in the *Metaphysics of Morals*, his clear intention was to understand punishment as a moral category, and this led him to try to connect it with the categorical imperative and to argue for retribution as its essential purpose. Thus, I do not think it is accurate to say that deterrence is the *only* justification for punishment and that retribution is not a duty to the criminal. I do, though, think that Tunick's interpretation of Kant's exceptions to the law of retribution has some merit. At one point, Kant seems to want to suggest that the exceptions he mentions are not really dispensations from the law of retribution. For example, he says regarding the cases of the duellist and the mother who kills her illegitimate baby that these two individuals find themselves faced with two competing and equally binding imperatives – the honour of their station and the prohibition against murder – and that this clash of imperatives causes each to be thrown back into the state of nature, where killing does not count as murder.[32] Thus, according to Kant, retribution would not have to be exacted since in the state of nature there was no law against which to transgress in the first place. But Tunick's interpretation of these exceptions seems better than Kant's, on the latter's own terms. Kant's appeal to the state of nature to explain these exceptions seems rather contrived. Is the conflict between a just law (i.e., against murder) and a "barbaric" sense of honour really an insoluble quandary? It would seem less contrary to morality to require a man to defend his honour in court (or in the court of public opinion) than to allow him to take another's life unnecessarily. Similarly, although it might require a hard choice, it seems less contrary to morality to hold a woman responsible for not having a child she would be unwilling to raise than to allow her to kill that child with impunity once that child is already born. Here, Kant seems to be trying to invent an ad hoc theoretical justification for a practical solution to the conflict between morality and competing political forces – namely, between the moral demand for retribution and the entrenched traditional sense of honour. The same seems true of Kant's discussion of the right of clemency, where his concern is clearly with the stability of the civil order.[33]

Thus, although I do not think that Tunick's ultimate conclusion – that for Kant, the purpose of punishment is deterrence – is warranted, I do think that he helpfully points to the fact that in certain details, Kant failed to adhere consistently to his basic position regarding the categorical character of the duty to punish retributively. On the one hand, Kant wanted to affirm that retribution is a strict duty; on the other, he wanted to balance this moral imperative against other concerns – although presumably a moral duty cannot really be thought of as categorical if it is subject to exceptions.[34] Nevertheless, it seems to me that despite this inconsistency Kant does articulate a basis upon which it may be possible to justify retribution in the strong sense, understood as a duty rather than as a mere side-constraint.

We have now traced the arguments by which Kant expounds the meaning of retribution and defends it as the essential purpose of punishment in a morally serious civil society. Nevertheless, the talk of "proportionality" and "likeness," as that which truly respects the criminal's choice, remains rather vague, however much it may appeal to commonplace assumptions. The cogency of Kant's argument for retributive punishment depends on whether or not his claim that retribution preserves the inner dignity of the offender as an autonomous being can be explained in clear terms. But so far, we have only accepted this as a formulaic premise. What proof is there that the offender himself really does experience his punishment as dignifying and morally elevating? We now turn to this question.

Conscience and the Basis of the Feeling of Guilt

What distinguishes human beings, according to Kant, is our capacity to act as beings subject to universal legislation. Thanks to this capacity, I may hold myself in the highest esteem and may claim a right to be respected by others on an equal footing, regardless of the status in which I have been placed by society, nature, or chance. Although Kant tends to emphasize this egalitarian basis of personal worth, he also acknowledges another source of worth for which we can be held in esteem: the goodness of our actions. An example of the latter may be found in the familiar case of Kant's world-weary and reluctant philanthropist who, "no longer moved by any inclination … tears himself out of this deadly insensibility and does the action [i.e., helping others in need] without any inclination for the sake of duty alone." At that moment and "for the first time his action has its genuine moral worth" (*Gr* 4:398–99 [66]). Although, as a human being, the reluctant philanthropist already deserves respect, his difficult and rare self-conquest elevates still higher his standing in our eyes and in his own, and it is responsible for the moral satisfaction he experiences. Kant's characterization of this feeling of moral satisfaction echoes unmistakably classical and biblical accounts of virtue. According to the *Rechtslehre*, "there is a subjective principle of ethical *reward*, that is, a susceptibility to being rewarded in accordance with laws of virtue: the reward, namely, of a moral pleasure that goes beyond mere contentment with oneself … and that is celebrated in the saying that, through consciousness of this pleasure, virtue is its own reward" (*MM* 6:391 [154]; emphasis in original). Although virtue is itself intrinsically choiceworthy, it also makes us deserving of reward, one form of which is the feeling of moral pleasure, because it essentially involves a painful struggle against one's natural inclinations.[35]

The case of self-reproach is analogous to that of self-esteem. When we believe ourselves to have done wrong in some way, we judge ourselves deserving of self-reproach. We experience this as "pangs of conscience." Kant seems to interpret this inner experience of self-reproach not as a mere habituated emotional response (or a biological reflex) but as an act of reason. For Kant, our pangs of conscience are the voice of our own reason as it judges us, refusing to allow us to forget our deserts and even forcing us to suffer the pain of remorse as a kind of inner judicial punishment. Granted, we are distressed by the pain of remorse and in a sense wish to be rid of it. But from the premise, Kant seems to infer that the pangs of conscience are the result of an act of reason and the fact that we cannot get rid of these pangs, no matter how much we may resist them – that we subject *ourselves* to such a trial voluntarily.

Kant uses the analogy of the judge quite extensively to describe the workings of the reproachful conscience. When the conscience passes judgment, it "pronounces the sentence of happiness or misery, as the moral results of the deed" (ibid., 6:439n [189n]). The conscience does not merely identify certain types of actions as morally good or bad; its judgment is also a "sentence" bearing consequences: it "either acquits or declares us guilty and deserving of punishment" (*LE*, "Conscience," 129). What is more, it is not enough that self-reproach and repentance follow this judicial pronouncement of the conscience; the conscience is satisfied only "if [its judicial verdict] is felt and enforced" (ibid., 131). According to Kant,

> the first effectual expression of this judicial verdict which has the force of law is moral repentance; the second, without which the sentence is inoperative, is action in accordance with the judicial verdict. If it does not result in *practical endeavor* to do what is demanded for the satisfaction of the moral law, the conscience is but an idle conscience, and however penitent we may be the penitence is vain so long as we do not *satisfy the debt we owe* to the moral law; for ... a *debt* is not satisfied by penitence, but by *payment*. (Ibid., my emphases)

By "payment" of the "debt" we owe to the moral law, as distinguished from mere "penitence," Kant seems to be referring to judicial punishment. Although he does not spell it out, his meaning seems to be that a person with a healthy conscience must be willing not only to accuse himself but also to submit to punishment, knowing this to be the morally necessary consequence of his actions. If he does not so submit, then he loses the basis for self-respect and is degraded in his own eyes.[36] To preserve his dignity as a moral being the offender must submit himself to retributive punishment.

We can see from Kant's remarks on the reproachful conscience that there is indeed some support in ordinary moral experience for his view of the dignifying effect of retributive punishment on the criminal himself. That there is no parallel to this account in the works of Hobbes, Montesquieu, or Beccaria – the classic defenders of deterrence-focused punishment – might be regarded as a serious weakness in their penal thought. Still, one wonders whether Kant's assumption that a rational basis exists for the reproachful conscience can be defended by critical reason itself, as distinguished from common practical experience. This work is done by Kant's concept of the highest good.

Retribution and the Highest Good

Kant's account of the highest good (or *summum bonum*) functions to restore harmony between the two aspects of our being: the rational and the empirical. As empirical beings, we are driven by the desire to fulfil our needs, the total satisfaction of which we call happiness. As moral beings we hold that we ought to pursue virtue – a good higher than happiness and choiceworthy for its own sake – above all else, regardless of whether it also contributes to our well-being. On the one hand, there is nothing intrinsic to the concept of virtue that requires the sacrifice of this-worldly happiness – Kant was not an ascetic. On the other, Kant acknowledges that there is no necessary correlation in nature between virtue and well-being, as both experience and natural science teach us.[37] It is all too common to find virtuous individuals suffering undeservedly and the unjust prospering. According to Kant, we cannot help but reject this "antinomy" of practical reason, which threatens to undermine morality's coherence. In order to reject that antinomy, reason demands that we postulate the conditions that would allow the convergence of happiness and morality – the highest good. Besides the postulate of the efficacy of rational freedom, there are two such conditions: (1) the existence of an omnipotent, intelligent, and just being that always acts in accordance with the laws of morality to reward the virtuous and punish the vicious, and (2) the immortality of the soul.[38] For, if it were otherwise, then "the moral law … must be fantastic, directed to empty imaginary ends, and consequently inherently false" (ibid., 5:114 [118]).

Contrary to the biblical view, the highest good cannot be construed as a gift of divine grace. Kant's God is not the mysterious God of the Bible, who will be gracious to whom he will be gracious and whose ways are beyond our ken, but the perfect agent of practical reason. If the highest good were to depend on grace, then virtue might not always be rewarded – an implication that practical reason rejects. If "virtue and happiness are thought of as necessarily combined, so that the one cannot be assumed by a practical reason without the other belonging to it," then this combination must be "as the connection of cause and effect" (ibid., 5:113 [117]). The only way we can conceive of the connection between virtue and happiness as *causal* is if we postulate the immortality of the soul and the existence of a just and omnipotent God, who could *never* will anything other than the highest good, as reason understands it.[39] Such a God would guarantee the "effect" of happiness as a consequence of moral goodness by distributing well-being to each in exact proportion to his desert, "for to be in need of happiness and also worthy of it and yet not to partake of it could not be in accordance with the complete volition of an omnipotent rational being" (ibid., 5:110 [114–15]). Only on the assumption of such postulates is morality possible, since only then can we allow ourselves to hope that human beings will be rewarded and punished in accordance with their worthiness by an unerring judge, if not in this life then in the next. According to Kant, rational faith in such postulates is unavoidable; we always affirm them when we are acting morally, even when we are not aware of it.

The notion that each person will be held to account by an omniscient and all-powerful judge for every one of his actions is at the same time terrifying and comforting. Kant's God is first and foremost not a compassionate and merciful God, but a just one. For in distributing happiness in accordance with the concept of the highest good, God does not will that all men should necessarily be perfectly happy, but rather that they should enjoy as much happiness as they have deserved through their deeds. In Kant's *Critique of Judgment*, he says that the final purpose of nature, as created by God, "can only be *man under moral laws*" (*CJ* 5:445 [334]; emphasis in original). But, Kant continues,

> I say deliberately: *under* moral laws. The final purpose of creation is not man [acting] *in accordance with* moral laws, i.e., a man whose behavior conforms to them ... And this agrees perfectly with the judgment that human reason makes when it reflects morally on the course of the world. Even in evil we believe we perceive the traces of a wise reference to a purpose, provided we see that the wanton villain does not die until he has suffered the punishment he deserves for his misdeeds ... The highest wisdom in the government of the world we posit in this: that the opportunity for good conduct, but the consequence of both good and bad conduct, is ordained according to moral laws. In the latter consists, properly speaking, the glory of God, and hence it is not unfitting if theologians call it the ultimate purpose of creation. (Ibid., 5:449n [338n]; emphases in original)

According to Kant, then, the ultimate end of divine providence is not necessarily men acting in complete conformity with moral laws. Rather, the end of providence is perfect justice: the proportional distribution of happiness in accordance with moral worthiness.[40]

This ringing endorsement of divine retribution is striking, and significant for our understanding of Kant's view not only of divine retribution but also of the significance of retribution, as such.[41] Recall that in the *Rechtslehre*, Kant had argued that judges duly constituted by the state must embody the principle of retribution in order to protect the dignity and autonomy of criminals. To that account of the political function of punishment – as imposing a strict duty on the state – we now add the present account of the wider moral significance of retributive punishment as it emerges in the context of Kant's second and third critiques. If one focuses on the *Rechtslehre* alone, it is easy to see how one might get the impression that deterrence is the fundamental aim and justification of punishment as an institution and that the principle of retribution is only a necessary, but not a sufficient, reason for punishing crime. We have now seen that for Kant, retribution is an aspect of the ultimate end of practical reason, the highest good.

It can now be said, after a review of the evidence, that Kant understood retributive punishment of the guilty as an intrinsic moral good. This helps explain why he regarded it as a strict moral duty of the state (as distinguished from a limitation or side-constraint).[42] Furthermore, we can now also better appreciate the extent to which the principle of retribution resonates with ordinary moral experience, even after that experience has been shaped historically by the idea of modern natural right. Finally, and most importantly, we can now see how Kant understood retribution to be grounded in pure reason, as an extension of the highest good.

What, then, can be said about the merits of Kant's demonstration of the rational basis of the principle of retribution? Some commentators have pointed out several difficulties with Kant's linking of virtue and happiness in the concept of the highest good. Shell, for example, has observed that Kant's argument seems to blur together two distinct issues: *moral worth* as an unconditioned good, on the one hand, and *moral worthiness* as the condition of entitlement to happiness, on the other.[43] How exactly does reason make the transition from the former to the latter?[44]

Furthermore, in our earlier discussion of Plato's penal thought we saw the Athenian Stranger raise the question of the coherence of retributive punishment precisely from the point of view of the commonsense moral opinions to which retributivists like Kant try to appeal. There we saw that the question of retributive punishment points to the more fundamental question of the goodness of moral virtue itself. Retributive punishment, as Kant and most people understand it, assumes that an unjust action diminishes the unjust person's worthiness to be happy, since we say that the unjust person "got away" with some portion of happiness to which he was not entitled (e.g., stolen property, or illicit self-gratification). The punishment that follows is thought to restore the imbalance between worthiness and well-being. But if moral virtue is something intrinsically good and self-sufficient, and if it brings its own rewards of pleasure and inner well-being (in the conscience), while guilt is accompanied by pangs of self-reproach, then retributive punishment must be irrational, since the unjust man would have to be considered already unhappy in spite of his ill-gotten gains, and thus need not be subjected to further suffering. Likewise, it would follow from the implications of this commonsense view that just or law-abiding individuals are already so completely fulfilled that they ought not to feel any indignation or envy towards the criminal, but should rather pity him. Kant insists that moral virtue is an unconditional (self-sufficient) good and that it is accompanied by inner well-being, and he *also* wishes to affirm the justice and reasonableness of retribution. Yet I do not believe that Kant's arguments in support of retributive punishment are sufficient to defend its coherence in light of the Platonic–Socratic critique.[45] That happiness ought to be dependent on virtue, and that we must believe in the existence of a divine dispenser of retribution, had been judged by Kant to follow from the facts of the moral consciousness. But is the moral consciousness as unequivocal about what constitutes just punishment as Kant claims? Rather, does not the moral consciousness itself under certain circumstances approve of the departure from strict justice in favour of justice in another sense – as expressed, for example, in the principles of equity and mercy? In other words, is it not possible that the moral consciousness itself is much more divided as to the goodness of retribution than Kant had admitted? Whereas Kant had ascribed our concern with happiness exclusively to our empirical natures, is it not possible that he did not sufficiently consider whether, or to what extent, this concern is essentially bound up with our concern with justice itself?

Conclusion

One of the most important implications of Kant's penal thought is that modern societies continue to find the connection between punishment and desert deeply compelling, notwithstanding their abiding concern with security. For Kant, this meant that just deserts and retribution must be accommodated within any modern theory of punishment. Kant was able to formulate a retributive theory of punishment on modern principles – that is, without returning to the classical analysis of punishment – and in this respect Kant's achievement may be admired. As a retributive theory of punishment, Kant's account avoids the morally shocking implications of the essentially consequentialist theories of earlier modern thinkers, especially the implication that the interests of criminals must bow to the interest of the greater number. The sort of retributive punishment Kant imagined would not, therefore, be the kind of vengeful, harsh, and even brutal punishment that one might have observed practised in the austere classical republics. Rather, Kantian retribution would serve as a measure of proportionality that would, in many cases, *limit* the severity of the penalty in a manner that should make it more fitting to the gravity of the crime, its circumstances, the intention of the criminal, and so on. In short, in the modern context the principle of retribution could be expected to *moderate* punishment by helping to avoid the excesses of utilitarian calculation. At the same time, the retributive aim of Kantian punishment is also intended to do honour to our enduring concern with justice, understood as both a political and a moral virtue.

Although we had occasion to raise questions about the ultimate coherence of the popular concern with retribution to which Kant appeals, drawing on certain Socratic reflections that we have gleaned from our examination of Plato, there is also much in Kant's solution to the problem of punishment to recommend it as a political compromise. With the benefit of hindsight, however, we can say that the historical success of Kant's theoretical achievement has been mixed. On the one hand, many Western democracies continue to express their support for retribution as an appropriate aim of punishment, distinct from deterrence, rehabilitation, and other accepted aims. Some countries – particularly the United States – even acknowledge retribution as an aim of their criminal justice system in their statutes and in the judicial opinions of their courts. On the other hand, the laws and governments of most Western countries have ceased to regard retribution as an appropriate aim of punishment, and there are currently several activist movements (such as Amnesty International and the Restorative Justice movement) that are opposed to retribution on principle. Moreover, there is more intellectual opposition to retribution in Western societies than there is principled support for it. In the next chapter we will turn to perhaps the best-known attack on the modern criminal justice tradition, one that criticizes not only its retributive element but indeed the whole edifice: Foucault's *Discipline and Punish*.

Chapter 5

Foucault and the Crisis of Modern Criminal Justice

All of the modern thinkers we have examined up to now shared a sense of optimism about the modern penal reform project as a whole. The discoveries made by Enlightenment science and philosophy concerning man's nature and his rights, when applied to criminal justice, promised to purge all of the prejudice and barbarism that had plagued traditional criminal justice institutions. According to Foucault, however, the optimism of these thinkers, and of the penal reformers inspired by them, was misplaced. While the Enlightenment had indeed ushered in an age of unprecedented order and security, the new "penality" that would come to enforce and sustain this order could not be described as humane (mild and benevolent), despite being technically sophisticated. Foucault's account of the institutional and intellectual history of modern punishment is intended to show that the Enlightenment's penal reform project took an unexpected turn, ushering in an unprecedented mode of social control that Foucault calls "discipline." This new form of correction, according to Foucault, does not rehabilitate, does not deter, and is not a milder form of punishment than its historical precedents. Indeed, the new mode of correction has the *appearance* of mildness, having exchanged corporal punishments for incarceration, when in fact it has only adopted new methods that are the more oppressive for being insidious.

The characteristic techniques of modern discipline have been firmly entrenched in our institutions for a long time, according to Foucault, but we are only now beginning to understand their nature and dimensions and to appreciate their relation to the original modern idea of punishment. It is this insidious modern penality that Foucault purports to analyse, and it is in relation to this historical examination that he first announces the crisis of modern criminal justice.

Contractarianism in Theory vs Practice

Foucault acknowledges that to a significant extent the ambitions of the early penal reformers were fulfilled. Towards the latter part of the eighteenth century, violent crimes substantially declined, while punishments became milder (*Discipline and Punish*, 75). In the popular understanding, as among the intellectual and political elites of the time, it became a widely accepted principle that no matter how horrific the crime, society must continue to respect the humanity inherent in the criminal. "In the worst of murderers," the spirit of Enlightenment proclaimed, "there is one thing, at least, to be respected when one punishes: his 'humanity'" (74). The new humanizing spirit in criminal justice was not so much a theoretical doctrine, according to Foucault, as "a cry from the heart of an outraged nature," one that was expressed in a "lyrical" rhetoric by the Enlightenment *philosophes* (74, 90–1). This is not to say that crime declined altogether; rather, the drop in violent crime coincided with a rise in property crime, according to contemporary reports cited by Foucault. Nor did law enforcement become less strict in every respect, according to this account: although it became less corporal in most cases, it also became more intrusive and far-reaching as more categories of crime were established in law – particularly those against property, reflecting the "bourgeois" class's conception of justice – and as the police apparatus began to grow and take on more of a surveillance role.

The "lyrical" rhetoric in terms of which the appeal to humanity as the limit of punishment was framed tended, however, to obscure the theoretical paradox underlying that noble sentiment. According to "the general theory of the contract," citizens are presumed to have consented to the established laws, since these protect the lives and property of all. In light of this principle, any violation of the lawful order is a sure sign of the offender's dangerousness and thus gives society a right on contractarian grounds ("since the defense of each individual is involved" in the defence of the whole) to use any means it may deem necessary to protect itself against the threat (89). In his discussion of the theoretical basis of the modern punishing power, Foucault limits himself to a quote from Rousseau's *On the Social Contract*:

Every malefactor, by attacking the social rights, becomes, by his crimes, a rebel and a traitor to his country; by violating its laws he ceases to be a member of it; he even makes war upon it. In such a case the preservation of the state is inconsistent with his own, and one or the other must perish; in putting the guilty to death we slay not so much the citizen as the enemy. (quoted at 90)[1]

"Every malefactor" (however great or small his crime) gives the society whose laws he has violated an "absolute right" over his life, making himself liable to the full range of punishments, according to their discretion. Since every citizen is assumed to consent to everything that is enacted in the laws, the criminal himself must logically accept even the extreme penalty as the legitimate consequence of his deed, by virtue of which he becomes "worse than an enemy" and "nothing less than a traitor" and "a monster," even in his own eyes. The full consequence of contractarian punishment theory, then, according to Foucault, is that "the least crime attacks the whole of society; and the whole of society – including the criminal – is present in the least punishment" (ibid.). Where could one possibly find a moderating principle in such a theory of punishment?

But this very brief exposition of the foundational argument for a contractarian right to punish is incomplete, for it relies only on the most extreme, anti-liberal version of contractarianism – namely, Rousseau's. Recall that Hobbes denied that individuals transferred all of their rights to the sovereign and argued that they may, and must, retain their natural right to preserve their own lives. Hobbes even conceded to individuals in civil society a corresponding right to judge for themselves what is necessary for their preservation, and even a right to the means required for a comfortable existence. On the basis of these inalienable rights (which are not to be confused with entitlements), Hobbes deduced a substantial range of excuses and extenuations that may be reasons to exempt the criminal from the most extreme punishments if he committed his crime under some duress or restraint. In his exposition, Foucault does not take into account this (or any other) alternative version of contractarianism, and this weakens his conclusion that even the least crime makes the offender a rebel and a traitor so that "the preservation of the state is inconsistent with [the preservation of the criminal], and one or the other must perish."

Our investigations in preceding chapters can help us understand that Foucault's conclusion – that according to modern contractarianism the least criminal becomes the property of the state – is true only as a formal possibility, but it is not formally necessary, nor is it necessary for it to become common practice, given modern conditions. We will be able to confirm this if we focus on two elements of the Hobbesian deduction of the right of sovereignty. According to Hobbes's deduction (which the Rousseau passage quoted by Foucault closely parallels), the only secure way for individuals to escape the violent state of nature is to recognize (1) that the sovereign authority established by the social contract is absolute, and (2) that the fundamental guarantee of the political union's continued existence is the continued consent of its members. The consent of citizens – be it motivated by fear of violent death (as in Hobbes) or by respect for the general will (as in Rousseau) – is of the utmost importance in practice because, if it should ever lapse, there would be no other power on earth to take over the task of maintaining the civil order. It is formally true that any crime, however minor, may be regarded as a threat to the unity of the political will, since in every criminal action the offender takes it upon himself to decide what is permissible, which is the definition of the state of nature, where each is his own judge.[2] However, nothing in this contractarian deduction *requires* that the least criminal be put to death or transformed into property of the state, since in the state of nature there is no justice, and therefore no guilt or liability to punishment. It is therefore not true that the least criminal loses all his rights against civil society and is to be dealt with at society's absolute discretion. What is more, it is not true given actual conditions (at least in a Hobbesian political system) that civil society would find it useful to punish a minor crime with any great severity, since the lapse of consent on the part of one subject is practically negligible in the face of a powerful sovereign who enjoys the support of the vast majority of his subjects.

Nevertheless, Foucault's conclusion remains correct as a formal possibility, since civil society retains an absolute right to defend itself, and since it (or its constituted representative) remains the sole arbiter of what is necessary and useful to its preservation. Hobbes, as we saw, had unambiguously affirmed this formal possibility again and again. Everything then comes to depend upon the actual political conditions that inform criminal law and administration in a given contractarian society. Hobbes, as we know, preferred monarchy as a form of government, and therefore in an ideal Hobbesian state we might expect the sovereign to favour an enlightened policy where severe punishments are reserved for only the most dangerous offences. But conditions are significantly different in a regime governed by democratic majorities of small property owners. Simply put, a democratic majority consisting of small property owners living under a regime that is concerned with preserving individual security and protecting commerce will tend to favour stricter law enforcement and more punitive corrections – not because the property-owning majority is vengeful, but because its intense fear for the security of private persons and property will incline it to exaggerate the threat of crime and the means thought to be necessary to contain it. As we know from experience, when crime rates rise

– or are perceived to rise (cf. 76–7) – an apprehensive public will often demand the enactment of laws that are "tough on crime," even if this goes against the enlightened opinion of policy-makers. And this fearful preoccupation with the maximum possible security of our persons and property will continue to predominate in liberal societies, at least according to Foucault's analysis.

The most massive proof of this that is adduced by Foucault is the steady and seemingly inevitable expansion of carceral punishment. In every modern nation today, hundreds of thousands – and in some countries, millions – of criminals have been warehoused for long, sometimes indefinite terms. This is a punishment whose conditions can hardly be considered humane and that has little hope of correcting or returning offenders to law-abiding society. (More on this below.) What is more, Foucault claims that this outcome was inevitable and that it could have been foreseen even in the eighteenth century, since, according to his analysis, at that time it was the recently empowered economic middle class that had the greatest influence over the character of the new criminal law reforms, so that the economic (rather than humanitarian) concerns of the bourgeoisie were "the essential *raisons d'être* of penal reform" (89).

Against the perversely harsh modern criminal justice systems, the voice of humanity asserts itself as a "discourse of the heart." It is the voice of intellectuals, of political figures, of lawyers and judges, and of humanitarian activists. Yet Foucault argues that the impassioned character of this humanitarian objection of the heart, however sincere, is inherently unstable, since it depends not on the feelings of the one who is liable to punishment, but on "those of the men who … have the right of exercising against him the power of assembly" – namely, the judges, jurors, and legislators. While the sentiments of judges and political leaders may prove to be magnanimous on some occasions, they may just as easily be influenced by "all the hardness of heart induced by familiarity," as well as by the voting public to which they are accountable (91). The unflattering truth is that democratic majorities and their leaders can easily afford to wax eloquent about the humanity of the criminal; yet when it comes time to make policy decisions, fear of crime generally wins out against magnanimity and enlightened policy.

It is all to the good when the disciplines of criminology, sociology, and psychology make efforts to inform the public that the impact of "tough on crime" legislation may be less than anticipated and that punishment is less effective at preventing crime than less coercive methods, such as educational programs for juvenile offenders and psychiatric treatment for past offenders with psychological problems. In the final analysis, the contractarian theory of punishment – especially in democratic societies – implies that the ultimate judgment of the danger posed by crimes, and of the appropriate methods of crime prevention, rests with the public. For the entire edifice of the liberal state stands or falls with the public's opinion of its security – which, as we recall, Montesquieu took to be the core meaning of "liberty." To use Hobbes's formulation, "the greater crime is that where the damage, *in the common opinion of men*, is most sensible."[3] Thus, no matter how much I, as the offender, might appeal to the mercy of my fellows, or beg them to consider how negligible was the harm I caused, or how pressing my circumstances, or, again, how unreasonable is the law that I violated, I may justly be treated "as a *lion* or a *tiger*, one of those wild savage beasts, with whom men can have no society nor security," to use Locke's formulation.[4] Foucault is therefore right to this extent: that in modern liberal democracies, criminal justice practices will tend to be informed by the most fearful policy.

This in no way alters the fact that retribution remains invalid in the new correctional systems, since it remains true that by definition, retribution has no social utility. In this respect, one might argue, the new systems are humane, at least when compared with traditional penal practices. Yet perhaps the decline of retribution did not contribute to an advance towards moderation in punishment after all. The principle of retribution requires proportionality in punishments, and this means not only that the severity of punishments may not be decreased below what the crime deserves, but also that it may not be increased above that level. In modern penal theory, in which retribution has been discredited,[5] the way has been opened to disproportionally heavy punishment, which is justified on grounds of general utility and society's right to self-defence. This increased severity is reflected not so much in the length of individual prison sentences, but rather in the mode of punishment itself – namely, mass incarceration. It may be that incarceration was originally introduced as the primary mode of punishment for its mildness (as a non-corporal form of punishment) as well as for its utility, but it continues to be heavily relied upon even now that it has become clear that mass incarceration is often quite degrading and difficult to endure psychologically and even physically. Thus Foucault writes that while "the right to punish has been shifted from ... vengeance ... to the defense of society," it "now finds itself recombined with elements so strong that it becomes almost more to be feared" (90).

So we must therefore grant that Foucault has struck a serious blow against modern punishment theory and that in elucidating its contradictions he has made explicit the tensions that have existed in modern punishment theory since Hobbes. Foucault's analysis reveals that the supposed fortuitous harmony between general utility and moderation, which the penal reformers had taken for granted, has proved to be illusory. The Enlightenment *philosophes* believed that both of these goals could be achieved by the same reforms, but according to Foucault they had overestimated the bourgeois class's ability to judge its own best interests, rightly understood, as well as its capacity to act on its humanitarian aspirations.

Foucault on the Prison

We now turn from Foucault's analysis of modern punishment theory to his examination of carceral punishment itself. Foucault's historical account of the emergence of the prison is intended to show that what was, in the eighteenth century, only a theoretical possibility has over time become a reality, and is today an urgent problem – namely, the increasingly despotic character of the administration of punishment.[6] Foucault does not, however, regard the emergence of carceral punishment as a natural outgrowth of modern punishment theory. In the first place, he points out that the early penal reformers had maintained that the deterrent effect of punishment would be maximized if the penalty for a given crime resembled it in quality and quantity as much as possible, so that the association of the one with the other in the minds of citizens would be as clear as possible. According to that view, theft would best be punished by confiscation, abuse of public office by loss of civil rights, murder by execution, arson by burning, and so on. This resemblance of the punishment to the crime "is an advantage for the stability of the [mental] link, an advantage for the calculation [i.e., on the part of the criminal] of the proportions between crime and punishment and the quantitative reading of interests" (104–5; 114).[7] Such a scheme obviously could not be carried out if every punishment was reduced to one form – incarceration – with only the length of the prison term varied according to the severity of the crime. Foucault further observes that the early penal reformers had many of the same reservations about incarceration as the later critics of the prison would have: it is costly; it allows vices to be communicated from hardened criminals to petty and first-time offenders; it exposes inmates to the arbitrary will of guards and prison administrators; it hides convicts behind walls, thus preventing them from serving as a salutary example to the public; and so on (114–15). But "within a short space of time, detention became the essential form of punishment. In the [French] penal code of 1810, between death and fines it occupies, in a number of forms, almost the whole field of possible punishments." How did this come about?

According to Foucault, part of the reason for the rapid growth of prisons was enthusiasm about a technological advance of the nineteenth century – what Foucault calls "penitentiary science" (120–6). This was an effort to apply modern medical and psychological theories, as well as certain principles of architectural design (championed by Bentham in his *Panopticon*), to the creation of new prisons – penitentiaries – that would not only detain and punish but also cure and reform. The key innovations of penitentiary science were isolation of the individual prisoner and his constant observation. These innovations were immediately put into practice in a handful of model prisons. The most famous of these were in Philadelphia (the Walnut Street and Cherry Hill prisons) and Auburn, New York.[8] They were built to house inmates in individual cells, in order to remove them from the harmful influence of their fellow inmates and to encourage reflection and repentance. An inmate's life was to be strictly regimented, and his time was to be divided into periods of labour, isolation, and religious instruction, so that no idle habits or corrupting influences could interfere with his rehabilitation. This benefit was to be further ensured through constant surveillance by prison officials occupying conveniently located observatories. Foucault admits that these technical innovations were important, but he denies that they are sufficient by themselves to explain the rapid expansion of carceral punishment.

The deeper reason for this rapid expansion, according to Foucault, was the development of what he calls modern discipline (to be distinguished from punishment proper). In Foucault, this is a technical concept that is meant to capture a very broad range of practices and techniques that were already in use in the late eighteenth century in the military, hospitals, schools, monasteries, and workhouses. Punishment, as traditionally understood, and as the eighteenth-century penal reformers continued to understand it, was meant to operate on the minds or souls of the convicted through "signs" and "representations." Whether the emphasis of traditional punishment was retribution or deterrence, it was to be accomplished by communicating a message (a threat, a legal judgment, the assertion of a norm) to the criminal and to society as a whole. In contrast, modern discipline, which increasingly becomes the new "penality," targets not the soul, but the body:

> The point of application of the penalty is not the representation, but the body, time, everyday gestures and activities; the soul, too, but in so far as it is the seat of habits. The body and the soul, as principles of behavior, form

> the element that is now proposed for punitive intervention. Rather than on an art of representations, this punitive intervention must rest on a studied manipulation of the individual ... As for the instruments used, these are no longer complexes of representation, reinforced and circulated, but forms of coercion, schemata of constraint, applied and repeated. Exercises, not signs: time-tables, compulsory movements, regular activities, solitary meditation, work in common, silence, application, respect, good habits. (128)

The prison presented itself as an ideal opportunity to apply these techniques, and according to Foucault, this is what really drove the rapid increase in the use of incarceration as the primary mode of punishment, despite its inconsistency with the principles of punishment theory.

Once the penitentiary became established in the public understanding as a great advance in criminal justice, the wedge that had been driven between modern punishment theory and penitentiary practice began to widen, and it continued to widen as the logic of penitentiary science took its course. Whereas criminal justice theory requires judicial sentencing and punishment to follow clear legal standards known to all, disciplinary science calls for absolute discretion for prison administrators, which militates against determinate sentencing in accordance with fixed legal standards.[9] For while justice proclaims that all individuals are equal in the eyes of the law, and that they must be judged by their deeds alone, disciplinary science teaches that the effectiveness of correction is directly related to the extent to which disciplinary techniques are individualized – that is, the extent to which the qualities of body and soul of each individual, to the last minute detail, are taken into account when determining an appropriate corrective regimen.[10] Despite this contradiction, a fundamental change in orientation was soon accepted by courts and legislative assemblies, which were persuaded of the social utility of the penitentiary technique, and which began to cede more and more responsibility for penal administration to prison officials, who over time acquired a "despotic" power in this domain (108).[11] As a result, "what is now imposed on penal justice as its point of application, its 'useful object,' will no longer be ... the juridical subject of an ideal contract; it will be the disciplinary individual" (227).

Foucault's discussion of the emergence of modern discipline goes quite far, and much of it is speculative and unlikely to convince the most sceptical of readers. It denies that modern discipline – taken as a whole in all its practical effects – was ever intended as a constitutive element of any of the large-scale political projects conceived by seventeenth- or eighteenth-century political philosophy. He credits the mechanistic view of man introduced by Descartes as only partly responsible for opening up this new possibility of social organization and control (136–7). He goes on to argue that the genesis of what he calls modern discipline is in large part a mysterious process: a convergence of apparently unrelated institutions and techniques that together make up "a new micro-physics of power" that had for some time "constantly reached out to ever broader domains, as if they tended to cover the entire social body" (139).[12] Many questions can be raised about this general thesis, and many more can be raised about specific features of Foucault's argument.

In the first place, Foucault focuses his investigation of the history of modern criminal justice on France, and we may wonder whether all that applies to a state famous (or notorious) for its administrative centralization would also apply to countries with stronger traditions of federalism and local self-government. Moreover, when he does turn to examine prominent American penal reformers, Foucault reads them tendentiously. When discussing Benjamin Rush, for instance, he stresses Rush's interest in a medical approach to prisoner rehabilitation (Rush had been a physician) while neglecting his genuine piety and his concern for the moral reform and spiritual salvation of prisoners.[13] One could argue more generally that Foucault's analysis does not take sufficiently seriously the great hopes of many penitentiary advocates that their new prisons would have an unprecedented capacity to transform seemingly hardened criminals into responsible citizens and good Christians.[14] Foucault is strangely cynical about this aspiration of the penitentiary movement, dismissing it as mostly empty rhetoric.

Like some other observers, Foucault finds that the expectations of the early penal reformers for the penitentiary were excessive.[15] As a rule, penitentiary inmates have had high rates of recidivism throughout the long history of this institution – a fact that has been and continues to be a great embarrassment for the modern criminal justice system. What is worse, few if any of the costly subsequent reforms intended to address this basic problem have had any positive effect.[16] The ideals of penitentiary science could not be attained in the model prisons of Auburn and Cherry Hill, and they appear to be as far out of reach today as ever. Penitentiaries today hardly even deserve the name, since the primary purpose they continue to serve is incapacitation and deterrence (and even the effectiveness of the latter is challenged by some criminologists). Carceral punishment has thus largely failed to meet the goals that were its explicit original justification. Yet despite this, it continues to be the primary – indeed, all but exclusive – mode of punishment in the Western world. Some now take for granted that the prison system (one can hardly continue to call it a penitentiary system) is necessary, believing that one can no longer imagine any other way of dealing with convicted populations that in some Western countries numbers in the hundreds of thousands, and even in the millions. Those who are not convinced of the inevitability of mass carceral punishment, however, remain at a loss to justify it. The continued existence of this morally unaccountable institution thus looms as a massive indictment (perhaps not fatal, but embarrassing nonetheless) of liberalism itself. For all the questionable claims of Foucault's account, it is difficult to deny this, its main thrust, just as it is difficult to ignore the problem of carceral punishment once one becomes aware of its dimensions.

The Present State of Modern Criminal Justice

The greatest contribution of *Discipline and Punish* is its analysis of the collapse of the modern theory of criminal justice at its very heart: its attempt to justify punishment in light of a rational standard of natural right. As we argued in earlier chapters, this collapse was always inevitable. Although it took some time (and several transformations in, and iterations of, the theoretical framework) for this process to work itself out, its conclusion could no longer be ignored or denied after the historical emergence and failure (from the point of view of its original intention) of mass carceral punishment. "In becoming a legal punishment, it [i.e., carceral punishment] weighted the old juridico-political question of the right to punish with all the problems, all the agitations that have surrounded the corrective technologies of the individual" (235). The "problems" and "agitations" of which Foucault speaks are the troubling signs of unregulated coercion in the midst of liberal society – signs that threaten to undermine our feeling of individual freedom and security.[17] In spite of his very different philosophical orientation, in his concern with this phenomenon Foucault may be said to continue in the spirit of the Montesquieuan liberal-republican tradition.

The most urgent question that remains concerns the present status and future prospects of the embattled carceral penal system. For Foucault, the outlook is bleak, since he regards that system both as indispensable (at least within the limits of the prevailing political order) and as incapable of being salvaged from his critique, given that for him, the insinuation of modern disciplinary techniques into the carceral penal system is a consequence of the logic of liberal institutions. Foucault impugned the intentions of the original penal reformers as tied up with the economic interests of the bourgeois class. In his words, "humanity [was] the respectable name given to ... economy and to its meticulous calculations" (92). Similarly, Foucault claims that the penal system as it now exists is a means to perpetuate the political domination of that same class over the working class, and the exploitation of the latter by the former. The "peasant illegality" that developed after the French Revolution was in fact, according to Foucault, a political protest against the new regime of bourgeois property holders (273–4). But instead of acknowledging this illegality as a political challenge, the new regime criminalized it as a "delinquency" (a term that, for Foucault, captures the sorts of offences typical of the poor classes: "petty theft, minor acts of violence, routine acts of law-breaking" – 278–9). This "legal" strategy of neutralizing the greatest political threat to the new regime had to be perpetuated, and this was accomplished by means of the prison, according to Foucault. Here, the failure of the penitentiary technique to lower recidivism rates turned out to be an unexpected political advantage to the ruling classes. "Delinquency" initially seems ideally suited for penitentiary correction, and any failure of such correction is likely to be attributed to extrinsic causes (imperfect institutional design, maladministration, etc.). In fact, however, "the prison, apparently 'failing,' does not miss its target; on the contrary, it reaches it, in so far as it gives rise to" delinquency, which is "secretly useful" since it is at once "refractory and docile" (276–7). In short, Foucault's provocative claim is that the carceral penal system continues to exist – not despite its failings, but *because* of them – in order to create a permanent illegal underclass whose offences are tolerable and whose continued existence serves the interests of the property-owning majority.

The argument we have just summarized is nothing if not provocative, albeit also speculative and, it must be admitted, somewhat theoretically extravagant. Nevertheless, aside from calling further into question the true motives of political majorities in liberal-democratic countries, it is in fact somewhat misleading, since, on the terms of Foucault's own analysis, it gives the ruling economic classes too much credit. That is because, as we have already seen, Foucault's basic claim is that the development of modern disciplinary techniques is a historical process that has always escaped human control.[18] The ultimate cause of this historical development is not human agency but technology, understood as a quasi-autonomous force in human affairs. Thus when the penitentiary came to dominate criminal justice, it did so *in spite of* the wishes of the public and its representatives (whether those wishes were noble or, as Foucault alleges, base). As Foucault himself puts it, "if the penitentiary, in so far as it went well beyond mere detention, was able not only to establish itself, but to entrap the whole of penal justice and to imprison the judges themselves, it was because it was able to introduce criminal justice into relations of knowledge that have since become its infinite labyrinth" (248–9). Foucault seems to be saying that the "relations of knowledge" into which criminal justice was thus fatefully introduced were none other than the technical sciences of the psychological and physiological mechanisms that underlie illegal behaviour, which Foucault associates with penitentiary science.

But how does the discovery of a mechanistic science of criminal behaviour "entrap" the criminal justice system, and in such a way as to elude human control? Foucault's answer to this question is twofold. In the first place, penitentiary technique is indispensable because of its utility. The utility Foucault has in mind cannot be tied to the effectiveness of penal correction, since according to him, the penitentiary not only fails to correct but also *creates* delinquency. Rather, the utility of the carceral penal system is evidently political in nature. For Foucault this means, as we have seen, that the creation and maintenance of a delinquent class blunts the political threat that the propertyless classes would otherwise pose to the regime of the propertied majority. Even if we doubt the truth of this particular imputation, however, it is hard not to suspect that some of the public's inertia regarding the carceral penal system (despite its dissatisfaction with that system) has some political dimension. Critics point out that modern criminal justice's exclusive reliance on mass incarceration could be replaced with some combination of incarceration and community-based correction (especially for less hardened offenders).[19] Essentially, this would mean transferring a substantial portion of the correctional and crime prevention functions from government agencies to local communities, where they might take the form of community reintegration programs, neighbourhood watch groups, or even informal mechanisms such as neighbourly vigilance and the sharing of parenting duties.[20] This strong shift of responsibility for crime prevention from governmental institutions and processes to communities has been, and may remain, politically unpopular because of its many inconveniences from the point of view of modern societies, which are accustomed to extensive protections (supported by statutes and by cultural consensus) of individual privacy and autonomy. All of us hesitate to mind our neighbour's business, lest the next time our own private doings become the focus of neighbourly scrutiny. The existence of this *laissez-faire* cultural consensus seems to favour mass incarceration, for all its problems, over more communal methods of crime prevention. This point would seem to receive support from our earlier discussion of Plato's analysis of the limits of criminal justice in the republican context. According to Plato, what one might call informal community-based methods of crime prevention all require a vigilant, public-spirited citizenry whose moral outlook is informed by a demanding conception of self-denying virtue. Yet the qualities that make human beings fit for an austere republican life are precisely the same ones that also make them less fit for modern liberal institutions, which presuppose an overriding concern for individual security, property, and freedom of expression. For these deep-seated reasons, community-based methods of crime prevention would be difficult to introduce into liberal society.[21]

The second part of Foucault's answer to the question of the intractability of penitentiary technique has to do with what the discoveries of the sciences of criminal behaviour imply for the "juridical" status of crime and of the criminal. The individualizing knowledge of penitentiary technique focuses less on the criminal deed and its circumstances than on the criminal himself – on his psychology, social position, and upbringing. This leads to "a curious substitution: from the hands of justice, [the penitentiary system] certainly receives a convicted person but what it must apply itself to is not, of course, the offence, nor even exactly the offender, but a rather different object, one defined by variables which at the outset at least were not taken into account in the sentence, for they were relevant only for a corrective technology" (251–2). In fact, juridical determinations of an offender's culpability (the gravity of his offence, and so on) are not simply irrelevant to penitentiary technique – they actually contradict it by the terms by which they are understood. The psychological reductionism that is characteristic of modern criminology leaves no room for stock legal or moral concepts such as premeditation, responsibility, free will, and the conscience; nor can it be in any way reconciled with these concepts (unless, that is, one fully subscribes to Kantian compatibilism). In the face of this positivist scepticism, a retreat from the carceral penal system in the direction of any non-penitentiary approach to criminal justice would be difficult to justify. Foucault calls this dilemma a "criminological labyrinth from which we have certainly not yet emerged" (252 and context).

Conclusion

Foucault's critique of modern criminal justice theory brings its various tensions and contradictions to a crisis point. As we saw in earlier chapters, the major theorists of that tradition were sufficiently aware of its problems. Even when their attempted solutions were not all that might have been desired, the earlier penal theorists made every effort to "soften" the remaining difficulties through doctrinal or rhetorical means (thus, Hobbesian "authorization" and Beccaria's humanitarianism). Foucault, by contrast, explodes all such stopgap devices. He directs his attack especially against the equivocation of liberals about the true aim of the modern criminal justice system by asking whether its fundamental aim is just and humane or whether it amounts to a project for extending the political and economic advantage of the propertied majority. The defenders of modern criminal justice have always claimed that justice, humanity, and the security of life and property always go together under a regime of enlightened criminal laws; Foucault rejects this stance on the basis of his understanding of the character of liberalism and of bourgeois society.

The strongest piece of evidence that Foucault advances in support of his thesis about modern criminal justice in crisis is his analysis of carceral punishment. According to that analysis, penitentiary technique individualizes punishment, replaces the juridical subject with the object of disciplinary science, and reduces all punishment to a single mode (thus destroying any semblance of proportionality). These consequences run contrary to the explicit principles of modern penal theory, yet they were made possible by that theory. Since the principles of the original penal reformers are defied by the carceral penal system we have today in its operation, we must somehow explain that system's rapid emergence as well as the near-universal acceptance of its necessity. The explanation Foucault offers is at times extravagant, yet some of its chief points cannot be denied. In the first place, despite the public's dissatisfaction with mass incarceration, its political utility for contemporary liberal societies makes it difficult to abandon for otherwise more attractive methods of crime prevention. Furthermore, the discoveries of the behavioural sciences, which are so integral to modern criminology, have helped undermine the credibility of traditional moral and juridical concepts, thereby making the status quo appear unavoidable.

Discipline and Punish has its fair share of critics, and indeed, there is much that deserves to be criticized. Yet once one gets beyond the general objections to Foucault's opaque formulations, his sometimes unnecessary neologisms, and his occasionally tendentious use of historical facts, one begins to see that his critics are not actually challenging his critique of the principles of modern criminal justice – and it is not clear whether they always fully understand that critique. (It bears repeating that the critique of the theory of modern criminal justice should not be confused with Foucault's broader arguments and claims about modern discipline.) Given its faults, *Discipline and Punish* has been easy to ignore for contemporary penal theory and scholarship, especially in the English-speaking world. But perhaps the key reason why Foucault is often too easily dismissed by criminologists and punishment theorists is that he makes politics central to his analysis. Contemporary criminology and punishment theory have tended to treat their respective subject matters as independent of politics, perhaps with the intention of forestalling further controversy in an already controversial field. Yet it has been one of the claims of this study that the political context is essential for understanding the various problems of criminal justice. Although no longer himself in the tradition of modern political philosophy, Foucault remains our most direct link to that tradition's teaching on crime and punishment. Having done the work of connecting Foucault to the development of Western rationalist penal thought, and having traced the key moments in that development leading up to its present crisis, this study has perhaps made possible a rethinking of the most challenging criminal justice issues facing us, as citizens of liberal-democratic societies, in ways that are more fully informed about what is truly at stake.

Punishment and Liberalism

The discipline of criminology currently understands itself as a value-free science, like economics and sociology, with which it shares many of its methods. While examining the rise and fall of crime rates and their underlying causes, modern criminology has thus far left questions of policy aims to political theorists, and ultimately to legislators and democratic majorities. Public debates, however, have been largely unsuccessful in sorting through some of the difficult normative issues implicit in questions about the competing aims of punishment. In fact, it has become routine for the public simply to look away. There is little reason to hope there will be a spontaneous change in the lamentable public inaction regarding the fundamental problems of modern criminal justice. Political theory for its part has so far ignored criminal justice. As political theorist Albert Dzur recently wrote, "Anglo-American political theory has hardly registered mass incarceration and has done little to analyze any incongruity with core democratic commitments."[1] The present study has attempted to remedy this gap in the scholarship by uncovering the original debates in Western political thought surrounding the principles of punishment. This, however, is still only a beginning, one that clarifies the terms of the debate but that by itself cannot give rise to real policy decisions. An extensive empirical knowledge of the dimensions of crime in a large society, which is the proper sphere of criminology, is indispensable to any serious attempt to formulate practical proposals for criminal justice policy. Such expertise must inform the practical application of the normative principles and must in turn be informed by those principles.

Criminologists cannot afford to keep neglecting the essentially political task of weighing and adjudicating among competing aims of criminal justice. Criminologists often trace the origin of their discipline to

Beccaria's *On Crimes and Punishments*, which they understand as having established the empirical study of the causes of crime and the effects of punishment. But as we have seen, unlike later criminologists Beccaria was no less concerned with the normative questions of punishment than he was with the empirical ones. In fact, *all* of the intellectual forerunners of modern criminology we have discussed – Hobbes and Montesquieu, as well as Beccaria – believed that the question of the proper aim of punishment was a matter for serious dispute and debate, having serious moral implications, and that this question could not be resolved simply by a popular vote for one or another set of preferred policy objectives. Criminologists, and not just political theorists, must concern themselves with the *ends* of punishment.

The present study might help criminologists identify some of the outstanding questions their discipline must begin to answer. First, up to what point is the unprecedented security we enjoy worth the corrosive effect that mass incarceration has on our sense of civic unity? Given that security must rank quite high as a priority in a liberal political order, how much must we moderate our noblest aspirations to apply the institutions of punishment to the rehabilitation of criminals and the reconstitution of civic community? Importantly, our investigations have implied that some such tradeoff among the competing ends of criminal justice must be accepted – since no perfect harmony of ends is possible in this sphere – and that it is better to accept a reflective compromise of our aspirations than to delude ourselves either with a policy of utility that poses as morality or with a moral formalism that remains deaf to political necessities (both physical and psychological). Second, criminology must be able to tell us what kinds of offences can be criminalized or decriminalized in a liberal political order and to what extent, given that liberal societies are naturally quite tolerant of what Montesquieu called crimes against mores and public tranquillity, *but only up to a point*. Can recreational drug use be decriminalized without seriously undermining some minimum level of public decency and self-respect? Can punishment of certain severe crimes – such as rape and murder – be carried out without any accommodation of public sentiments of moral indignation and retribution? To be sure, these are difficult questions, the answers to which would depend on extensive knowledge of many complicated dimensions of society, including demography, the family, and what sociologists call "social capital." But if such answers are to have any value, they must come from criminologists who have thoroughly informed themselves about the normative aspects of these questions.

Specific questions about mass incarceration (with various moral and political implications) would also need to be addressed. The many grievances typically levelled against mass incarceration include the following: that it is ineffective in the performance of its corrective function, as evidenced by high rates of recidivism; that it is ineffective in the performance of its deterrence function, due to low or unpredictable conviction rates; that it results in inhumane conditions for inmates, especially overcrowding and rampant violence; that the courts rely too heavily on prison sentences, as opposed to community-based corrections; and that prison sentences are excessively punitive (a charge made by critics on the left) or excessively short or arbitrary (a consequence of indeterminate sentencing and early release laws, according to critics on the right).[2] Certain other charges commonly levelled against the modern penal system – for example, that it discriminates by race in sentencing, and that it criminalizes poverty and mental illness – are strictly speaking not criticisms of mass incarceration per se; nevertheless, it is sometimes suggested or implied that incarceration somehow exacerbates these injustices. Some of these criticisms presuppose that crime prevention is the sole proper aim of punishment and demand the reform of carceral punishment with a view to enhancing its effectiveness; other criticisms on this list presuppose other ends, such as humanitarian benevolence, equality, rule of law, justice, or civic solidarity. To address these criticisms squarely, it will be important for criminologists to make all such presuppositions explicit.

Because of the empirical orientation of contemporary criminology, whenever current debates do touch on normative issues they have a strikingly disoriented character. One prominent debate may serve as an illustration. Over the past two generations, the discipline of criminology has been preoccupied with questions surrounding an unprecedented crime wave in many Western countries. In the 1960s and 1970s alone, the rates of homicide in Canada and the United States more than doubled (according to Statistics Canada and the FBI's Uniform Crime Reports), while property offence rates approximately tripled in both countries. This sharp increase in crime drew much public attention, which paved the way for batteries of studies of many aspects of crime and criminal justice policy. At that time, various explanations for the sharp increase in crime were offered.[3] The most common and least controversial of these focused on the sudden increase in the numbers of young people following the postwar baby boom. Since young males are overwhelmingly the group most at risk of falling into crime, the sudden influx of young men in the postwar decades was in itself a highly significant factor in the rise of crime rates, according to this explanation. The discovery of this age effect did not by itself satisfy criminologists, however, since it did not provide any insights as to what might be done to curb soaring crime (short of getting rid of young men). Furthermore, as a theoretical explanation of crime, it was obviously incomplete, since youth by itself cannot explain criminality. It is true that a large proportion of "career" criminals (those with high offence rates and long criminal careers) start their careers as young men, but overall, most young men never commit a serious offence in their lives. So the question of what could lead certain young men (and individuals from other groups) to take the fatal step of committing a serious crime remained.

From the criminologists' point of view, there was yet another reason to be dissatisfied with the age-effect explanation of the crime boom. They noted that while this explanation was consistent with similar spikes in crime rates in many other Western countries, it could not account for the relatively low crime rates during the same postwar period in some non-Western countries, such as Japan. If culturally conservative nations like Japan could keep crime under control when the age of their populations fluctuated, could it be that Western culture, or certain characteristic institutions of Western societies, were somehow responsible for the rising crime rates?

Numerous attempts were made to come up with "structural" explanations to supplement the age-effect theory of crime. Among conservatives, the eminent criminologist James Q. Wilson pointed to the "counterculture" movements of the 1960s and 1970s, which attacked "middle-class values" and promoted self-expression, free love, and recreational drug use.[4] If young people – Wilson's argument ran – had embraced the standards of responsibility and industry inherited from their parents, they would have been less tempted to turn to crime; but flouting these standards became acceptable and even admirable among Western youth, with the result that internal controls on illicit behaviour were weakened.[5] Yet Wilson proposed this explanation only as a plausible account, not as a demonstrable scientific theory; indeed, he took other criminologists to task for seeking "fundamental causes" of criminal behaviour, which Wilson himself regarded as impossible to find. He advocated, instead, taking a "citizen's" perspective when analysing criminal justice policy. Such a perspective would be sceptical of extravagant or radical theoretical explanations and would favour commonsense assumptions about individual agency and motivation. (Wilson evidently believed that his own account, which emphasized cultural factors in the crime boom of the 1960s and 1970s, would be compelling to a commonsense, civic perspective.) Notwithstanding this scepticism towards fundamental causal explanations, Wilson later proposed a kind of fundamental theory of criminality in *Crime and Human Nature* (which he co-authored with psychologist Richard Herrnstein). In this landmark work, he presented an extensive review of criminological and psychological studies and concluded that individual biology (especially factors such as body type and a genetic predisposition to psychopathology) contributed just as much to criminal behaviour as did an individual's social environment. On these grounds, *Crime and Human Nature* favoured more traditional methods of crime prevention, arguing in support of deterrents such as incarceration and stronger policing. Wilson was particularly influential in the United States, where he popularized his "Broken Windows" theory of crime control, with its emphasis on stricter policing of minor offences – "order maintenance" – as an indirect means to prevent more serious crimes.[6] He was also a strong advocate for the expansion of the prison system that has been under way since the 1980s – an expansion that, according to some, has substantially lowered crime rates (although this remains a hotly debated issue among criminologists).

Wilson became a controversial figure because of his efforts to defend the traditional approach to crime. Some at the time viewed that approach as having failed to prevent the crime boom of the 1960s and 1970s; others contended that it exaggerated the crime boom. A very different explanation for violence and criminality than Wilson's was championed by liberals and progressives. According to President Lyndon Johnson's attorney general, Ramsey Clark, the traditional approach to crime, which for the causes of criminality in the individual, was misguided, and the true causes were to be found in deeper, systemic social ills. Among those systemic ills were Americans' individualism, their national predisposition to violence, and their selfish acquisitiveness. High crime rates could never, according to Clark, be reduced sufficiently by getting "tough on crime"; this could only happen through sweeping social, economic, and educational reforms. According to Clark's *Crime in America*, only relief from poverty and mutual fear could prevent young men living in urban slums from falling into a life of crime, and this could only be accomplished if reason and science were brought to bear on the "old instincts" of the nation as a whole so that the "reflex to violence" and the "acquisitive instinct" (responsible for the injustice of steep economic inequality) were "conditioned out of the American character." Clark's call to address the systemic causes of crime was meant to appeal to Americans'

interest in their own security, but at the same time it clearly and elo-
quently spoke to his audience's nobler sensibilities. Clark was implying
that the modern criminal justice system's methods were failing because
they were both ineffective and unjust. But in spite of its high moral tone,
the book contained not even the rudiments of a theory of what justice
demands (or any reference to any such existing theory). Thus Clark's
vague assumptions that justice, security, social equality, and political
solidarity had always gone together could not be considered more than
mere speculations. Clark's book paid almost no attention to the higher-
order political questions of criminal justice that it implicitly raised; and
it remained entirely oblivious to the tradition of Western penal thought,
which had for a long time wrestled with those very questions. Without
an adequate understanding of those questions, it is impossible to grasp
the political status of security or its relation to other political priorities
in a liberal-democratic order. Thus, Clark's call for wholesale criminal
justice reform seemed at once confused, utopian, and partisan.[7]

Although Wilson found himself on the opposite side of the debate
over the appropriate response to rising crime rates, his work did not
quite avoid the problems that affected his opponents. Whatever the
merit of his preferred policies from the narrow point of view of effective
crime control, his arguments for those policies rarely if ever addressed
his opponents' more radical contention that the traditional approach to
criminal justice was fundamentally unjust. Moreover, Wilson did not
realize that his appeal to the civic perspective (which he made partly in
order to avoid the hard systemic questions and to counter the sociological theories of crime of some of his colleagues) *required* an answer to the
basic question of the justice of the traditional approach to crime, since
as citizens we demand fairness, proportionality, and humanity from our
penal institutions no less than we demand security. The criminological
studies of recent decades are of no help here; indeed, as Wilson himself
argued in *Thinking About Crime*, we cannot reasonably hope that such
studies will ever establish the "fundamental causes" of crime,[8] which
means that as citizens, we ought not to abandon our collective responsibility of thinking about the basic questions of criminal justice on the
pretext that such questions might safely be left to value-free positivist
science. As Thacher has recently put it, "strong causal arguments [in
criminology] rarely succeed to the degree needed," since "causal analysis that aims to identify large indirect effects produced through complex causal chains is unlikely to offer clear-cut advice for policy."[9] We
have no choice but to use our theoretically informed *political* judgment

to decide whether to continue to rely heavily on traditional criminal justice approaches, or whether to begin to emphasize welfare spending, medical treatment programs, community correction, and various other methods as means of crime control.

Unfortunately, the current theoretical debates about punishment, which tend to be conducted in legal and ethics journals, are drawn largely from the sorts of political arguments that had originally been used to found modern criminal justice theory. When present-day liberals draw on the tradition of modern political theory, they limit themselves to two attenuated strands of that tradition: a utilitarianism handed down from Beccaria and Bentham on the one hand, and a neo-Kantianism favoured by leading liberals like John Rawls, H.L.A. Hart, and Joel Feinberg on the other.[10] As we noted in our introduction, in recent decades neo-Kantian theories of punishment have won prominence, now that utilitarian punishment theories have fallen out of favour due to what has generally been regarded as their moral reductionism. Liberal thinkers who have helped redefine the recent punishment debate tend to agree with Kant that there is a real need to restore to punishment its retributive dimension in some form, in order to account for our respect for the dignity and rights of individuals in the face of the frequently overwhelming popular pressure to advance the greatest happiness of the greatest number. These liberal punishment theorists have tried to argue that retributive punishment is fully compatible with liberalism and that there is no real tension between the backward-looking concern with desert that characterizes retribution and liberals' forward-looking commitment to external liberty and physical security.[11]

Yet a recent friendly critic of liberalism, Stanley Brubaker, has argued to the contrary – that contemporary liberals *cannot* justify retributive punishment on their principles and that they do not even fully understand what punishment is.[12] Like Kant, Brubaker believes that proportionality is central to what most people think makes punishment just and that ordinary, practical knowledge of the appropriateness of retribution is as common in liberal societies as it is in any healthy political community. As one explanation of the preponderance in political life of the retributive outlook, Brubaker suggests that retributive punishment performs an important expressive function: through it, a political community emphatically affirms its shared conception of the human good and the rank-ordering of virtues and vices by rewarding men it admires and punishing those whose actions it condemns as immoral. Contemporary liberals, by contrast, cannot justify retributive punishment because of their basic theoretical commitments, according to Brubaker's account. Most prominent strands of contemporary liberalism (Brubaker cites Lockean, neo-Kantian, and utilitarian versions in particular) insist on maintaining a strict neutrality towards the various conflicting views of the human good, as a result of their scepticism regarding that good. Constrained by this neutrality, liberals can impose "penalties" (which Brubaker distinguishes from "punishment"), which are intended to deter crime and to compensate victims for their losses, since this can be accomplished without requiring individuals to obey the law for what some might hold to be the morally right reasons. But liberalism's neutrality towards the good denies the right to punish in order to express moral condemnation of criminal acts, since doing so would presuppose some standard of the human good.[13] Thus, according to Brubaker, while liberals may deter, compensate, and rehabilitate, they cannot punish in the sense that most resonates with ordinary moral experience.

On Brubaker's account, when contemporary liberals try to make room for retribution in their penal schemes, they do so either inconsistently or by way of emptying the notion of retribution of its essential meaning. When societies punish, they surely do so for the sake of deterrence, but they also punish for the sake of retribution because they see it as a legitimate and independent end of punishment. On this basis, Brubaker criticizes Hart and Rawls, who deny that we ever punish *because* we want the guilty to "pay" for their actions. They claim that we only punish for the sake of deterrence and that when we invoke the notion of just deserts we only mean to set an upper limit, or side-constraint, on public coercion in order to forestall punishment of the innocent and disproportionate punishment of the guilty. While such a limiting principle could well be desirable on humanitarian grounds, it would not, according to Brubaker, entirely satisfy our concern for retribution, since, contrary to Hart and Rawls, we do in fact tend to believe that punishing the guilty is an end in itself.[14] Since liberal societies do punish retributively (in Brubaker's sense), liberalism's failure to justify retribution creates a troubling dissonance between liberal theory and practice.[15]

This failure of neo-Kantian liberalism to make sense of the enduring appeal of retribution, or even to take seriously the suggestion that retribution may constitute a proper aim of punishment, is, I would argue, a reflection of its failure to think through the questions and problems of punishment in light of the tradition of political philosophy. Thus contemporary liberals would do well to give more serious thought to the classic liberal approach to retribution found in Montesquieu. Like contemporary liberals, Montesquieu is sceptical of retribution, but because he eschews the formalism of Hobbes, he is more sensitive to the fact that even thoroughly liberal societies partly depend on institutions that do not neatly harmonize with liberalism, such as the family and republican virtue (or an attenuated form thereof). Montesquieu helps us see how these institutions themselves contain the origins of the concern for retributive justice and how a moderated retributive element might (and must) be accommodated by a liberal criminal law. Nevertheless, for the deeper meaning of the concern for retributive justice, contemporary liberals would have to turn not to Montesquieu, or Hobbes, or even Kant, but to Plato. Our discussion of Plato's *Laws* showed that the appeal of retribution could be explained as originating most powerfully in the moral demands of republican political life. In the tradition of Western political philosophy, classical republicanism was understood to be one of several fundamental alternative ways of organizing politics – and indeed human life as a whole – that would always remain a profoundly appealing possibility. The way of life represented by classical republicanism – its commitment to the public good and at the same time to individual human excellence – must therefore be reckoned with, even by its opponents.[16] Plato himself was in some ways critical of classical republican life and of the intellectually confused punitive attitude to which it was prone, yet he found the latter to be inseparable from the former when he considered the nature and limits of political life.

This study has admittedly posed more challenges than it has offered concrete solutions, and some of these challenges are daunting. Continuing to ignore these challenges, however, is not an option, while facing them squarely promises great rewards in the form of a richer, more engaged civic life in which punishment is not an injustice to the offender and an embarrassment to society, but a reconciliation of the two.

Notes

Introduction

1 Braithwaite, *Restorative Justice*, 11 ff., 45, 74, 100–3, 129; see also Hahn, *Emerging Criminal Justice*; Christie, "Conflicts as Property"; Schneider, *Refocusing Crime Prevention*, ch. 1; Sutton et al., *Crime Prevention*.

2 Thus restorative justice advocates propose to return some of the control over the administration of criminal justice to local communities by introducing "community conferences" into the criminal justice process. Such conferences would deter and correct at the local level through "reintegrative shaming" rather than through traditional punishments, thereby healing frayed social bonds and reviving a sense of community. Advocates of restorative justice claim to embrace traditional goals of incarceration – namely, rehabilitation, deterrence, and victim satisfaction – while rejecting it as a means to that end. See Braithwaite, *Restorative Justice*, 80–8, 129–32. See also 95 ff.

3 *Furman v. Georgia*, 408 U.S. 239.

4 Ibid., 270.

5 Ibid., 286.

6 Ibid., 296.

7 *Gregg v. Georgia*, 428 U.S. 183–7 (1976).

8 As Emile Durkheim shows, a purely utilitarian understanding of wrongdoing and punishment can be rejected even on purely empirical grounds. See Durkheim, *Sociology and Philosophy*, 40–9.

9 See Morris, "Persons and Punishment"; C.S. Lewis, "The Humanitarian Theory of Punishment"; Murphy, "Marxism and Retribution," 242–3; Feinberg, *Doing and Deserving*, ch. 5. The position against which these critics are reacting is defended by Smart in Part I of his essay in Smart and Williams, *Utilitarianism*. See also Benn, "An Approach," 331–4.

10 See Dagger, "Playing Fair"; Morris, "Persons and Punishment."

11 Feinberg in *Doing and Deserving*, ch. 5, provides a clear account of the "expressivist" conception of retribution. See also Primoratz, "Punishment as Language."

12 For a review of the objections made against the various types of retributivism and the rebuttals to those objections, see Boonin, *The Problem of Punishment*, ch. 3.

13 See Rawls, "Two Concepts of Rules," and Hart, "Prolegomenon." The difference between the two is that while Rawls tries to defend the principle of retribution as a rule within a rule-utilitarian framework, Hart defends retribution as independently grounded in the principle of fairness. Later, though, Rawls adopts the principle of justice as fairness and explicitly follows Hart's view of punishment. See Rawls, *A Theory of Justice*, 211–12 and 276–7.

14 Rawls, "Two Concepts of Rules," 5–6.

15 Hart, "Prolegomenon," 1–4, 10–11. Hart calls this political actors' "oversimplifying tendency."

16 See Corlett, "Making Sense of Retributivism," 81–3. See also Boonin, *The Problem of Punishment*, 63–77, for a critique of Rawls's rule-utilitarian version of the argument.

17 Moore, *Placing Blame*, chs. 3–4; Corlett, "Making Sense of Retributivism"; Brubaker, "Can Liberals Punish?," 822–5 and 827–31.

18 Brubaker, "Can Liberals Punish?," 829–30. But see also Brubaker and Terchek, "Punishing Liberals?," 1315–16. On the distinctions we commonly draw between punishment and other kinds of coercive measures, see Feinberg, *Doing and Deserving*, ch. 5.

19 With the exception of Koritansky's *The Philosophy of Punishment*, I know of no scholarship that makes its theme the connection between criminal justice theory and political philosophy. The present book goes beyond Koritansky's (a collected volume) in that it not only links penological ideas to political principles in the works of individual thinkers (as the essays in Koritansky's volume do) but also attempts to map the historical transformations of criminal justice theory onto the parallel history of political philosophy in the West.

20 See Mackenzie, *Plato on Punishment*; Saunders, *Plato's Penal Code*; L. Pangle, "Moral and Criminal Responsibility."

21 Important exceptions are Cattaneo, "Hobbes's Theory of Punishment"; Norrie, "Thomas Hobbes"; Schrock, "The Right to Punish."

Chapter 1

1 Braithwaite and Pettit, *Not Just Deserts: A Republican Theory of Criminal Justice*. See also the Introduction to this volume and the sources cited there in note 1.

2 See Braithwaite, *Restorative Justice*, 17–18, 73–8.

3 Braithwaite and Pettit, *Not Just Deserts*, ch. 6, esp. 88–92.

4 Braithwaite and Pettit, *Not Just Deserts*, 54, 59–60.

5 This, of course, is not to say one way or the other whether such a demand on the part of republican citizens would be right.

6 Thus, in my view, the relation between the two dialogues is complementary, and their respective teachings cohere to comprise a greater whole (as argued by Bruell in "On Plato's Political Philosophy"). I am less inclined than some scholars to regard the *Laws* as a "late" work in Plato's intellectual development that gives evidence of a break with his teacher, Socrates, or of a great mind in decline (or both).

7 Adkins, in *Merit and Responsibility*, ch. 14, esp. 293–5, gives a somewhat different explanation for why Plato's thematic discussion of wrongdoing, moral responsibility, and punishment belongs in the *Laws* rather than in one of Plato's "earlier" political works.

8 By contrast, philosophy asks "What is law?," thus proclaiming its ignorance of its nature and power. Cf. beginning of the *Minos*.

9 At 702b–702e, Kleinias announces that he has been appointed by his native city of Knossos to serve on a committee of legislators to draw up a comprehensive legal code for a new Greek colony, Magnesia, and it is on his behalf that the Stranger elaborates his system of laws, as well as its underlying principles. For the original Greek text of the *Laws*, I have relied on the Oxford critical edition and consulted the Loeb and E.B. England editions. Some of the shorter translations are my own, but for longer translations I have relied on T. Pangle.

10 The other two alternatives are much too radical to be implemented. The first would require that the few "just" should somehow overpower the many "unjust" (see 627b), while the second option (the enslavement of the vicious to the virtuous) might be possible only in the city in speech – not in deed – presented in the *Republic*, where philosophers rule autocratically over willing subjects.

11 The ancient Greek word *timōria* (one of the common words for punishment) is related to *timē*, which translates as "honour," "status," or "wealth" – all of which may be understood as types of property. Hence *timōria* comes to mean the restoration of *timē* to one who has lost it by taking it away from the offender responsible for inflicting the loss. Cf. Saunders, *Plato's Penal Code*, 3–4, 20. See below, 49 (and n37), for a comment on Aristotle's discussion of reciprocity, a branch of corrective justice that is believed to be the return of harm for harm, and that is modelled on commercial exchange.

12 The Stranger seems to speak with some truth here. Hesiod writes (*Works and Days*, 270–2): "I would not myself be just, nor have my son be just

among bad men: for it is bad to be an honest man where felons rule; I trust wise Zeus to save me from this pass."

13 There is some controversy over the correct interpretation of this ambiguous passage. I am inclined to agree with England (in Plato, *Laws of Plato*, vol. 2, 476–8), who reads *timōria* as referring only to the criminal's acquisition of a bad character and bad associates, not to the destruction of the criminal that the city may deliberately cause "in order that many others may be saved." Mackenzie's reading of *timōria* as referring to both the capital punishment imposed by the city for purposes of deterrence and the wretched condition of the soul of the criminal as a consequence of his assimilation to bad men seems logical, insofar as both fail to make the criminal better. See Mackenzie, *Plato on Punishment*, 196n62. Yet the Stranger may have reason for his reluctance to call deterrent punishment *timōria*. The general preamble clearly intends to disparage retribution, on the ground that it produces no positive effects to redeem the harm it does. Deterrence, on the other hand, does benefit others, though it does nothing good for the offender himself, and therefore from the point of view of political necessity can claim to be a certain kind of justice. Yet the Stranger refuses to call deterrence a *dikē* in the strict sense, and so allows it to occupy a kind of moral middle ground. This seems to be in keeping with the Stranger's civic or statesmanlike orientation, alluded to earlier. As we will see later, the penal code elaborated in Book 9 contains a number of features explicitly designed with a view to deterrence.

14 Lewis goes so far as to write that "[t]he nerve of the problem of punishment in the *Laws* is the tension between reason and spiritedness." Lewis, "The Limits of Reform," in Koritansky, *The Philosophy of Punishment*, 29. The passion of spiritedness (*thumos*) plays a very important political role in Plato's dialogues. Its central character – the concern with one's own – lies at the heart of a number of distinctively human emotions and mental states, some noble and some base, that include love of honour, civic and familial loyalty, courage, shame, and indignation. Cf. T. Pangle, "The Political Psychology," 1062–4. Spiritedness is *the* political passion because without it political life would not be possible: one cannot have a city without loyal citizens, brave soldiers, and attentive parents. But despite, or rather because of, the intense concern with one's own that it fuels, spiritedness can too narrowly focus our view on what is our own – especially our honour or dignity – so much so as to blind us to reason and to what is truly good for us, for our friends, and for our city (cf. 731e–732b). The self-assertive tendency of spiritedness that causes us to demand the respect we are owed and to lose sight of the good leads us to want to harm those who

have dishonoured us, even if this would not advance our true interests in any way. From the spirited point of view, every unlawful or undeserved injury is viewed as a loss of honour for the victim and as a "gain" of honour for the offender. Spirited indignation is guided by the thought that it can restore this loss of honour by inflicting an equivalent injury, and thus dishonour, on the original offender. From the point of view of spirited indignation, it is no matter that the future interests of the two parties are lost sight of in the course of this retributive settling of accounts. By indicating that the man declared by the city to be virtuous will be punishing out of spirited anger, the prelude shows its awareness of the fact that its authoritative affirmation of the absolute benevolence of justice will not be able to transform the essentially spirited character of the citizenry. It thereby acknowledges the need to tolerate to some extent the retributive manifestation of spiritedness, even while it tries to temper this manifestation as much as possible.

15 From 730d1 the Athenian never uses *dike*, but only *kolasis* (or a cognate) to designate punishment (730d8, 731b7). This word can mean to punish, chastise, or correct, and does not carry with it the sense of being necessarily in accordance with right.

16 For an extensive discussion of the various ways in which the Stranger's institutions in the *Laws* are designed to temper spirited anger, see L. Pangle, "Moral and Criminal Responsibility in Plato's *Laws*."

17 Cf. *Apology* 25c–26a, as well as Socrates's long discussion of the "measuring art" in *Protagoras* 351b–360d, esp. 358c–d.

18 Mackenzie, in *Plato on Punishment*, at 134–6, 197–8, overlooks this inconsistency in the text and reads the general preamble as simply repeating the Socratic refutations of voluntary wrongdoing that can be found in the *Protagoras* and the *Gorgias*.

19 Regarding the greatest crimes, the Stranger proposes to show "in each single case what retribution [*timōriai*] should be attached" (853a). This is a noteworthy mention of retributive punishments (*timōriai*) as a subset of judicial penalties (*dikai*). It is peculiar because, as we recall, the general preamble had clearly denied that *timōriai* were *dikai* (on the ground that justice, *dike*, always confers a benefit, whereas retribution only intends harm). This blurring of the difference between *timōria* and *dikē* echoes the equivocal status of retribution that we observed in our discussion of the general preamble.

20 If a domestic servant or a resident alien is caught committing one of the three mentioned capital crimes, he is to be whipped as much as the judges should decide is appropriate and thrown naked beyond the borders of the

country, but not killed, since it is possible that by undergoing punishment
he will become better, "for no judicial punishment that takes place according to law aims at what is bad" (854d).

21 As Saunders's *Plato's Penal Code*, 139–40, suggests.

22 This is the first instance of the word "philosophy" or one of its cognates in
the whole work, which further marks the dialogue's ascent from the more
mundane subjects of legislation to a theoretical plane. Cf. Strauss, *The
Argument and Action*, 128–9.

23 Examining the opinions of the celebrated Greek legislators is not quite the
same thing as examining what is best concerning legislation, which is what
the Stranger had actually proposed he and Kleinias do. The Stranger appears to assume that the famous legislators had left behind them written
preludes explaining the wisdom of their laws, a possibility he had ruled
out moments earlier when he asserted that human beings living under *all
actual legislation* live as slaves being doctored by slaves (cf. again 857c).

24 Cf. Strauss, *The Argument and Action*, 130.

25 This may explain the reason for the Stranger's implausible argument that
actions are always suffered in the same manner as they are performed. In
proceeding this way, the Stranger makes his own position (i.e., punishment
is both just and noble) more awkward, and thus easier for Kleinias
to dispute. He thus makes Kleinias's refusal to dispute it even more puzzling, inviting us to reflect on the reasons for that refusal. On these grounds
I disagree with Saunders's interpretation of this passage as merely a prepa-
ratory "lesson in predication." See Saunders, "The Socratic Paradoxes," 422.

26 See L. Pangle, "Moral and Criminal Responsibility," 459.

27 Plato's Socrates's knowledge consisted of his awareness of our ignorance
about the "noble and good" things (cf. *Apology* 21b–22e). Through his
many conversations with men and women in all walks of life, Socrates
was able to learn that the greatest obstacle preventing most people from
gaining a greater awareness of their ignorance about the most important
things is not their indifference about these things, but rather the great
power they hold over our hearts, a power that often prevents us from sub-
jecting our conflicted opinions about these things to thorough examination
for fear that such an examination might lead to the disappointment of our
fondest hopes. Thus most men, according to Socrates's view, remain deeply conflicted throughout their lives about justice, the noble, and the good,
while only a few, like Socrates himself, are able to acknowledge to themselves the seriousness of their condition of ignorance, even if only for a
few brief moments in their lives (cf. *Alcibiades I* 116e–118b). See also Bruell,
"On Plato's Political Philosophy," 97–102. This view is echoed by the

Stranger in the passage we are presently considering when he attributes the confusion about the identity of the just and the noble things not only to themselves, as legislators, but to "the many" as well.

28 Cf. again 626b: "For … nothing is really beneficial, neither possessions nor customs, unless one triumphs in war. For then all the good things of the defeated belong to the victors."

29 Aristotle, *Nicomachean Ethics*, 1132b21–1133a2.

30 For Socrates's full reflections on this subject, see again the texts sited in n17, above.

31 See *Protagoras*, 352c–357d; *Gorgias*, 466e ff. For a very thorough discussion of the Socratic critique of retributive punishment in the context of the *Gorgias*, see Stauffer *The Unity of Plato's Gorgias*. See also the commentary of Mackenzie, *Plato on Punishment*, ch. 9.

32 Other commentators would be inclined to classify the psychological state I have described as just one of many kinds of ignorance, which would not be functionally different from the other types – for example, a non-vacillating, erroneous conviction that injustice is superior to justice. Both these forms of ignorance would look functionally the same, from their point of view, since both would equally exculpate an offender of any guilt. There is a significant difference, however, between the Socratic argument that all injustice is involuntary, and the results of the Stranger's examination of Kleinias's opinions about punishment. The former is a purely hypothetical deduction – depending on several assumptions (that all men choose what is good for them; that justice is the greatest good for us) – that does not necessarily reflect what human beings living in political society actually believe. On the other hand, Plato's depiction of the Stranger's examination of Kleinias does point to a plausible view of what most people actually believe. One of the ways in which this is helpful is by making it possible to explain some of the phenomena we are investigating: for example, why criminals can appear to commit injustice deliberately, and then later repent of their actions.

33 Examples of such characters in Plato are Thrasymachus, Polus, and Callicles. See *Republic* 336b; *Gorgias* 484a–b, 485b–c.

34 C. Zuckert, *Plato's Philosophers*, 117, notes that restoring friendship is a distinct aim of punishment, but does not go far enough in drawing out the implications of this.

35 Cf. Saunders, *Plato's Penal Code*, 356. The traditional distinction between voluntary and involuntary crimes, which the Stranger is about to re-establish, may – to the extent that it is persuasive – make it possible in practice to give a kind of publicly convincing justification for adding a desert-based dimension to penalties.

36 See also Shorey, *What Plato Said*, 342–3.

37 One might also consider the example of the Roman Coriolanus. The Stranger's view of the problematic connection between motivations and deeds recalls the theme of the *Theaetetus* regarding the problematic connection between our opinions about things and the things themselves (i.e., the problem of knowledge).

38 See Shuchman, "Comments," 36–7.

39 To draw distinctions based on any effects *other* than one's own greatest good would be extrinsic to what the Stranger means by voluntary action. The Stranger seems to anticipate that such incidental considerations could not affect what he means by the voluntary when he suggests (in perfect Socratic fashion) that the voluntary in one sense cannot differ from the voluntary in some other sense by virtue of being voluntary: "But in what way are they two, if they don't differ from one another by being … voluntary?" – 861d. Compare Socrates's arguments in the *Protagoras* about the "calculating art," where considerations of pleasure and the noble are excluded as extrinsic to that calculation of one's greatest advantage, which saves our lives. See also the *Hipparchus*, as well as commentary on this dialogue by Bloom in T. Pangle, *The Roots of Political Philosophy*, 32–52.

40 See O'Brien, "Plato and the 'Good Conscience,'" 195n17; Mackenzie, *Plato on Punishment*, 144, 201–2; Saunders, "The Socratic Paradoxes," 422–4; but cf. Strauss, *The Argument and Action*, 132 and context. Aristotle, too, rejects on political grounds the Socratic thesis regarding voluntary injustice. See *Nicomachean Ethics* 1099b12–25; 1114a31–b25. In his discussion of the legal conception of "intention" as a requirement for criminal liability, Duff observes that "courts and commentators seem to agree" on "a central notion of … intention or 'purpose'; but they differ on whether that notion need be defined at all; and on whether, if it needs defining, it should be defined in terms of 'desire' (or 'want'), or of 'decision,' or of acting 'in order' to bring a result about"; yet such theoretical confusion apparently does not prevent juries or judges from applying the concept of intentionality in practice. See Duff, *Intention, Agency and Criminal Liability*, 27, 31–2.

41 The Stranger's law itself makes it explicit that justice demands that the worst criminals suffer in return exactly that harm which they wrongfully inflicted: "If someone ever kills his father, he must endure to suffer violently this same thing at the hands of his children at some time; if he should kill his mother, it is necessary that he himself be born partaking of female nature, and having become such, must at a later time depart life at the hands of the offspring. For there is no other purification for the shared polluted blood, nor is the pollution willing to be washed away, until the

soul that perpetrated the deed pays for murder with murder, like for like, and thus, by appeasing, lays to rest the spiritedness of the entire family" (872e–873a).

42 See also L. Pangle, "Moral and Criminal Responsibility," 467: "But whereas most people see [voluntary murders] as deserving more harm, the Athenian sees them as calling for more help. And although most people view them as in every respect voluntary, the Athenian's argument taken as a whole suggests that crimes committed "voluntarily" are at the deepest level even more *involuntary* than harm inflicted accidentally, for in corrupting one's own soul one acts more against one's true wishes than in making a simple mistake."

43 In this respect, the Stranger's approach is similar to Aristotle's. Like Plato's Stranger and Socrates, Aristotle defines justice as directed to some good – or more precisely, the common advantage of the city – but he differs from Plato in defining the common advantage as consisting in mutual exchange among citizens. Aristotle argues that for mutual exchange to occur, *all* the things exchanged must be somehow made commensurable. Thus "in communities concerned with exchange, the just in this [i.e., corrective] sense … holds them together … For either people seek to reciprocate harm for harm – if they do not, that is held to be slavish – or they seek to reciprocate good for good. And if they do not do this, there is no mutual exchange, and people stay together through mutual exchange." *Nicomachean Ethics* 1132b31–1133a2.

44 Mackenzie, *Plato on Punishment*, 173–5, and Saunders, *Plato's Penal Code*, 145–7, do not take this important qualification into account, and thus take the tripartite psychology presented by the Stranger unproblematically as his own view.

45 Note that the Greek word *hamartēma* is ambiguous, in that it could mean either a (morally culpable) wrong, or a failing or error that occurs through no fault of our own. The use of this ambiguous term (instead of the less ambiguous *adikia*) forces us to recall the Stranger's own understanding of all injustice as involuntary, which has now been all but abandoned.

46 We might already wonder, however, whether the Stranger is right to assume that the simple, self-aware sort of ignorance will always be less dangerous to society than the presumptuous sort of ignorance. Is it not possible that a consistent sceptic – who knows that he does not know whether justice is or is not human virtue – could choose to publicly dissimulate his knowledge of ignorance for the sake of his private ends? Later (in Book 10), when the Stranger addresses the crime of heresy, he appears to come close to the latter conclusion. There, he argues that the men who do not hesitate

to speak their impious and unjust opinions publicly, and who openly ridicule conventional piety and morality, would be *less* harmful to the city than the "ironical" men who (perhaps because they are more consistent in their opinions about justice) hide their true opinions and deceitfully adopt the forms of conventional piety and become diviners, tyrants, demagogues, and sophists (908a–e).

47 This seems consistent with the Stranger's image of the human being as a puppet of the gods, who is pulled in different directions by certain cords (reason and the passions), but who can also "assist" the pull of certain cords against others (644d–645b). See also Adkins, *Merit and Responsibility*, 302–3.

48 "If a man's reason and desires are not in conflict, *whatever his basic view of life*, he is to be termed *dikaios* [just], provided that his actions are based on reason, not passion or desire." Adkins, *Merit and Responsibility*, 307–8; italics in original.

49 For this reason, O'Brien, Saunders, and Mackenzie all deny Adkins's thesis and favour the interpretation of *kan sphalletai ti* (at 864a) as referring only to errors regarding circumstances that lead to harm, not to fundamental errors in moral understanding. See Saunders, "The Socratic Paradoxes," 430–2; Mackenzie, *Plato on Punishment*, 247–9; O'Brien, "Plato and the 'Good Conscience,'" 84–5.

50 This seems to imply that the ultimate and highest authority in the city will not be the law itself (to say nothing of consent), but either reason or divine revelation.

51 We must still wonder why the Stranger would ever state his "true" opinion at all, and in such an unqualified manner that the tension between it and the spurious public doctrine becomes palpable and troubling. Consider, in this regard, Strauss, *The Argument and Action*, 128–9.

52 See Morrow, *Plato's Cretan City*, 241–96; Saunders, *Plato's Penal Code*, chs. 7–14.

53 Adkins, *Merit and Responsibility*, has shown to what extent the traditional (heroic and pre-Socratic) notions of Greek morality – including pollution, shame, and heroic virtue – are in tension with the Socratic or Platonic emphasis on moral responsibility. See chs. 5 and 8, with chs. 13–14.

54 For an excellent discussion of the various details of Magnesia's penal code, and their relation to the Stranger's theoretical views, see Saunders, *Plato's Penal Code*.

55 Regarding some crucial difficulties with the Stranger's refutation of the heresies, see Strauss, *The Argument and Action*, 146–9.

56 Even the unrestrained heretics are punished less severely than they would be in a more traditional society. Although they are ruled by unrestrained

passion and are said to be incurable, they are not executed to prevent them from falling deeper into psychic corruption, as one might have expected from earlier discussions. Furthermore, the claim that they deserve "neither one nor two deaths" is ambiguous. See Strauss, *The Argument and Action*, 156.

57 Given the possibility that even after five years the perplexed heretic may remain unreformed, the Stranger must legislate that those convicted of heresy a second time must be punished with death (909a).

58 Saunders, *Plato's Penal Code*, 168–78, provides an ingenious account (based on passages in the *Timaeus*) of how conventional punishments might still effectively serve the cause of moral reform. Briefly, he argues that, since the underlying condition of an unjust character is an unhealthy arrangement of physiological forces (whether due to habit or to strong passion), the penalty creates a physical disturbance that "unsettles" the unhealthy arrangement, making moral reform possible. In other words, this sort of reform seems to follow the model of electroshock therapy. I remain unpersuaded of the effectiveness of such a process to produce genuine moral reform, as it seems to me more likely that, after the disturbance, an unhealthy soul would lapse back into its unhealthy habits than that it would spontaneously take on healthy ones. It seems to me that the Stranger is right, that genuine moral reform would require a much lighter touch, informed by extensive knowledge of the individual case – like the sort of treatment that would take place in Magnesia's *sōphronisterion*.

59 See, again, Adkins's excellent work on the differences between classical Greek and modern morality.

Chapter 2

1 See Machiavelli, *The Prince*, ch. 7; *Discourses on Livy*, III.1.

2 The fundamental importance of Hobbes for modern punishment theory is acknowledged by Cattaneo ("Hobbes's Theory of Punishment") and Norrie ("Thomas Hobbes and the Philosophy of Punishment").

3 All references to the *Leviathan* (given as chapter and paragraph) are to the Edwin Curley edition and its pagination.

4 See *De Cive* 1.2, first note.

5 One view, championed by Taylor and by Warrender, is that Hobbes's political teaching is entirely independent of his philosophical materialism and that the former is in fact grounded upon a kind of proto-Kantian conception of duty. (See Taylor, "The Ethical Doctrine of Hobbes," and Warrender, *The Political Philosophy of Hobbes*.) Strauss (*The Political Philosophy of Hobbes*, chs. 2

and 7) maintains that the moral attitude informing Hobbes's political teaching developed before his turn to modern natural science and that it (the moral basis) consists in Hobbes's view of the antithesis between the rational passion of fear and the irrational passion of vanity. Hampton (*Hobbes and the Social Contract Tradition*), Gauthier (*The Logic of Leviathan*, ch. 2), and Macpherson (*The Political Theory of Possessive Individualism*, 70–5) argue in various ways that Hobbes intended to ground his political teaching on a moral basis, but failed. Goldsmith (*Hobbes's Science of Politics*, 93–109) and Watkins (*Hobbes's System of Ideas*, ch. 5) have argued that Hobbes is a straightforward materialist whose political science is a descriptive account of the consequences of human psychology. My view is closer to that of Strauss, and I briefly indicate the textual evidence for it in the discussion.

6 Utilitarian punishment theory has its origins not in Hobbes but in Cesare Beccaria's *On Crimes and Punishments*, which followed the *Leviathan* by about a century. See chapter 4 of the present study.

7 Hence, Heyd ("Hobbes on Capital Punishment"), who views Hobbes's political teaching as grounded in materialism, assumes that his argument for a subject's right to resist punishment rests on naturalistic premises, which I will show it does not. Or, at any rate, Hobbes did not intend for it to rest merely on naturalistic premises.

8 It is helpful in this regard to contrast Hobbes's theory of natural right with that of his contemporary Spinoza. Although the two may seem similar, only the latter unambiguously developed a theory of right that was thoroughly naturalistic. See Spinoza's *Theologico-Political Treatise*, ch. 16, beginning.

9 *De Cive*, Preface to the readers (18–19).

10 See also *De Corpore* (in Molesworth, *The English Works of Thomas Hobbes*, vol. I) part I, ch. 6.7: "*Civil* and *moral philosophy* do not so adhere to one another, but that they may be severed." "For the causes of the motions of the mind are known, not only by ratiocination, but also by the experience of every man that takes the pains to observe those motions within himself." Italics in original.

11 Strauss, *The Political Philosophy of Hobbes*. See, again, the chapters cited in note 5 above.

12 See also *De Cive* 1.7: "Amid so many dangers therefore from men's natural cupidity, that threaten every man every day, *we cannot be blamed* for looking out for ourselves" (my emphasis).

13 *De Cive* 1.4.

14 The issue of the status of the laws of nature in Hobbes's works has been discussed at length by other commentators. I follow Johnston (*The Rhetoric of "Leviathan"*) in reading Hobbes's occasionally contradictory statements

on this subject as rhetorically useful for advancing the moral transformations Hobbes wished to bring about. Consider, for example, the marked difference in tone between chs. 13 and 15 of the *Leviathan*. Whereas in the former the laws of nature are called "convenient articles of peace," in the latter they are connected to virtue and the conscience (see especially 15.36–40). Similarly, in ch. 17 Hobbes goes so far as to write concerning the fundamental covenant by individuals to constitute the sovereign authority that "it is more than consent, or concord; it is a real unity of them all" (17.13). Although it is possible to give such statements too much weight – as both Taylor and Warrender do – it is important not to dismiss them simply as failed arguments.

15 Contrast with Aristotle, *Nicomachean Ethics* 1138a6: "Whatever the law does not command, it forbids."

16 Recall that the Stranger's thesis about the involuntariness of all injustice was in some tension with the traditionalist penal legislation he enacts for the republic of Magnesia.

17 Consider, for example, *Laws* 853c–d.

18 This has indeed been the trend historically in the development of modern criminal law.

19 That publicity is an important desideratum of democratic governance has been argued – for example, by Habermas, in *The Structural Transformation of the Public Sphere*, ch. 25.

20 In this, Hobbes may be said to anticipate later criminological theories that locate the causes of crime in the institutional structures of the surrounding society.

21 One might still question whether Hobbes has underestimated the impulsiveness of individuals who are prone to crime (such as drug addicts and psychotics) and who therefore cannot help giving in to immediate self-gratification, even while they fear severe, but remote, punishment. Perhaps Hobbes had not anticipated the truly dysfunctional social conditions in some of the Western world's most crime-ridden cities.

22 Compare with Hobbes's own individualistic conception of the family in *Leviathan* ch. 20 and *De Cive* ch. 9, and see Hampton's commentary in *Hobbes and the Social Contract Tradition*, 9–11.

23 It is an interesting sign of Hobbes's rigorous thinking, or perhaps of his egalitarianism, that he even suggests that robbery of a poor man might be considered a greater crime than robbery of a rich one, since "it is to the poor [one] a more sensible damage."

24 Thus, if we understand the rightful end of government as Hobbes does – as the preservation of peace – then we cannot accept the argument

commonly advanced by retributivists like Morris (or quasi-retributivists like Rawls) that while political society might come into being for the sake of mutual benefit and defence, the laws and institutions created to enact this aim can have an independent justification of their own, such as fairness. See Rawls, "Two Concepts of Rules," 4–8; Morris, "Persons and Punishment," 477–9. If the right to self-preservation is the foundation and source of all other rights and obligations, then any duty of fairness would have to be understood in just these terms. Hobbes shows with perfect clarity that retributive punishment cannot be understood to be just in a society founded on a pact of mutual defence and benefit. To attempt to establish retribution on contractarian grounds is already to move in the direction of Kant (see chapter 4).

25 Hence Heyd, "Hobbes on Capital Punishment," 122, is clearly mistaken when he claims that the Hobbesian right to punish is founded on the social contract.

26 Hobbes was therefore the founder of yet another truism for criminologists: that the effectiveness of punishment depends on its certainty just as much as, if not more than, on its severity (see 27.18).

27 Cf. Thomas Aquinas, *Summa Theologiae* II–II, Q. 64, A. 6 (in Baumgarth et al., *On Law, Morality, and Politics*), where it is maintained that one ought to disobey one's sovereign when he commands the killing of an innocent. See also the *Nicomachean Ethics* 1110a26–8, where Aristotle suggests (though he does not absolutely affirm) that it might be better to die rather than to be compelled to do very shameful things; Plato, *Laws* 869b9–c7, has the Athenian stranger legislate that one may not kill a parent, even in self-defence.

28 Jeremy Bentham indicates his awareness of this tension between utilitarian punishment on the one hand and the proportionality or "fittingness" of penalties according to the ordinary moral understanding on the other. "Authors of celebrity," Bentham writes, "have … said that the greatness of temptation is a reason for lessening the punishment; because it lessens the fault; because the more powerful the seduction, the less reason is there for concluding that the offender is depraved. Those, therefore, who are overcome, in this case, naturally inspire us with commiseration. *This may all be very true, and yet afford no reason for departing from the rule.* That it may prove effectual, the punishment must be more dreaded than the profit of the crime desired. Besides, an inefficacious punishment is doubly mischievous; – mischievous to the public, since it permits the crime to be committed; – mischievous to the delinquent, since the punishment inflicted upon him is just so much misery in waste. What should we say to the surgeon, who, that he might save his patient a small degree of pain, should only

half cure him? What should we think of his humanity, if he should add to his disease the torment of a useless operation? It is therefore desirable that punishment should correspond to every degree of temptation" (my emphasis; original paragraph divisions have been omitted for the sake of simplicity). Bentham, *The Rationale of Punishment*, ch. 6 (70; cf. 74, "Rule IX").

29 Pitkin, "Hobbes's Concept of Representation," I and II; Orwin, "On the Sovereign Authorization"; Tuck, *Natural Rights Theories*, ch. 6; Hampton, *Hobbes and the Social Contract Tradition*, chs. 5 and 8; Martinich, *Hobbes*, ch. 4.

30 Hobbes conceived of the natural right to defend one's life as quite expansive. We can no more alienate our right to resist wounds or imprisonment than we can alienate our right to self-defence, "because a man cannot tell, when he seeth men proceed against him by violence, whether they intend his death or not," and since "the motive and end for which this renouncing and transferring is introduced, is nothing else but the security of a man's person, in his life and in the means of so preserving life as not to be weary of it" (14.8). This is as much as to say that the criminal who is sentenced to any substantial corporal, carceral, or in some cases even pecuniary punishment immediately regains his original natural right to all things and so returns to the state of nature vis-à-vis his former sovereign and fellow-subjects.

In the earlier *Elements of Law* (see I.19.10 and II.20.7), Hobbes had maintained that each subject *does* renounce his right to defend himself against his sovereign; this allowed Hobbes to avoid the conflict between natural right and the right to punish. But, in a different way, that strategy was even more damaging to Hobbes's overall purpose, since it compromised the privileged moral status of self-preservation. Hobbes was therefore forced to revise his view in the later *De Cive* and the *Leviathan*. With this expansive definition of the right to self-preservation, Hobbes anticipates Locke.

31 I therefore believe that Schrock ("The Right to Punish") and Norrie ("Thomas Hobbes") go too far in concluding that this clash of rights undermines Hobbes's whole theoretical framework. In Norrie's words, it "leads to the immanent collapse of, and implicit denial of the possibility of, the social state and the institution of punishment" (307). In my view, Gauthier and Martinich are more correct to argue that the clash of rights (of the criminal and of civil society, respectively) implied by punishment does not create an inconsistency in Hobbes's political theory, although it does reveal the limits of the social contract. See Gauthier, *The Logic of Leviathan*, 146–9; Martinich, *Hobbes*, 115–18. Hampton, *Hobbes*, 197–207, argues that although this does not cause Hobbes's theory to fail theoretically, it does make it impracticable or utopian: "Hobbes's argument does not fail because he cannot establish the rationality of creating an absolute sovereign, nonetheless it

fails because he cannot establish, given his psychology, that men and women are *able* to do what is required to create a ruler satisfying his definition of an absolute sovereign" (197; emphasis in original).

32 Johnston, *The Rhetoric*, 80–2, points out that the Hobbesian sovereign's authority is "curiously negative" in that it is established only by the subjects divesting themselves of their natural rights. It would be "difficult to convince oneself," Johnston continues, that this "rather hollow conception of power is really adequate to do the work Hobbes's theory requires it to do." Accordingly, "Hobbes's increased sensitivity to the importance of public opinion as an element of sovereign power had led him to be more concerned than ever before that the rights of sovereignty should be recognized, in a widespread and public manner, as legitimate. The concept of authorization helped meet this concern."

33 Thus Hampton (*Hobbes*, 206) draws the conclusion that "Hobbesian people empower a ruler by obeying his punishment commands, and they do so whenever *they decide* such obedience is conducive to their best interests" (emphasis in original).

34 See also Schrock, "The Right to Punish," 853–68. Cattaneo and Norrie both believe that the subject's unconditional authorization of his sovereign's actions *is* necessitated by Hobbes's principles, but I do not think that either gives sufficient reasons for this. Both rely too much on Hobbes's assertions but do not consider whether those assertions are substantiated on Hobbes's own terms. See Cattaneo, "Hobbes's Theory of Punishment," 293; Norrie, "Thomas Hobbes," 304–6. Tuck gives a somewhat stronger defence of the necessity of unconditional authorization. According to Tuck, the sovereign's natural right only permits him to act in *his own* defence, and this appears to Tuck not to give him the right to punish in order to defend civil society as a whole. Unconditional authorization therefore becomes necessary to justify punishment. Tuck, *Natural Rights Theories*, 129–30. But the problem Tuck focuses on is not as great as he believes, for the sovereign's personal safety and the security of civil society are mutually dependent; thus, punishing the guilty is *also* an act of self-preservation by the sovereign.

35 Orwin and Johnston make the best case for the view that Hobbes's theory of authorization is essentially a rhetorical device that emerges only in the *Leviathan* – the most rhetorical of Hobbes's three major political works – and is absent in the earlier *Elements of Law* and *De Cive*, which already contain Hobbes's political thought in its mature form. See Orwin, "On the Sovereign Authorization," 28–32; Johnston, *The Rhetoric*, 80–2. As we will see in the next chapter, this particular inconsistency in Hobbes's position was successfully attacked by Beccaria.

36 The humanizing features of Hobbes's punishment theory continue to inform modern penal thought and practice. As an illustration of this, one
might consider the passionate appeals to the decency and humanity of
modern democratic societies by recent penal reformers like psychologist
Karl Menninger and former US Attorney General Ramsey Clark, whose
moralizing eloquence appears side by side with their calls for modern
societies to consider their own safety and security. See Ramsey Clark,
Crime in America; Karl Menninger, *The Crime of Punishment*.

Chapter 3

1 Montesquieu, *The Spirit of the Laws*, trans. Cohler, 12.2 (emphasis added).
Henceforth all references unaccompanied by a title are to this text. I have
consulted the *Oeuvres complètes de Montesquieu* (ed. André Masson) for the
original French.
2 Prior to Montesquieu, modern thinkers had focused on those threats to individual security that stemmed from religious dispute, disputes about the
best regime, or natural scarcity. Montesquieu himself was far from denying the importance of these issues as fundamental political problems. In
fact, it is the success of his predecessors (consider Montesquieu's praise
of the "great men" of France, England, and Germany in the "Preface," xlv)
that made it possible for him to turn his attention to such specific questions as the criminal law. See also Carrese, *The Cloaking of Power*, 18–25.
3 Thus, for example, although family life is natural to human beings, the
structure of the family is not necessarily (that is, by nature) monogamous.
See 26.3–7 and 14.
4 For a more extensive discussion of human nature as malleable and non-
teleological, see T. Pangle, *Montesquieu's Philosophy of Liberalism*, 28–37.
5 Nevertheless, in the decisive respect despotism remains a legitimate form
of government for Montesquieu, since it satisfies the minimum requirement
of human nature, which is preservation. In this respect, he is in complete
agreement with Hobbes. See 1.2: "Peace would be the first natural law."
6 See T. Pangle, *Montesquieu's Philosophy of Liberalism*, 107: "In his presentation of the traditional forms of government [which takes up the first eight
books of *The Spirit of The Laws*], Montesquieu has revealed the inadequa-
cies of their particular principles and the aims that derive from those principles. He has thereby pointed to the desirability of a government having
no other purpose than the security and comfort of its citizens."
7 As Carrese puts it, "a complex judging power becomes the crux of
[Montesquieu's] moderate constitutionalism because its rules and

procedures stymie excesses of raw power, or of high idealism, that could damage individual interests and tranquility." *The Cloaking of Power*, 35.

8 Montesquieu was not so naive as to believe that no harsh punishments of any sort would ever be needed. His intention was not to call for the complete abolition of corporal punishments. See 6.10, 18.

9 For examples of mild republican penal practices, see pp. 83, 84, and 88; for examples of harsh republican practices, see pp. 11, 16, and 93; for ambiguous cases, see pp. 85–6, 89, and 92.

10 See Livy, 3.34.

11 Cf. 12.11n29 and context. In the text cited by Montesquieu, Livy's point seems to be that the Valerian and Porcian laws were introduced in order to protect the *political* rights of the plebs rather than to moderate the severity of punishments for its own sake (as Montesquieu claims).

12 See 6.15, where Montesquieu describes the types of penalties imposed on the different orders when Rome under the emperors "drew somewhat nearer to monarchy." See also 6.21, where Montesquieu remarks that it is in the nature of monarchy to take an interest in the security of "important men" but remains silent about men of common status.

13 See pp. 83, 84–5, 90, and 92. Consider also the ambiguity of 6.9: "It would be easy to prove that in all or nearly all the states of Europe penalties have decreased or increased in proportion as one has approached or departed from liberty."

14 See Book 24; but cf. 25.13.

15 According to both T. Pangle and Schaub, Montesquieu uses the theme of despotic (human) government extensively in *The Spirit of the Laws* and in the *Persian Letters* as an allegory for the government over men by the God of the Bible. See Pangle, *The Theological Basis*, ch. 2; Schaub, *Erotic Liberalism*, ch. 5. See also Krause, "Despotism in *The Spirit of Laws*," in *Montesquieu's Science of Politics*, ed. Carrithers, Mosher, and Rahe, 252–3.

16 Montesquieu distinguishes the passion of shame – which has in it an element of self-love – from the much more self-denying love of virtue that one finds in republics. For this reason, the love of honour and the feeling of shame that accompanies loss of reputation are not anti-liberal passions. In discussing Montesquieu's account of honour, Krause writes that, although there are tensions between democracy and the love of honour, and although "democratic forms of honour are bound to be weak … still democratic societies need some form of honor" to sustain "the capacity for political agency." "The Politics of Distinction and Disobedience," 490–1.

17 See below.

18 12.19. See also 12.10 and 22.

19 Blackstone, *Commentaries*, IV.1 (pp. 18–19).

20 See, again, 12.4 (p. 190); cf. Hobbes, *Leviathan*, ch. 15. Thus, like Hobbes, Montesquieu believed that the character of criminal laws is deeply connected to prevailing popular ideas about justice and desert. To regard traditional penal practices as merely limited by technological backwardness is to misunderstand the phenomenon. Modernization of criminal law depends fundamentally on popular *moral* enlightenment.

21 Cf. 19.16, especially n16.

22 See also Carrese, *The Cloaking of Power*, 64–9.

23 According to Locke, a church is "a voluntary Society of Men, joining themselves together of their own accord, in order to the publick worshipping of God, in such a manner as they judge acceptable to him, and effectual to the Salvation of their Souls" (*A Letter Concerning Toleration*, 28).

24 This might seem paradoxical from the point of view of today's liberal-democratic societies, which experience very high levels of violent crime. However, the pronounced increase in violent crime is a relatively recent phenomenon in modern democracies (dating to the 1960s or 1970s in most Western countries) and appears to be connected to the erosion of the traditional family. See, for example, Francis Fukuyama, *The Great Disruption*. For evidence of the statistical relationship between family dysfunction and crime, see Farrington, "Families and Crime," in Wilson and Petersilia, eds., *Crime and Public Policy*. It is an important question whether Montesquieu's understanding of the conditions of liberalism could have allowed him to anticipate this problem.

25 See 6.19, and again 6.2 and 12. See also 5.14.

26 Consider, again, the formulation of the principle of retribution at 1.1.

27 Consider these statements at 1.3: "Since nature has established paternal power …," and "Political power necessarily includes the union of many families." On the character of the passions and moral qualities established in the family – especially, the shame and love of dependants on the one hand, and the jealousy of fathers on the other – see 10.10, 12. In the context of his endorsement of the law of retaliation against violent crimes, Montesquieu states that this law is "drawn from reason *and* from the sources of good and evil" 12.4 (my emphasis). This statement may imply that "the sources of good and evil" may be distinct from reason and thus not necessarily rational. Since the earliest – and in a sense the foundational – moral education we receive is in the family (cf. 4.4), it may well be said to be a "source of good and evil." In European societies, the paternalistic morality that originates in the family seems to be reinforced by biblical religion. The virtues natural to dependent members of the family listed in 16.10 are also Christian virtues.

28 See, again, 20.1.

29 Later liberals like Joel Feinberg argue that all of the most serious crimes can
be shown to harm the individual (thus violating the "harm principle," as
originally conceived by John Stuart Mill) and that this obviates the need for
criminal law to appeal to the alleged inviolability of any independent moral
standards, cherished for their own sake by the community, apart from the
harm they cause to individuals. Yet Feinberg is able to do this only by defining "harm" to the individual (the "thwarting of an interest") in a very broad
sense that goes well beyond physical harm ("interests in the continuance
of a foreseeable interval of one's life and the interests in one's own physical
health and vigor") to include any actions that would undermine "emotional
stability" by producing "groundless anxieties and resentments," and even
actions that would thwart "ultimate goals and aspirations" held by the individual. See Feinberg, *Harm to Others*, ch. 1; cf. his *Harmless Wrongdoing*,
ch. 30 (esp. his discussion of James Fitzjames Stephen at 155–9).

30 See Calvin, *Institutes*, VI (in the F.L. Battles translation, see 212, 216–19);
Augustine, *The City of God*, I.21.

31 Thus, rape is now generally punished by prison terms of ten or more years
– with about half of this time regularly waived for good behavior – which
is arguably less severe than traditional penalties for the same crime, such
as death or castration.

32 Beccaria's treatise also had its opponents among both jurists and the
Catholic clergy. See Maestro, *Cesare Beccaria*, ch. 3.

33 Before Beccaria, Rousseau had elaborated a contractarian argument for the
right to punish (in *On the Social Contract*). But Rousseau's social contract is
not a liberal one, since for Rousseau each party to the contract must alienate the entirety of his natural right to the sovereign (the general will) and
thus retains no rights against the sovereign.

34 Beccaria's psychology also leads him to reject as erroneous the view – typical of retributivism – that the true measure of crimes is to be found in the
evil intention or intrinsic injustice of the persons who commit them.
Human beings are not ultimately responsible for their intentions, which
are actually "contingent on the impression caused by the [external] objects
at the time and the preceding disposition of the mind"; these dispositions,
in turn, "vary from man to man and in the same man according to the
very swift succession of ideas, emotions and circumstances."

35 Cf. Beccaria's brief comments (in his preface, "To the Reader") on "natural
justice," which is, along with divine justice, "of [its] essence constant and
unchangeable," but which, Beccaria insists, has no more bearing than the
latter on actual political life, since political life is infinitely variable.

36 I have not encountered any commentary on Beccaria that shows awareness
    of this serious theoretical difficulty, although in contemporary punishment
    debates it is very common to find utilitarianism being criticized for subor-
    dinating the interests of the individual to those of the majority. Thus, for
    example, Hostettler in *Cesare Beccaria* (72) somehow reads Beccaria as hold-
    ing that "justice has nothing to do with physical power," when in fact it is
    said to be nothing but the power of the majority used in the service of its
    advantage. Crimmins notes that Beccaria's assumption that individuals
    enter into the social contract for the sake of self-preservation (a right they
    never lay down) "sounds much like Hobbes's justification of resistance to
    a punishing sovereign." Yet Crimmins never even suggests that this may
    potentially be in tension with Beccaria's principle of general utility. See
    Crimmins, "The Principles of Utilitarian Penal Law in Beccaria, Bentham,
    and J.S. Mill," in Koritansky, *The Philosophy of Punishment*, 141–4.
37 But how reliable are the enlightened sentiments to which Beccaria appeals
    when it comes to precisely those cases in which the interests of the majori-
    ty are believed to conflict with the integrity of the life and limb of the of-
    fender? As we will see in chapter 5, below, Foucault rightly discerned that
    the principle of compassion as a limit on the punishing power is essential-
    ly a selfish principle, since it respects the sentiments of the law-abiding
    majority and thus is quite susceptible to being overridden by the casuist-
    ries of prudential reason, especially when the fear of danger is compelling.
38 William Bradford, a leading penal reformer in the United States at the time
    of the founding, testifies to this in his report to the governor of
    Pennsylvania ("An Enquiry"). The report opens with the claim that "the
    general principles upon which penal laws ought to be founded appear to
    be fully settled." "Among these principles some have obtained the force
    of axioms, and are no longer considered to be the subjects of doubt or
    of demonstration." These axioms include the principle that prevention of
    crimes ought to be the sole purpose of punishment and that every punish-
    ment that is not absolutely necessary for this "is a cruel and tyrannical
    act." All that remained to be done, according to Bradford, was to show
    how these principles might be applied effectively in practice. Cf. Thomas
    Jefferson, *The Complete Jefferson*, 61.
39 For comprehensive historical accounts, see Hirsch, *The Rise of the
    Penitentiary*; Rothman, *The Discovery of the Asylum*.
40 They observe that "there are in America as well as in Europe, estimable
    men whose minds feed upon philosophical reveries, and whose extreme
    sensibility feels the want of some illusion. These men, for whom philan-
    thropy has become a matter of necessity, find in the penitentiary system

a nourishment for this generous passion." Beaumont and Tocqueville, *On the Penitentiary System in the United States.*

41 See Rush, *A Plan for the Punishment of Crime*, 6–7, 12.

42 Lev 24:10–23; Gen 9:6.

43 Pestritto (*Founding the Criminal Law*, chs. 1–3) likewise argues that the remarkable consensus then existing regarding the overall program of penal reform allowed many unresolved theoretical problems and questions to remain obscured.

Chapter 4

1 In addition to the thinkers whose penal thought we have already discussed, see Locke, *Second Treatise of Government*, s. 8; Mill, *On Liberty*, 9.

2 See Merle, *German Idealism*, chs. 1–3; Sussman, "Shame and Punishment"; Hill, "Kant on Wrongdoing"; Tunick, "Is Kant a Retributivist?"; Byrd, "Kant's Theory of Punishment"; and Scheid, "Kant's Retributivism."

3 Kant, *Metaphysics of Morals* (henceforward *MM*), 6: 305–13 (84–90). Whenever possible, the pagination of the standard German edition of Kant's works will be given as the first set of page numbers (along with the volume number); the numbers in parentheses that follow refer to the corresponding pages in the cited English translation. Other works by Kant frequently cited in the text have been identified by the following abbreviations: *Critique of Judgment* (*CJ*); *Critique of Practical Reason* (*CPr*); *Groundwork of the Metaphysics of Morals* (*Gr*); and *Lectures on Ethics* (*LE*).

4 Cf. Hegel, *The Philosophy of Right*, s. 100. In the decisive respect, Hegel follows Kant in his understanding of retribution as essential to punishment. Hegel's derivation of the principle of retribution differs somewhat from that of Kant. According to Hegel, a crime is a "negatively infinite judgment" that negates not only the particular – that is, the property right of the victim – but the universal as well – namely, right as such. To allow a crime to go without retribution is to allow the negation of right, and of freedom along with it, to stand. Retributive punishment is therefore to be understood as the negation of a negation. See ibid., ss. 95, 99–101.

5 Consider Kant's illustration of the formulation of the categorical imperative to treat human beings as ends in themselves in the case of making a false promise. Kant argues that a false promise could never be understood as being compatible with the choice of the person whom we have deceived. Even if lying were necessary for the other's own good, it would still be incompatible with his autonomy, and thus would amount to treating him as a mere means to our ends. See *Gr* 4:429–30 (97).

6 See *Gr* 4:403–5 (71–3).

7 See Uleman, "External Freedom in Kant's 'Rechtslehre,'" 585–91.

8 6:227–8 (19–20). If one's actions fall short of what one can be constrained by law to do – that is, if they are morally culpable – then their "rightful effect" is punishment. Conversely, if one does more than what the law requires, this is meritorious, and the rightful effect of meritorious action is reward.

9 Cf. *MM* 6:335 (108).

10 This view has been revived more recently by neo-Kantians like Morris (see "Persons and Punishment"), and Murphy (see "Marxism and Retribution").

11 In the context, Kant anticipates the objection that equal retribution "is not possible in terms of the letter" in every single case. No one can demand an eye for an eye from a blind man. Kant argues, however, that it is possible to remain true to the spirit of the principle, if not always to its letter. In his example, Kant suggests that when an innocent person has been insulted, the punishment of the offender can satisfy the demand of retributive justice, even if it does not take the exact same form as the original insult, as long as the offender is made to feel shame in proportion to the outrage he caused his victim. See *MM* 6:332–3 (105–6).

12 Cf. Kant's note at *Gr* 4:430 (97), where he clearly implies that punishment is a strict duty to others.

13 See Kant's essay, "An Answer to the Question: 'What is Enlightenment?'" in *Political Writings*.

14 See, for example, Jeffrie Murphy, "Does Kant Have a Theory of Punishment?"

15 *MM* 6:218–19 (20); cf. *MM* 6:214 (14).

16 One might object that in the *Rechtslehre*, retributive punishment is concerned not with the *ends* of a criminal's choices, but merely with their "form" as they relate to the choices of others, as Kant appears to state in the context of his discussion of the principle of reciprocity (*MM* 6:230 [23–4]). But in that context, Kant seems to be speaking only about reciprocal relations between persons insofar as their actions, "as facts," can have influence on each other – that is, wholly as external phenomena – and does not intend to say anything about imputation, a subject with which he had already dealt earlier. (Cf. translator Mary Gregor's note c, on page 24.) It is hard to imagine what Kant could have in mind, if not the criminal's immoral ends, when he speaks of his "inner wickedness."

An issue to which I cannot give adequate treatment here is why retribution must follow some immoral actions but not others. The answer, I believe, has to do with Kant's distinction between perfect and imperfect duties. Human beings are competent to punish transgressions of perfect duties, knowing that such transgressions are always morally culpable, whereas imperfect duties need not be violated just because our actions do not appear to conform to them.

17 See Kant, *Critique of Pure Reason*, A 551–2/B 579–80 (475).

18 I must therefore disagree with Herbert's and with Fleischacker's attempts to interpret Kant's use of "desert" as signifying something that does not relate to moral motivations. See Herbert, "Immanuel Kant," 67–72; Fleischacker, "Kant's Theory of Punishment," 202–5.

19 As Hegel would later argue, some amount of uncertainty and contingency must be accepted in all action, and therefore (perhaps somewhat paradoxically) we can be held responsible for consequences we did not intend or anticipate. See *The Philosophy of Right* s. 118. See also Herbert, "Immanuel Kant," 67–8.

20 Cf. *CJ* 5:429–31 (317–19) with *MM* 6:246–7 (40–1).

21 *MM* 6:230–32 (24–6).

22 See again *MM* 6:307 ff. (86 ff.).

23 *MM* 6:219–20 (21).

24 Hill, "Kant on Wrongdoing," 409.

25 Hill, "Kant on Wrongdoing," 429.

26 Hill, "Kant on Wrongdoing," 428–31. In his interpretation, Hill follows Byrd's "Kant's Theory of Punishment" and Scheid's "Kant's Retributivism." Byrd reads Kant's basic position as virtually identical with that of H.L.A. Hart (see Byrd, "Kant's Theory of Punishment," 183).

27 Cf. Hill, "Kant on Wrongdoing," 433–4, 438.

28 Tunick, "Is Kant a Retributivist?," 60–78.

29 Cf. *MM* 6:235–6 (28).

30 Tunick, "Is Kant a Retributivist?," 64.

31 Tunick, "Is Kant a Retributivist?," 65–6. Cf. *MM* 6:336–7 (108–9).

32 *MM* 6:336 (109).

33 See *MM* 6:334 (107–8), 6:337 (109–10). Cf. Tunick, "Is Kant a Retributivist?," 63–4.

34 There is another passage that is often cited by Kant scholars as showing him to be espousing what is essentially a deterrence theory of punishment. In his posthumously published *Lectures on Ethics*, Kant says that "all punishments imposed by sovereigns and governments are pragmatic; they are designed either to correct or to make an example" (*LE*, "Reward and Punishment," 55). It may be that Kant changed his mind about punishment from the time his lectures were composed to the time of the writing of his *Rechtslehre*. In any case, if in the final analysis there remains a real

discrepancy between the two texts, more weight should be given to the *Metaphysics of Morals*, which was published in Kant's lifetime and therefore represents his mature view, than to his lectures, which were published without his supervision.

35 Cf. *MM* 6:379–80 (145–6).

36 As an illustration of what Kant may have in mind in this passage, consider the example of the titular character in Thomas Hardy's *The Mayor of Casterbridge*.

37 *CPr* 5:110–14 (114–18).

38 *CPr* 5:110 ff. (114 ff.).

39 *CPr* 5:114–32 (118–36).

40 See also *MM* 6:488–90 (230–2); and "On the Miscarriage of all Philosophical Theodicies" 8:260n (28n), in Allen Wood and George di Giovanni, eds., *Religion and Rational Theology*. Cf. Byrne, *Kant on God*, 110–17; and Beck, *Commentary*, 270–1.

41 The idea that divine retribution and human punishment follow the same principle is suggested by Fleischacker, "Kant's Theory of Punishment," 203–6.

42 See also *CPr* 5:61 (63): "When … someone who delights in annoying and vexing peace-loving folk receives at last a right good beating, it is certainly an ill, *but everyone approves of it and considers it as good in itself even if nothing further results from it*; nay, even he who gets the beating must acknowledge, in his reason, that justice has been done to him, because he sees the proportion between welfare and well-doing, which reason inevitably holds before him, here put into practice" (my emphasis).

43 See Shell, *The Rights of Reason*, 94.

44 Similarly, Beck has argued that Kant does not adequately show how the highest good might be derived from the categorical imperative, considering that the latter omits any reference to happiness. Beck speculates that Kant's synthesis of virtue and happiness might perhaps be defended on the ground that "it is important for the architectonic purpose of reason in uniting under one Idea the two legislations of reason, the theoretical and the practical … [since r]eason cannot tolerate a chaos of ends." Yet Beck himself finds no such argument in Kant's writings. See Beck, *Commentary*, 242–5. Taylor raises a similar doubt in "Kant's Political Religion," 11–12.

45 Fackenheim attempts to save Kant from inconsistency by arguing that the key to understanding his many contradictions lies in grasping his new kind of metaphysics. "Kant destroys the metaphysics which is based on speculation and replaces it with a metaphysics which is based on moral consciousness." Kant "seeks to prove, not immortality and God, but that

the belief in immortality and God is implicit in finite moral consciousness." We should therefore attribute the tensions and ambiguities we find
in Kant's arguments – such as the ambiguity of the *summum bonum* – not
to Kant's incompetent philosophizing, but to finite moral consciousness.
"The philosopher too is a finite moral agent; and it is in his latter rather
than his former capacity that he is in touch with ultimate moral reality:
and as philosopher he recognizes this fact." See Fackenheim, "Kant's
Philosophy of Religion," 9, 15–18. Thus, according to this line of argument,
Kant would urge us to embrace retribution, despite the unanswered questions we have raised regarding the relation between happiness and virtue,
because it is a product of our finite moral consciousness. This does not
seem persuasive to me. Kant's fundamental intention is to show how morality is rational; he can do so by demonstrating its coherence to speculative reason, but certainly not by allowing speculative reason to dissolve
into a mysterious metaphysics of moral consciousness.

Chapter 5

1 The passage is from Rousseau, *On the Social Contract*, 2.5.
2 See also White's brief discussion of this point in Foucault, in "Le pouvoir
  et la parole," in Artières et al., *Surveiller et Punir de Michel Foucault*, 291–2.
3 See, again, the *Leviathan*, 27.41. Emphasis added.
4 Locke, *Second Treatise of Government*, 2.11.
5 Given Foucault's philosophical commitments, it would no longer be possible for him to have recourse to the principle of retribution along Kantian
  lines, as a way of solving the problem of the unlimited modern punishing
  power. Foucault does not even entertain this as a possibility, since the
  Kantian concept of punishment relies on a view of man as constituted by a
  transcendental ("noumenal") autonomous self – a view that, from Foucault's
  point of view, has been widely discredited as a historical artefact of the Age
  of Enlightenment. See Foucault, *The Order of Things*, ch. 9; "Nietzsche,
  Genealogy, History," in *The Foucault Reader*, 76–100. Foucault's historicism
  appears to presuppose and to depend on the vast success (and subsequent
  developments) of Rousseau's critique of rationalism in the name of what
  Rousseau called natural goodness. (See especially the *Discourse on the Origins
  and Foundation of Inequality among Men*, in *The First and Second Discourses*, ed.
  Masters and Masters.) According to that epoch-making critique, rationality
  is only an acquired faculty – one that, as such, cannot serve as the source of
  natural right. On the contrary, it is the essentially non-rational passions of
  self-love and love of liberty (which are themselves crucially shaped by

society in all of its forms) that express the "perfectibility" of our nature – or, more accurately, its malleable and non-teleological character. Modern society has become more prosperous and secure, but at the cost of the self-alienation of the individual, whose reason and passions forever remain in contradiction. One might say that, in a certain sense, Foucault's *Discipline and Punish* draws out the implications of this Rousseauan analysis for liberal criminal justice. While liberal citizens have been sufficiently enlightened (as to the causes of crime and the corrupting effects of society itself on the individual) to feel pity for the criminal, they nevertheless cannot help constantly considering their own self-interest, which teaches that the criminal is a dangerous threat that needs to be incapacitated or destroyed altogether.

6 See also Boulant, *Michel Foucault et les prisons*, 106–24.

7 Cf. Beccaria, *On Crimes and Punishments*, ch. 19; Montesquieu, *The Spirit of the Laws*, 12.4.

8 See also Adam J. Hirsch, *The Rise of the Penitentiary*.

9 In this respect, Foucault's account of prison administration closely parallels Weber's theory of bureaucratic administration.

10 This fact about penitentiary science has been admitted even by Foucault's staunchest critics. See Pinatel, "Philosophie carcérale, technologie politique, et criminologie clinique," in Artières et al., *Surveiller et Punir de Michel Foucault*, 115. See also, more generally, Saleilles, *L'individualisation de la peine*.

11 See also Foucault, *Discipline and Punish*, 129–30, 183, 245–7.

12 Cf. Foucault, *Discipline and Punish*, 199, 249. White, in Artières et al., *Surveiller et Punir de Michel Foucault*, 286–90, discusses Foucault's penchant for ascribing causality to obscure forces, and links this feature of *Discipline and Punish* to the earlier *Words and Things*.

13 See Foucault, *Discipline and Punish*, 128–9, and contrast with our discussion of Rush's pamphlet on the penitentiary in chapter 3.

14 Pinatel observes that Foucault understates the influence of Catholicism on the European penitentiary movement. See "Philosophie carcérale," 103–4.

15 See Foucault, *Discipline and Punish*, 264–71. See also Rothman, *The Discovery of the Asylum*; Hirsch, *The Rise of the Penitentiary*.

16 The criticism of the effectiveness of the carceral penal system is quite extensive. Those who claim that the penal system cannot be salvaged as an instrument of correction or deterrence, and that it must be abandoned root and branch, include Knopp et al., *Instead of Prisons*; Cohen, *Against Criminology*; West and Morris, *The Case for Penal Abolition*; and Irwin and Austin, *It's About Time*. Others argue that the effectiveness of prisons in their corrective and deterrent capacities is marginal, but believe this problem can be remedied with further reforms. See, for example, Dilulio,

Governing Prisons. It should be noted that no one denies that prisons are effective at *incapacitating* offenders.

17 Foucault concerns himself with manifestations of despotic disciplinary structures in all aspects of modern life, and his focus on the modern penal system in particular is explained by the fact that it represents the furthest development of this phenomenon. The question of this broader claim in *Discipline and Punish* is beyond the scope of the present study.

18 Polet, too, observes this inconsistency in the argument of *Discipline and Punish*. See "Punishing Some, Disciplining All," in Koritansky, *The Philosophy of Punishment*, 214.

19 See the note on the restorative justice movement in our Introduction, 6–7 and n2.

20 Stuntz argues that in previous generations, local communities in the United States had significantly more control over criminal justice than they do today. See *The Collapse of American Criminal Justice*, chs. 3–4, 7.

21 Thus Stuntz, in *The Collapse* (283, 307–8), recommends "decentralization" and "local democracy" as a way of fixing the broken criminal justice system. But he does not regard these changes as probable, since they would depend on a political majority that lives in relatively safe neighbourhoods and thus has no incentive to support extensive reforms. See also the findings in Schneider, *Refocusing Crime Prevention*, regarding the non-participation of residents of a Vancouver neighbourhood in local community crime prevention programs.

Conclusion

1 Dzur, "An Introduction," 1.

2 For an overview of the issues, see Piehl and Useem, "Prisons," in Wilson and Petersilia, *Crime and Public Policy*, 532–58.

3 For an overview of the competing theories of this phenomenon, see for example Siegel and McCormick, *Criminology in Canada*, ch. 3; Rosenfeld, "Changing Crime Rates," in Wilson and Petersilia, *Crime and Public Policy*, 559–88.

4 See, especially, Wilson's *Thinking About Crime*.

5 Versions of this explanation have since been proposed by political scientist Francis Fukuyama (in *The Great Disruption*) as well as, more recently, by psychologist Steven Pinker. In *The Better Angels of Our Nature: Why Violence Has Declined*, Pinker attributes the sharp spike in crime in the 1960s to a "decivilization" of society, and the subsequent decline of crime in the 1990s to a "recivilization" brought about by a collective reaction against the radicalism of preceding decades, a concern in urban and economically

disadvantaged communities about their declining conditions, and (in the United States) the resurgence of social conservative movements such as Christian evangelicalism. On the other hand, Stuntz, in *The Collapse of American Criminal Justice*, attributes the late-twentieth-century crime boom to "pendulum justice": according to Stuntz, the crime boom was a consequence of the excessive leniency of American criminal justice immediately following the Second World War (see esp. ch. 9).

6 See the March 1982 *Atlantic Monthly* article, "Broken Windows," authored by Wilson and George L. Kelling.

7 Similar problems can be identified in another book popular at that time, which also criticized the traditional approach to criminal justice: psychiatrist Karl Menninger's provocatively titled *The Crime of Punishment*.

8 See also Zimring, *Perspectives on Deterrence* (esp. 32–107) for an overview of the wide range of factors that may affect the efficacy of deterrence and thus infinitely complicate the search for an exhaustive theory of the fundamental causes of crime.

9 Thacher, "Order Maintenance Reconsidered," 412–13.

10 As Koritansky also notes. See his "Introduction" in *The Philosophy of Punishment*.

11 Rawls, "Two Concepts of Rules," 3–32; Rawls, *A Theory of Justice*, 211–12, 276–7; Hart, "Prolegomenon," 1–27; Feinberg, *Doing and Deserving*, ch. 5. See again our discussion above, 10–12.

12 Brubaker, "Can Liberals Punish?" 821–36.

13 Brubaker, "Can Liberals Punish?" 821–2, 825.

14 Brubaker, "Can Liberals Punish?" 828–31. See also Corlett's criticism of Rawls in "Making Sense of Retributivism," 81–3.

15 Brubaker, "Can Liberals Punish?" 833.

16 On the controversy in the scholarly literature over the extent of the break between modern political thought and classical republicanism, compare Pocock, *The Machiavellian Moment*, with criticism of Pocock in T. Pangle, *The Spirit of Modern Republicanism*, and M. Zuckert, *The Natural Rights Republic*.

Bibliography

Primary Sources

Aristotle. *Nicomachean Ethics*. Trans. Robert C. Bartlett and Susan D. Collins. Chicago: University of Chicago Press, 2011. http://dx.doi.org/10.7208/chicago/9780226026763.001.0001.
– *Politics*. Trans. Carnes Lord. Chicago: University of Chicago Press, 1984. http://dx.doi.org/10.7208/chicago/9780226026701.001.0001.
Aquinas, Thomas. *On Law, Morality, and Politics*. Ed. William P. Baumgarth and Richard J. Regan. Indianapolis: Hackett, 1988.
Augustine. *The City of God against the Pagans*. Trans. Robert Dyson. Cambridge: Cambridge University Press, 1998.
Beaumont, Gustave de, and Alexis de Tocqueville. *On the Penitentiary System in the United States and Its Application in France*. Trans. Francis Lieber. Carbondale: Southern Illinois University Press, 1979.
Beccaria, Cesare. *On Crimes and Punishments*. Trans. David Young. Indianapolis: Hackett, 1984.
Benn, S.I. "An Approach to the Problems of Punishment." *Philosophy* 33, no. 127 (1958): 325–41. http://dx.doi.org/10.1017/S0031819100055017.
Bentham, Jeremy. *The Rationale of Punishment*. Ed. James McHugh. Amherst: Prometheus Books, 2009.
Blackstone, William. *Commentaries on the Laws of England*. Facsimile of the 1st ed. in 4 vols. Chicago: University of Chicago Press, 1979.
Boonin, David. *The Problem of Punishment*. New York: Cambridge University Press, 2008. http://dx.doi.org/10.1017/CBO9780511819254.
Bradford, William. "An Enquiry How Far the Punishment of Death Is Necessary […]" In *Pennsylvania*. Philadelphia: Dobson 1793, 1–73.

Braithwaite, John. *Restorative Justice and Responsive Regulation*. New York: Oxford University Press, 2002.

Braitwaite, John, and Pettit Philip. *Not Just Deserts: A Republican Theory of Criminal Justice*. New York: Oxford University Press, 1990.

Brubaker, Stanley C. "Can Liberals Punish?" *American Political Science Review* 82, no. 3 (1988): 821–36. http://dx.doi.org/10.2307/1962493.

Brubaker, Stanley C., and Ronald J. Terchek. "Punishing Liberals or Rehabilitating Liberalism." *American Political Science Review* 83, no. 4 (1989): 1309–16. http://dx.doi.org/10.2307/1961671.

Calvin, John. *Institutes of the Christian Religion*. Grand Rapids, MI: W.B. Eerdmans, 1995.

Christie, Nils. "Conflicts as Property." *British Journal of Criminology* 17 (1977): 1–26.

Clark, Ramsey. *Crime in America*. New York: Simon and Schuster, 1970.

Cohen, S. *Against Criminology*. Englewood Cliffs: Transaction, 1993.

Corlett, J. Angelo. "Making Sense of Retributivism." *Philosophy* 76, no. 295 (2001): 77–110.

Dagger, Richard. "Playing Fair with Punishment." *Ethics* 103, no. 3 (1993): 473–88. http://dx.doi.org/10.1086/293522.

Dilulio, John J. *Governing Prisons: A Comparative Study of Correctional Management*. New York: The Free Press, 1987.

Duff, R.A. *Intention, Agency, and Criminal Liability: Philosophy of Action and the Criminal Law*. Oxford: Basil Blackwell, 1990.

Durkheim, Emile. *Sociology and Philosophy*. Trans. D.F. Pocock. Glencoe: The Free Press, 1953.

Dzur, Albert. "An Introduction: Penal Democracy: *Good Society* Symposium on 'Democratic Theory and Mass Incarceration.'" *Good Society* 23, no. 1 (2014): 1–5. http://dx.doi.org/10.5325/goodsociety.23.1.0001.

Feinberg, Joel. *Doing and Deserving*. Princeton: Princeton University Press, 1970.

– *Harm to Others*. Oxford: Oxford University Press, 1984.

– *Harmless Wrongdoing*. Oxford: Oxford University Press, 1988.

Foucault, Michel. *Discipline and Punish*. Trans. Alan Sheridan. New York: Vintage Books, 1995.

– *The Foucault Reader*. Ed. Paul Rabinow. New York: Vintage Books, 2010.

– *The Order of Things*. [Trans. anon.] New York: Vintage Books, 1994.

Fukuyama, Francis. *The Great Disruption: Human Nature and the Reconstitution of Social Order*. New York: Simon and Schuster, 2000.

Furman v. Georgia. 408 U.S. 238 (1972).

Gregg v. Georgia. 428 U.S. 153 (1976).

Habermas, Jürgen. *The Structural Transformation of the Public Sphere: An Inquiry into a Category of Bourgeois Society*. Trans. Thomas Burger. Boston: MIT Press, 1989.

Hahn, Paul. *Emerging Criminal Justice: Three Pillars for a Proactive Justice System*. Thousand Oaks: Sage Publications, 1998.

Hart, H.L.A. "Prolegomenon to the Principles of Punishment." In *Punishment and Responsibility*. Oxford: Clarendon Press, 1968, 1–27.

Hegel, G.W.F. *The Philosophy of Right*. Trans. Alan White. Newburyport: Focus Publishing, 2002.

Hesiod and Theognis. *Theogony, Works and Days, and Elegies*. New York: Penguin Books, 1973.

Hirsch, Adam J. *The Rise of the Penitentiary: Prisons and Punishment in Early America*. New Haven: Yale University Press, 1992.

Hobbes, Thomas. *De Cive*. Trans. Richard Tuck and Michael Silverthorne. Cambridge: Cambridge University Press, 1998.

– *Elements of Law*. Ed. J.C.A. Gaskin. Oxford: Oxford University Press, 1994.

– *The English Works of Thomas Hobbes*. Ed. Sir William Molesworth. Elibron Classics, 2005.

– *Leviathan*. Ed. Edwin Curley. Indianapolis: Hackett, 1994.

The Holy Bible: King James Version. New York: Ivy Books, 1991.

Irwin, John, and James Austin. *It's About Time: America's Imprisonment Binge*. Belmont: Wadsworth, 1997.

Jefferson, Thomas. *The Complete Jefferson*. Ed. Saul Padover. New York: Duell, Sloan, and Pierce, 1943.

Kant, Immanuel. *Critique of Judgment*. Trans. Werner S. Pluhar. Indianapolis: Hackett, 1987.

– *Critique of Practical Reason*. Trans. Lewis White Beck. New York: Liberal Arts Press, 1956.

– *Critique of Pure Reason*. Trans. Norman Kemp Smith. New York: St Martin's Press, 1965.

– *Groundwork for the Metaphysics of Morals*. Trans. H.J. Paton. New York: Harper & Row, 1964.

– *Lectures on Ethics*. Trans. Louis Infield. Indianapolis: Hackett, 1980.

– *Political Writings*. Ed. H.S. Reiss. New York: Cambridge University Press, 1991.

– *Metaphysics of Morals*. Trans. Mary Gregor. Cambridge: Cambridge University Press, 1996. http://dx.doi.org/10.1017/CBO9780511809644.

– *Religion within the Bounds of Reason Alone*. Trans. Allen Wood and George di Giovanni. In *Religion and Rational Theology*. New York: Cambridge University Press, 1996.

Knopp, F.H., B. Boward, and M.O. Morris. *Instead of Prisons: A Handbook for Abolitionists*. Syracuse: Prison Research Education Project, 1976.

Lewis, C.S. "The Humanitarian Theory of Punishment." In *God in the Dock: Essays on Theology and Ethics*. Grand Rapids: W.B. Eerdmans, 1970, 287–300.

Livy. *The Rise of Rome*. Ed. T.J. Luce. New York: Oxford University Press, 1998.

Locke, John. *A Letter Concerning Toleration*. Ed. James Tully. Indianapolis: Hackett, 1983.

– *Second Treatise of Government*. Ed. Richard Cox. Wheeling: Harlan Davidson, 1982.

Machiavelli, Niccolo. 1996. *Discourses on Livy*. Trans. Harvey Mansfield and Nathan Tarcov. Chicago: University of Chicago Press, 1996. http://dx.doi.org/10.7208/chicago/9780226500331.001.0001.

– *The Prince*. Trans. Harvey Mansfield. Chicago: University of Chicago Press, 1985.

Menninger, Karl. *The Crime of Punishment*. New York: Viking Press, 1996.

Mill, John Stuart. "April 1866 Speech on Capital Punishment." In *Utilitarianism*, 2nd ed. Ed. George Sher. Indianapolis: Hackett, 2001.

– *On Liberty*. Indianapolis: Hackett, 1978.

Montesquieu, Charles Louis de Secondat, Baron de. *The Spirit of the Laws*. Trans. Anne Cohler. New York: Cambridge University Press, 1989.

– *Oeuvres complètes de Montesquieu*. Ed. André Masson. Paris: Nagel, 1950–5.

Morris, Herbert. "Persons and Punishment." *Monist* 52, no. 4 (1968): 475–501. http://dx.doi.org/10.5840/monist196852436.

Murphy, Jeffrie G. "Marxism and Retribution." *Philosophy and Public Affairs* 2, no. 3 (1973): 217–43.

Pangle, Thomas L., ed. *The Roots of Political Philosophy: Ten Forgotten Socratic Dialogues*. Ithaca: Cornell University Press, 1987.

Pestritto, Ronald J. *Founding the Criminal Law: Punishment and Political Thought in the Origins of America*. DeKalb: Northern Illinois University Press, 2000.

Pinker, Steven. *The Better Angels of Our Nature: Why Violence Has Declined*. New York: Penguin Books, 2011.

Plato. *Alcibiades I*. Trans. Carnes Lord. In T. Pangle, *The Roots of Political Philosophy*, 175–221.

– "Apology of Socrates." In West and West, *Four Texts on Socrates*, 63–97.

– *Euthyphro*. In West and West, *Four Texts on Socrates*, 41–61.

– *Gorgias*. Trans. James H. Nichols, Jr. Ithaca: Cornell University Press, 1998.

– *Laws*. Ed. Jeffrey Henderson. Cambridge, MA: Harvard University Press, 1926. http://dx.doi.org/10.4159/DLCL.plato_philosopher-laws.1926.

– *Laws of Plato*. 2 vols. Ed. E.B. England. Manchester: University of Manchester Press, 1921.

- *The Laws of Plato*. Trans. Thomas L. Pangle. Chicago: University of Chicago Press, 1980.
- *Lesser Hippias*. Trans. James Leake. In T. Pangle, *The Roots of Political Philosophy*, 281–99.
- *Lovers*. Trans. James Leake. In T. Pangle, *The Roots of Political Philosophy*, 80–90.
- *Minos*. Trans. Thomas L. Pangle. In T. Pangle, *The Roots of Political Philosophy*, 53–66.
- *The Republic of Plato*. Trans. Allan Bloom. New York: Basic Books, 1980.
- *Works*, vol. 5. Ed. John Burnet. Oxford: Oxford University Press, 1907.

Primoratz, Igor. "Punishment as Language." *Philosophy* 64, no. 248 (1989): 187–205. http://dx.doi.org/10.1017/S0031819100044478.

Rawls, John. *A Theory of Justice*, rev. ed. Cambridge, MA: Harvard University Press, 1999.
- "Two Concepts of Rules." *Philosophical Review* 64, no. 1 (1955): 3–32. http://dx.doi.org/10.2307/2182230.

Rothman, David J. *The Discovery of the Asylum*. Toronto: Little, Brown, 1971.

Rousseau, Jean-Jacques. *Collected Writings of Rousseau*. 11 vols. Ed. Roger Masters and Christopher Kelly. Hanover: University Press of New England, 1990.
- *The First and Second Discourses*. Trans. Roger D. Masters and Judith R. Masters. New York: St Martin's Press, 1964.
- *On the Social Contract*. Trans. Roger D. Masters and Judith R. Masters. New York: St Martin's Press, 1978.

Rush, Benjamin. *A Plan for the Punishment of Crime: Two Essays*. Ed. Negley Teeters. Philadelphia: Pennsylvania Prison Society, 1954.

Saleilles, Raymond. *L'individualisation de la peine*, 3rd ed. Paris: F. Alcan, 1927.

Schneider, Stephen. *Refocusing Crime Prevention: Collective Action and the Quest for Community*. Toronto: University of Toronto Press, 2007.

Siegel, Larry J., and Chris McCormick, eds. *Criminology in Canada: Theories, Patterns, and Typologies*, 4th ed. Toronto: Nelson, 2010.

Smart, J.C.C., and Bernard Williams. *Utilitarianism, For and Against*. Cambridge: Cambridge University Press, 2007.

Spinoza, Benedict. *Theologico-Political Treatise*. Trans. Martin D. Yaffe. Newburyport: Focus Publishing, 2004.

Stuntz, William J. *The Collapse of American Criminal Justice*. Cambridge, MA: Harvard University Press, 2011. http://dx.doi.org/10.4159/harvard.9780674062603.

Sutton, Adam, Adrian Cherney, and Rob White. *Crime Prevention: Principles, Perspectives, and Practices*. Port Melbourne: Cambridge University Press, 2008. http://dx.doi.org/10.1017/CBO9780511804601.

Templeton, Laura J., and Timothy F. Hartnagel. "Casual Attributions of Crime and the Public's Sentencing Goals." *Canadian Journal of Criminology and Criminal Justice* 54, no. 1 (2012): 45–65. http://dx.doi.org/10.3138/cjccj.2010 .E.29.

Thacher, David. "Order Maintenance Reconsidered: Moving beyond Strong Causal Reasoning." *Journal of Criminal Law and Criminology* 94, no. 2 (2004): 381–414. http://dx.doi.org/10.2307/3491374.

West, Gordon, and Ruth Morris, eds. *The Case for Penal Abolition*. Toronto: Canadian Scholars' Press, 2000.

West, Thomas G., and Grace Starry West. *Four Texts on Socrates*. Ithaca: Cornell University Press, 1984.

Wilson, James Q. *Thinking About Crime*, rev. ed. New York: Basic Books, 2013.

Wilson, James Q., and George L. Kelling. "Broken Windows." *The Atlantic*, March 1982.

Wilson, James Q., and Joan Petersilia, eds. *Crime and Public Policy*, 2nd ed. New York: Oxford University Press, 2011.

Zimring, Franklin E. *Perspectives on Deterrence*. Washington, D.C.: National Institute of Mental Health, Center for Studies of Crime and Delinquency, 1971.

Secondary Sources

Adkins, Arthur. *Merit and Responsibility*. Oxford: Clarendon Press, 1960.

Artières, Philippe, et al. *Surveiller et Punir de Michel Foucault: Regards critiques 1975–1979*. Maquette: Presses universitaires de Caen, 2010.

Beck, Lewis White. *Commentary on Kant's Critique of Practical Reason*. Chicago: University of Chicago Press, 1960.

Boulant, François. *Michel Foucault et les prisons*. Vendôme: Vendôme Impressions, Groupe Landais, 2003. http://dx.doi.org/10.3917/puf.boull.2003.01.

Brown, Keith C., ed. *Hobbes Studies*. Oxford: Basil Blackwell, 1965.

Bruell, Christopher. "On Plato's Political Philosophy." *Review of Politics* 56, no. 2 (1994): 261–82. http://dx.doi.org/10.1017/S003467050001843X.

– *On the Socratic Education*. Lanham, MD: Rowman and Littlefield, 1999.

Byrd, B. Sharon. "Kant's Theory of Punishment: Deterrence in Its Threat, Retribution in Its Execution." *Law and Philosophy* 8, no. 2 (1989): 151–200. http://dx.doi.org/10.1007/BF00160010.

Byrne, Peter. *Kant on God*. Burlington: Ashgate Publishing, 2007.

Carrese, Paul O. *The Cloaking of Power: Montesquieu, Blackstone, and the Rise of Judicial Activism*. Chicago: University of Chicago Press, 2003. http://dx.doi .org/10.7208/chicago/9780226094830.001.0001.

Carrithers, David W., Michael Mosher, and Paul A. Rahe, eds. *Montesquieu's Science of Politics: Essays on "The Spirit of the Laws."* Lanham: Rowman and Littlefield, 2001.

Cattaneo, Mario A. "Hobbes's Theory of Punishment." In Brown, *Hobbes Studies*, 275–97.

Fackenheim, Emil. "Kant's Philosophy of Religion." In *The God Within: Kant, Schelling, and Historicity*. Toronto: University of Toronto Press, 1996, 3–19.

Fleischacker, Samuel. "Kant's Theory of Punishment." In Williams, *Essays on Kant's Political Philosophy*, 191–212.

Galston, William A. *Kant and the Problem of History*. Chicago: University of Chicago Press, 1975.

Gauthier, David. *The Logic of Leviathan*. Oxford: Clarendon Press, 1969.

Goldsmith, M.M. *Hobbes's Science of Politics*. New York: Columbia University Press, 1966.

Hampton, Jean. *Hobbes and the Social Contract Tradition*. Cambridge: Cambridge University Press, 1986.

Herbert, Gary. "Immanuel Kant: Punishment and the Political Preconditions of Moral Existence." *Interpretation* 23, no. 1 (1995): 61–76.

Heyd, David. "Hobbes on Capital Punishment." *History of Philosophy Quarterly* 8, no. 2 (1991): 119–34.

Hill, Thomas E., Jr. "Kant on Wrongdoing, Desert, and Punishment." *Law and Philosophy* 18, no. 4 (1999): 407–41.

Hostettler, John. *Cesare Beccaria: The Genius of "On Crimes and Punishments."* Hampshire: Waterside Press, 2010.

Johnston, David. *The Rhetoric of "Leviathan."* Princeton: Princeton University Press, 1986.

Koritansky, Peter, ed. *The Philosophy of Punishment and the History of Political Thought*. Columbia: University of Missouri Press, 2011.

Krause, Sharon. "Despotism in *The Spirit of the Laws*." In Carrithers, Mosher, and Rahe, *Montesquieu's Science of Politics: Essays on "The Spirit of the Laws,"* 231–71.

– "The Politics of Distinction and Disobedience: Honor and the Defense of Liberty in Montesquieu." *Polity* 31, no. 3 (1999): 469–99. http://dx.doi.org/10.2307/3235250.

Mackenzie, Mary. *Plato on Punishment*. Berkeley: University of California Press, 1981.

Macpherson, C.B. *The Political Theory of Possessive Individualism: Hobbes to Locke*. Oxford: Clarendon Press, 1962.

Maestro, Marcello. *Cesare Beccaria and the Origins of Penal Reform*. Philadelphia: Temple University Press, 1973.

Martinich, Aloysius. *Hobbes*. New York: Routledge, 2005.

Merle, Jean-Christophe. *German Idealism and the Concept of Punishment*. New York: Cambridge University Press, 2009. http://dx.doi.org/10.1017/CBO9780511770425.

Moore, Michael. *Placing Blame: A General Theory of the Criminal Law*. Oxford: Oxford University Press, 1997.

Morrow, Glenn. *Plato's Cretan City: A Historical Interpretation of the "Laws."* Princeton: Princeton University Press, 1960.

Murphy, Jeffrie G. "Does Kant Have a Theory of Punishment?" *Columbia Law Review* 87, no. 3 (1987): 509–32. http://dx.doi.org/10.2307/1122669.

Norrie, Alan. "Thomas Hobbes and the Philosophy of Punishment." *Law and Philosophy* 3, no. 2 (1984): 299–320. http://dx.doi.org/10.1007/BF00144330.

O'Brien, Michael. "Plato and the 'Good Conscience': *Laws* 863E5–864B7." *Transactions and Proceedings of the American Philological Association* 88 (1957): 81–7.

– *The Socratic Paradoxes and the Greek Mind*. Chapel Hill: University of North Carolina Press, 1967.

Orwin, Clifford. "On the Sovereign Authorization." *Political Theory* 3, no. 1 (1975): 26–44.

Pangle, Lorraine. "Moral and Criminal Responsibility in Plato's *Laws*." *American Political Science Review* 103, no. 3 (2009): 456–73. http://dx.doi.org/10.1017/S0003055409990074.

Pangle, Thomas. *Montesquieu's Philosophy of Liberalism*. Chicago: University of Chicago Press, 1973.

– "The Political Psychology of Religion in Plato's *Laws*." *American Political Science Review* 70, no. 4 (1976): 1059–77. http://dx.doi.org/10.2307/1959374.

– *The Roots of Political Philosophy*. Ithaca: Cornell University Press, 1987.

– *The Spirit of Modern Republicanism*. Chicago: University of Chicago Press, 1988.

– *The Theological Basis of Liberal Modernity in Montesquieu's Spirit of the Laws*. Chicago: University of Chicago Press, 2010. http://dx.doi.org/10.7208/chicago/9780226645520.001.0001.

Pitkin, Hanna. "(a). "Hobbes's Concept of Representation – I." *American Political Science Review* 58, no. 2 (1964): 328–40. http://dx.doi.org/10.2307/1952865.

– "(b). "Hobbes's Concept of Representation – II." *American Political Science Review* 58, no. 4 (1964): 902–18. http://dx.doi.org/10.2307/1953289.

Pocock, J.G.A. *The Machiavellian Moment*. Princeton: Princeton University Press, 1975.

Saunders, Trevor. "The Socratic Paradoxes in Plato's *Laws*: A Commentary on 859c–864b." *Hermes* 96, no. 3 (1968): 421–34.

– *Plato's Penal Code*. New York: Oxford University Press, 1991.

Schaub, Diana J. *Erotic Liberalism: Women and Revolution in Montesquieu's "Persian Letters."* Lanham: Rowman and Littlefield, 1995.

Scheid, Don E. "Kant's Retributivism." *Ethics* 93, no. 2 (1983): 262–82. http://dx.doi.org/10.1086/292433.

Schrock, Thomas. "The Right to Punish and Resist Punishment in Hobbes's 'Leviathan.'" *Western Political Quarterly* 44, no. 4 (1991): 853–90. http://dx.doi.org/10.2307/448798.

Shell, Susan M. *The Rights of Reason: A Study of Kant's Philosophy and Politics.* Toronto: University of Toronto Press, 1980.

Shorey, Paul. *What Plato Said.* Chicago: University of Chicago Press, 1965.

Shuchman, Philip. "Comments on the Criminal Code of Plato's Laws." *Journal of the History of Ideas* 24, no. 1 (1963): 25–40. http://dx.doi.org/10.2307/2707857.

– "Kant on Punishment." *Kantian Review* 1 (1997): 116–24.

Stauffer, Devin. *The Unity of Plato's Gorgias.* Cambridge: Cambridge University Press, 2006. http://dx.doi.org/10.1017/CBO9780511499005.

Strauss, Leo. *Natural Right and History.* Chicago: University of Chicago Press, 1950.

– *The Political Philosophy of Hobbes: Its Basis and Its Genesis.* Trans. Elsa Sinclair. Chicago: University of Chicago Press, 1952.

– *The Argument and Action of Plato's "Laws."* Chicago: University of Chicago Press, 1975.

Sussman, David. "Shame and Punishment in Kant's *Doctrine of Right.*" *Philosophical Quarterly* 58, no. 231 (2008): 299–317. http://dx.doi.org/10.1111/j.1467-9213.2007.530.x.

Taylor, A.E. "The Ethical Doctrine of Hobbes." In Brown, *Hobbes Studies*, 35–55.

Taylor, Robert. "Kant's Political Religion: The Transparency of Perpetual Peace and the Highest Good." *Review of Politics* 72, no. 1 (2010): 1–24.

Tuck, Richard. *Natural Rights Theories.* New York: Cambridge University Press, 1979. http://dx.doi.org/10.1017/CBO9781139163569.

Tunick, Mark. "Is Kant a Retributivist?" *History of Political Thought* 17, no. 1 (1996): 60–78.

Uleman, Jennifer. "External Freedom in Kant's 'Rechtslehre': Political, Metaphysical." *Philosophy and Phenomenological Research* 68, no. 3 (2004): 578–601. http://dx.doi.org/10.1111/j.1933-1592.2004.tb00367.x.

Warrender, Howard. *The Political Philosophy of Hobbes: His Theory of Obligation.* Oxford: Oxford University Press, 1957.

Watkins, J.W.N. *Hobbes's System of Ideas*, 2nd ed. London: Hutchinson, 1973.

Weinrib, Ernest. "Law as Idea of Reason." In Williams, *Essays on Kant's Political Philosophy*, 15–49.

White Beck, Lewis. *Commentary on Kant's Critique of Practical Reason*. Chicago: University of Chicago Press, 1960.

Williams, Howard, ed. *Essays on Kant's Political Philosophy*. Cardiff: University of Wales Press, 1992.

Zuckert, Catherine. *Plato's Philosophers: The Coherence of the Dialogues*. Chicago: University of Chicago Press, 2012.

Zuckert, Michael. *The Natural Rights Republic*. Notre Dame: University of Notre Dame Press, 1996.